HARD LINE

HARD LINE

Life and Death on the U.S.-Mexico Border

KEN ELLINGWOOD

 PANTHEON BOOKS NEW YORK

Copyright © 2004 by Ken Ellingwood

All rights reserved under International and Pan-American
Copyright Conventions. Published in the United States by Pantheon
Books, a division of Random House, Inc., New York, and simultaneously
in Canada by Random House of Canada Limited, Toronto.

Pantheon Books and colophon are registered trademarks
of Random House, Inc.

Library of Congress Cataloging-in-Publication Data
Ellingwood, Ken.
Hard line : life and death on the U.S.-Mexico border / Ken Ellingwood.
p. cm.
Includes bibliographical references and index.
ISBN 0-375-42243-9
1. Alien labor, Mexican—Mexican-American Border Region. 2. Illegal
aliens—Mexican-American Border Region. I. Title.
HD8081.M6E4 2004
972'.1084—dc22   2003064694

www.pantheonbooks.com

Book design by Anthea Lingeman

Printed in the United States of America

First Edition

1 2 3 4 5 6 7 8 9

For my grandmother,

María del Socorro Sánchez,

with gratitude

Contents

Note on Accents

Because Americans, whatever their origin, tend to spell their names without accents, I have applied that style to the names of Mexican-Americans in this book; the names of Mexicans are spelled with the accents.

THE U.S.–MEXICO BORDER

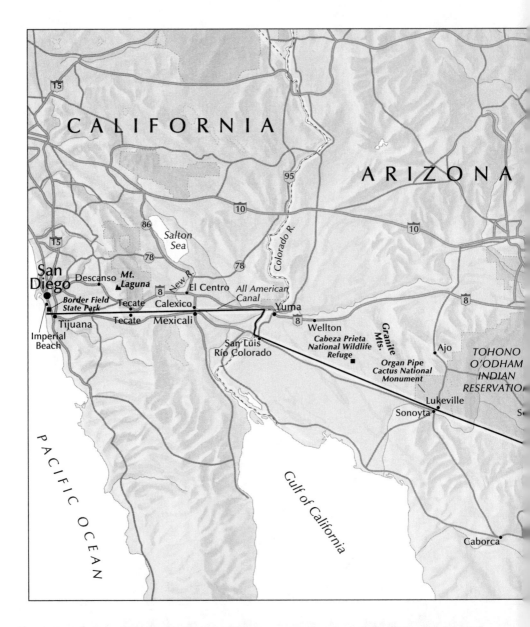

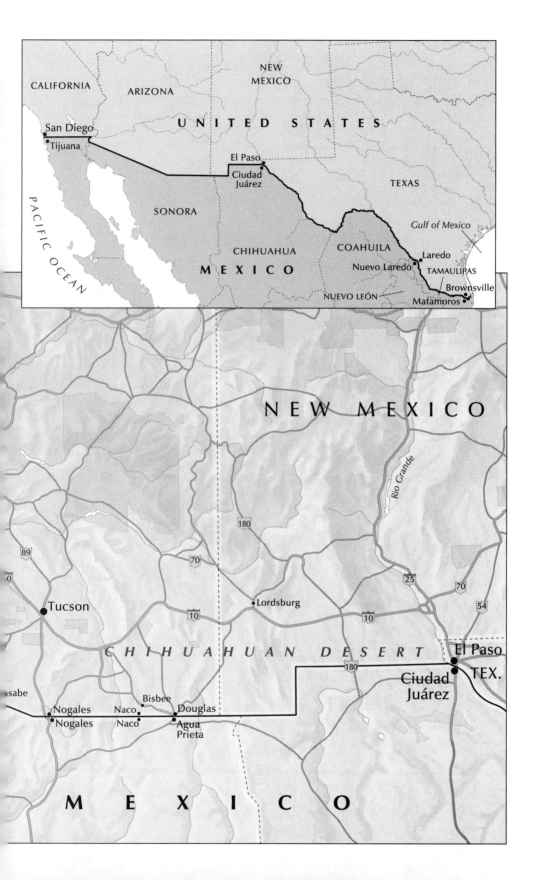

HARD LINE

PROLOGUE

The funeral is quick and dirty. The man is buried on a sunny California morning in much the same way he was found—alone and nameless and, from what anyone can tell, very far from home. His border-crossing journey ends in a pressed-wood box with screw-on plastic handles and a coroner's case number scrawled on the lid. Two of us look on as a trio of gravediggers with dour expressions and a pleasant fellow from a local funeral home lower the coffin into the slick Imperial County clay. They repeat the procedure with the boxed remains of a woman whose name also remains a mystery. With the addition of these two bodies, 133 undocumented immigrants now lie in this paupers' graveyard, their resting places designated by plain concrete loaves labeled "John Doe" or "Jane Doe."

The burial in this muddy graveyard in the town of Holtville represents the final step in this immigrant's ill-starred trip to the north. His remains were found three months earlier, in a creosote-specked wash deep in the California desert. During the peak of blistering summer temperatures, a deputy county coroner named Gary Hayes had to navigate his pickup miles into the parched countryside to reach the body. By the look of things, the migrant had succumbed first to the scorching heat and then, after death, to the messy work of scavenging animals. Coyotes, probably. As Hayes went about gathering the remains, the two men who had found the body, a pair of civilian contract workers who had been tending warning signs around the surrounding military bombing range, stood a healthy distance away from the tangle of clothes and skeletal remains and chatted with the handful of military officers and Border Patrol agents who had shown up. As Hayes searched the surroundings—one of the dead man's boots was missing—Richard Duarte, one of the sign tenders, squinted out over the seemingly endless desolation and contemplated the futility of the migrants' journey through this awful terrain. "These guys don't know what's happening out here," he mused. "The desert's a dangerous area. People just want to get across. They'll listen to whatever people say."

Indeed, the U.S.-Mexico border is a dangerous place, and always has been. It's home to criminal operators of every stripe—smugglers, drug lords, fugitives and crooked cops—and to some of the most unforgiving natural surroundings in either country. In years past, illegal border crossers had fallen prey to rapists and hardened killers, rain-engorged rivers, freeway traffic and their own ignorance and poor judgment. But by 2001, the number of fatalities across the nearly two-thousand-mile international boundary was hitting levels that dismayed even veteran border observers. More than three hundred were dying annually en route—enough to fill a passenger jetliner, as some pointed out. The difference now was that it was the border's brutal physical surroundings—not bandits or gunmen—that were doing the killing.

While past border media coverage had focused heavily on drug trafficking and the battle against runaway illegal immigration, this new death toll among undocumented migrants sneaking north into California and Arizona suddenly became a dominant theme at the border, as well as a disturbing problem for U.S. and Mexican officials far away in their nations' capitals. The safety issue grew more urgent with each new group of migrants that found itself in peril here in the deep desert sands of Imperial County, in the snow-topped mountains outside of San Diego and in the blast-furnace summertime heat of Arizona.

The reason for the deadly shift was man-made. A few years earlier, for the first time in its history, the U.S. government had made a sweeping effort to stave off illegal crossings in heavily populated areas that were well-known trouble spots—most prominently San Diego, California, and El Paso, Texas. These zones had once been virtual pedestrian highways for job-hungry immigrants lacking papers, but the huge buildup of Border Patrol agents in these places during the 1990s crackdown sent smugglers on an end run. They were soon leading their charges into the bleak and sparsely settled hinterlands—over mountains, across rivers and through merciless stretches of desert. Capture by the Border Patrol was less likely in these areas, but the risk of perishing rose dramatically.

Imperial County, occupying California's sparse southeastern corner just two hours from coastal San Diego, presents twin dangers: vast stretches of desert and treacherous irrigation channels. In 2001, the year of the migrant's burial, Imperial County was the deadliest spot on the U.S.-Mexico border for migrants. The death toll seemed to rise each day as the rural region became more popular as a crossing corridor. The fatalities placed heavier demands on the community as officials confronted the burden of identifying and burying the dead.

Imperial County is, like much of the U.S.-Mexico border, poor and overlooked. And it was but one setting for a wider drama playing out along various segments of the border during this period. As the U.S. enforcement crackdown took hold in 1994 and the years after, it brought long-coveted tranquility to urban areas like San Diego. But other, more rural areas on the border found themselves blindsided. The multi-part crackdown, whose California leg was called Operation Gatekeeper, created a shifting immigrant bulge, a sliding bubble such as that made by stepping on a balloon. It didn't take long for that bulge to reach unsuspecting border communities, altering life dramatically for many denizens of America's borderlands. Tensions rose. Impoverished rural counties faced financial crises as they coped with the sudden expense of having to jail, hospitalize or bury the immigrants whose northward trips now brought them to the countryside.

The moving migrant river, and the efforts by U.S. agents to corral it, disrupted the rhythms of small-town life, from horse country in eastern San Diego County to Imperial County's farms and beyond. Angry, gun-toting ranchers in Arizona scowled at the trails of trash left by hordes of immigrants trooping across their ranch lands. Fed up by the intrusion, some of the Arizonans, wearing badges that said "Ranch Patrol," had resorted to arresting the migrants and handing them over to Border Patrol agents, stirring fears of vigilantism. Elsewhere on Arizona's border, the Tohono O'odham nation, an Indian tribe with ancestral lands strad-dling the international divide, had a different problem. The stricter en-forcement along the border there had left tribal members on the U.S. side cut off from those on the Mexican side. The situation placed the tribe in technical violation of the law every time it sent one of its shuttle vans to pick up Mexican members and bring them back over the border through a gap in the border fence. The opening had once been a com-monly used crossing point for the tribe. Now it was a good place to get arrested by the Border Patrol.

That same period also saw three of the deadliest episodes to oc-cur on the Southwest border in modern times: a 1998 case in which eleven migrants perished in the Imperial County desert; the cold-related deaths of eight people during a snowstorm in the San Diego County mountains in 1999; and the horrific case of fourteen migrants who died in the Arizona desert near Yuma in May 2001. Twelve survived the Ari-zona tragedy, the worst involving cross-border hikers ever recorded. Winter and summer presented equally perilous conditions for those en-tering unlawfully on foot, but the dangers seemed to dissuade few from coming.

There was plenty of irony in this unusual period. In 2001, not long after the Yuma tragedy, *Time* magazine devoted a special issue to the border. It declared the border to be "vanishing before our eyes." But at a time when globalization and the North American Free Trade Agree-ment had begun to dissolve the U.S.-Mexico border as we knew it, that same frontier, in other ways, was hardened as never before.

The border has always been a site of conflict and of contradictory mean-ings. It is at once an exit and an entrance, the porous membrane between two cultures, a gateway and a wall. I came to know this fascinating and confounding zone by covering it as the San Diego–based border reporter for the *Los Angeles Times,* starting in 1998. The border assignment marked a strange sort of homecoming for me or, better put, it was like being in-troduced again to a relative I never had much of an opportunity to know. I was born on the border, in Laredo, Texas. That is where my father, a blue-eyed Maine Yankee stationed at the U.S. Air Force base there, met my mother, a spirited, ebony-haired girl from the Mexican side in

Nuevo Laredo. Except for a brief period living in my mother's former hometown as a child, I grew up almost entirely in Maine. My principal exposure to half my heritage was when Mexican relatives and family friends ventured north to take in our small-town New England existence, toting gifts of tortillas, mole sauce and goat-milk candy.

For my brother and me, the border was thus mainly the faraway setting for stories our mom told us about her youth on the Río Bravo—as the Rio Grande is known in Mexico—during the 1940s and 1950s. Most of her tales were about how young and crazy and full of life they all were and how innocent, too—the same stories American parents of that era told their children. But we also learned of our grandmother, who slipped across the border to work as a maid on a Texas ranch. And of the feared Texas Rangers, *los rinches,* whose swagger and bigotry sent many a Mexican's heart racing. There were wondrous accounts, too, of folk cures that worked, floods that frightened and tarantulas, of stern nuns and cross aunts and rancher uncles and the clamor of an unending procession of new cousins.

Outside our window in rural Maine, the evergreen forest where we cut our own firewood and hunted deer wore a parka of fresh snow. But inside, my curiosity about this other place was fired. In college, I studied Mexican history and worked on my Spanish. I gave my mother gray hairs by traveling around Latin America. My eventual return to the border—in California this time—had more to do with the newspaper's serendipitous staffing needs than any well-laid plan. But it was a chance to immerse myself in a world that was foreign and faintly familiar at the same time.

Over the next four years I would come to see this much-discussed but poorly understood zone as a reluctant stage for the playing out of hope and anger and governmental will. I would come to see it not just as the battleground for end-of-the-century politics, but also as the humble home of many decent people, buffeted by forces too distant and vague to control in any meaningful way.

The rest of America is now living what the Southwest and a handful of big cities had been witnessing for years. What happens on the U.S.-Mexico border matters now in St. Louis and Ames and Raleigh and

Nashua and Bozeman. Take a ride into the area where I grew up in rural Maine, where for many years my mother was sure to get a desperate call for translation help whenever a Spanish-speaking child showed up in the local schools, and you now run into Mexicans employed at the local egg farm. The same farm stand that sells sugar-and-gold corn to the natives also stocks jars of prepared mole and husks for making tamales.

Across the United States, longtime residents are rubbing elbows with immigrants from Mexico and elsewhere in Latin America. Radio airwaves carry Spanish across regions where the twang once ruled. In metropolitan Atlanta, the Latino population shot up nearly 400 percent during the 1990s. The number of Latinos grew even faster in other southern cities, like Charlotte and Winston-Salem, North Carolina. By 2003, police officers in rural Tennessee were being put through crash courses in Spanish.

The border is now everywhere. But out along the formal boundary between the two countries, the line has grown harder—harder to cross, harder to guard and, very often, harder to fathom.

Chapter One

SITTING ON AN X

U.S. Border Patrol agent Araceli Garcia gunned the truck's engine and reached the top of Spooner's Mesa, a broad field of daisies overlooking the ocean surf and the lowering sun. A sprawling wetlands stretches north toward San Diego's downtown, about fifteen miles in the distance. It is a stunning spot, providing the sort of wide-open coastal panorama that rapid development and protective landowners have rendered all but nonexistent in modern southern California. But in May 1999 we came for a different view. Spooner's Mesa happened to be an ideal vantage for seeing, up close, just how drastically the U.S.-Mexico border had been transformed along its westernmost stretch, as it slices between San Diego and Tijuana and kisses the Pacific Ocean here at Imperial Beach.

Atop the mesa, the change could be measured in the expensive new hardware installed in recent years. A mile-long row of border lights, mounted on poles and as powerful as those that illuminate sports stadiums, now extended to the rugged canyons on either side of the mesa. A ten-foot-high border fence provided a formidable barrier where a decade earlier immigrants had gathered by the hundreds in preparation for nighttime dashes to the other side. Buried in the ground at our feet were dozens of high-tech sensors that could detect movement and then transmit signals instantly to border agents in a control room at the Imperial Beach station.

The signs of change were also evident in what wasn't here. As Garcia showed me around the Imperial Beach region, she checked out the narrow canyons, washes and culverts that once were favored crossing points for migrants. All were deserted today. She wheeled onto the beach at Border Field State Park and pointed out the very spot where her mother had sneaked into the country illegally from Mexico twenty-seven years before. (Her mother was now a U.S. citizen.) The beachside park is just across the fence from a pleasant middle-class neighborhood on the Mexican side. In between stands the first stone border marker erected after the Treaty of Guadalupe Hidalgo ended the U.S.-Mexican war in 1848, granting modern-day California and much of the rest of the Southwest to the United States and creating what in these parts was the contemporary international boundary. Aside from the two of us, the park was empty.

The border fence had been labeled in orange paint with the names of nearby landmarks—a lighthouse, a yogurt shop on the Tijuana side—to help U.S. agents guide Mexican authorities on the south side when crowds gathered on Mexican soil and troublemakers heaved baseball-sized rocks over the fence at the American agents. Such cooperation was among the reasons officials in both countries insisted that crime on the border had dropped noticeably in recent years.

We slowly cruised along dirt roads where canyons finger across the international divide, undeterred by political boundaries. In the brushy reaches, the agent scanned sandy paths for footprints using a cobalt blue penlight. There were only squiggly snake trails and rabbit tracks, although a cluster of plastic water jugs told us that people had passed through recently. In a sobering reminder that serious trouble had not deserted this area altogether, Garcia pointed out the spot where a border agent had fatally shot a migrant the year before during an alleged rock-throwing attack. No charges were filed in the case.

The radio crackled, bringing word from the station's control room that someone had tripped one of the motion sensors. Garcia zoomed off to check. It was a false alarm, the first of several tripped by sunset strollers or children riding bicycles near their San Ysidro neighborhood. On this night the only radio call approaching urgency was a query from an agent who discovered a child locked in a parked car.

During an entire shift this evening, Garcia, an energetic twenty-three-year-old who had joined the Border Patrol four years earlier, did not make any arrests. She saw not a single illegal border crosser, not one suspicious footprint. Here on what was once the wildest stretch of the U.S.-Mexico border, the most stubborn foes that Garcia encountered were the undercooked potatoes she had brought for dinner. By shift's end, the forty-five or so Imperial Beach agents on duty would make a paltry twenty-four arrests, about half of the day's small total.

Night used to drop like a curse on Imperial Beach, turning the beaches and canyons into a pandemonium of illegal crossers, smugglers, bandits and the vastly outnumbered U.S. border agents who gave chase, mostly without success. Now, in the wide hollows where hundreds used to gather for the mad dash to neighborhoods and freeways on the U.S. side, only weeds clustered. Where enterprising Mexican vendors once dished up tacos to the hopeful hordes loomed not one but two strong fences and enough wattage to light up a Padres night game. Border Patrol agents were once in woeful supply. Now they were conspicuous in their trucks, parked a quarter-mile apart in a tidy string all the way to the sea. They were seeing fewer fence jumpers these days because migrants were more likely to try their luck in rural regions to the east than face almost certain capture here.

Agents now spent eight hours or more keeping watch this way. They called it "sitting on an X." With few migrants to chase, some passed the time scanning the newspaper. Others tapped out reports on laptop computers or jotted to-do lists. A few, contemplating life after the Border Patrol, even used the time to study for after-work classes. "A lot of the guys look at it as an eight-hour mobile office," one agent grumbled. Out on the line where mayhem once reigned, you could now hear an unexpected lament among the young, go-getter agents: the job had become dull. The stationary work gave rise to an acerbic job description: "human scarecrow."

As we sat in the night darkness, soft rock playing in Garcia's cab, the young agent recognized that the quiet hardly matched the adrenaline-stoked image of the Border Patrol's recruiting brochures. But it represented a measure of success that would have been inconceivable to her predecessors. "They thought they had no hope," she said. "They thought they'd never see the day. And the day is here."

· · ·

The new ennui in the Imperial Beach patrol zone, covering five miles from the San Ysidro port of entry—the nation's busiest—to the ocean, was the product of politics and provided testimony to the power of a hot-button issue to focus the will of policymakers when the perceived cost of inaction was even higher. By the outset of the 1990s, Imperial Beach had become the immigration equivalent of Three Mile Island, a disaster area of legendary lawlessness and, as a result, a handy rhetorical backdrop for Republicans and Democrats alike to decry a border out of control. Robberies and rapes of migrants were common in the ravines. Illegal border crossers overran the horse ranches of the rustic Tijuana River valley and the residential streets in the city of Imperial Beach. Some migrants were killed as they raced on foot across the two freeways leading north from the San Ysidro port of entry toward downtown San Diego. No more.

Presidential politics played a huge role in this transformation. At a time when Republicans were capitalizing on growing public fervor over illegal immigration, it was President Bill Clinton, a Democrat, who launched the unprecedented get-tough strategy, beginning in San Diego with Operation Gatekeeper. It was no accident that the effort would take root first in California, with its trove of electoral votes and years of chaos at the border. California also was the incubator in the early 1990s for an emerging movement of Americans expressing increased hostility toward undocumented immigrants. The Clinton administration unveiled Operation Gatekeeper in October 1994—one month before California voters were to vote on the controversial Proposition 187 ballot measure to cut off public services to illegal immigrants.

The border initiative first zeroed in on fourteen miles in San Diego, starting at the worst spot: Imperial Beach. National Guard troops helped erect fences made of steel construction panels handed down by the military. The barrier's final portion, a huge blade the length of a football field, jutted into the ocean at Imperial Beach to discourage swimmers. The number of agents assigned to Imperial Beach jumped immediately from 250 to about 400. One of the new hires was Garcia, who had grown up in the Los Angeles suburb of Artesia and was working as a manager in a discount clothing store before she decided to join the Border Patrol.

In the ensuing years, the San Diego contingent of the Border Patrol, covering sixty-six miles of the international boundary altogether, would continue to receive a huge infusion of funding and manpower. A similar push was launched in trouble spots across the country. Overall, the unprecedented expansion in five years doubled the number of border agents nationwide to about eight thousand. By 1999, arrests of undocumented immigrants in Imperial Beach had plummeted to a daily average of about forty-three, down from more than five hundred a day in 1994, when it was the leakiest spot on the Southwest border. Moreover, officials now figured those arrests included nearly all who still were foolish enough to try crossing. Before, even when arrests were far higher, most actually got away, sprinting north, often through residents' backyards toward the trolley and bus at San Ysidro, the Mexican-American neighborhood sitting at the border portal.

For the first time, officials said, they had achieved "control" over the border around San Diego. Arrests were at an eighteen-year low by the time Garcia was showing me around that area. "We're working without a net. We've never been where we are right now," a senior Border Patrol official claimed with obvious pride. Officials said the Imperial Beach experience had set a standard that others would come to demand elsewhere. Those appeals for help would soon become acute in places such as rural Arizona, as they became overwhelmed by undocumented migrants skirting this clampdown in San Diego and a similar one in El Paso.

Relying increasingly on paid smugglers, the undocumented border crossers were now traversing the countryside to the east of San Diego, first in the boulder-studded mountains an hour's drive from downtown and later, farther still, in the wide spaces of Imperial County. As new areas became overwhelmed, residents demanded more border control. And as more agents rushed to stanch the flow in these spots, immigrants streamed eastward yet again, to even more desolate terrain. The shifting flow—and the unwelcome new realities of this U.S.-Mexico border— were soon crashing down on quiet communities like Douglas, Arizona, that had long inhabited the border without great consequence or much notice from the outside world. Suddenly, they found themselves beset by hordes of border crossers and an instant influx of agents in hot pursuit.

. . .

Framed by a fence of steel grate, a fourteen-foot-tall white obelisk sculpted from Italian marble makes the border official at its western terminus, just steps from the Pacific Ocean. On the north side is the state park where Araceli Garcia and I enjoyed a stunning view of the coastline but no people. Just to the south is Playas de Tijuana, a middle-class enclave with a majestic beachside bullring, medical clinics offering alternative cancer cures to American patients and a string of seafood shacks along the sandy beach. It is a stretch favored by Tijuana weekenders seeking refuge from the crowded city. It also is believed home to a suspected drug lord, whose house sits just feet from the fence—maddeningly just out of reach for the U.S. prosecutors who would love to get their hands on him.

Border Field State Park sits out of the way, miles from the nearest freeway, and hence draws few visitors. Occupying the southwestern corner of the continental United States, it is a gorgeous, bluff-top spot for gazing at bobbing surfers and an assortment of seabirds, like the light-footed clapper rail, that inhabit the massive estuary at the foot of the mesa.

But the park also encapsulates as clearly as any spot can the utter strangeness of the border, how sharply and unapologetically it delineates and divides, even while cinching the two sides together. Through a two-hundred-yard stretch of grated fence—a rare interruption in the ten-foot solid-steel barrier separating the two sides here—you can chat with people in Mexico. Since it got so hard to cross in Imperial Beach without papers, some couples who have found themselves estranged by circumstance now come on weekends to visit, show off their newborns to relatives, share a lover's kiss. With one person on each side of the international boundary, it is one of the strangest romantic rituals you'll ever see.

Residents of Imperial Beach recall a time not so long ago when families from Tijuana strolled freely across a fenceless border to join relatives on the U.S. side for Sunday afternoon picnics in the park and then return home. A plaque mounted near the fence notes that the spot was dedicated in 1974 as a symbol of friendship between the people of the United States and Mexico.

Now, nearly three decades later, the park was the site of a controversy over plans to build a second, backup border fence ordered by Congress in 1996. The second fence, parallel to the first, would cut across the top of the grassy mesa, effectively chopping the picnic area in two. Entombed inside the planned double wall would be the border monument, whose original version was erected in 1851 as the first formal marker along this odd and troubled international boundary.

Running 1,952 miles from the Pacific Ocean to the Gulf of Mexico, the U.S.-Mexico border is unique in the world because it separates two countries with such wildly disparate standards of living. Here, the First and Third Worlds lie pressed together, cheek to cheek.

From Border Field State Park, the line runs overland across the bottom of California, Arizona and New Mexico, then southeast along Texas's Rio Grande before ending at Brownsville, on the Gulf of Mexico. It's a long and varied seam of boulder-crowned mountains, giant farms, the hottest desert in America, vast stretches of emptiness and a dozen or so important nodes of population—twin cities linked by language, history and commerce. Opposite the four American border states are six Mexican states, from Baja California and Sonora in the west to Tamaulipas and Nuevo León on the eastern end and, in the middle, Chihuahua and Coahuila.

This ten-state border strip is a magnet for newcomers from each country and therefore has grown at a galloping pace. The U.S. city of Calexico, California, and its much larger Mexican sibling, Mexicali, for example, grew by nearly 75 percent during the 1990s. Some demographers predict its population of about 12 million—those living in U.S. border counties and their equivalents, known as *municipios,* on the Mexican side—will double to 24 million by 2020. That would be an astounding increase that far exceeds average growth in either country as a whole. In fact, many border experts see the region as a zone unto itself—not the United States entirely, nor exactly Mexico, but a third country, with some characteristics of each and many others all its own.

The border also has tremendous symbolic power, which is one reason it has so often been depicted in noir-tinted movies, sung about in Mexican *corridos,* argued about on talk radio. It means very different things depending upon which side you're standing.

From the north, the border appears woebegone, home to some of the poorest communities in America. It is beset with high incidences of breathing disorders—the four U.S. border states account for nearly a third of the nation's cases of tuberculosis—and other health troubles, like diabetes. In many spots, the American side bears unnerving resemblance to its neighbor to the south, lacking even basic infrastructure such as sewage treatment.

But from Mexico, *la frontera* is a near-mythical promised land, a souped-up economic dynamo whose humming electronics plants, political inventiveness and proximity to the United States make it seem the very picture of Mexico's hoped-for future: vibrant, relatively well-to-do, forward-leaning. It is why so many villagers from Mexico's interior abandon the countryside for the border—and then head farther north into the United States. And it is part of the reason today you can spot families visiting through the fence at Border Field State Park.

There was little notice here when the border celebrated its 150th birthday in 1998. It was an anniversary many people preferred to ignore, marking as it did an especially painful moment in the history of relations between the two countries. American high school history students might pinpoint 1846 as the start of the Mexican-American War, which erupted over how much of Texas the United States could rightfully claim. The Treaty of Guadalupe Hidalgo ended the two-year conflict. That agreement, signed on February 2, 1848, created the modern American Southwest, shifting about half of Mexico's territory into U.S. hands. It delineated most of what we know today as the Mexican border, though maps used in Mexican schools as late as the 1940s labeled those lands as "temporarily" in American hands.

After the war, marking the border was the first joint project for the two countries. It went remarkably smoothly, considering how recently the nations had been at war. A pair of American boundary commissioners, John B. Weller and Andrew B. Gray, met their Mexican counterparts in San Diego in July 1849, two months later than the treaty prescribed; the late start was caused by shipping delays due to the throngs of travelers heading for California, where the gold rush had begun the previous year. The group set to work in San Diego and by October had agreed upon an end point for the new border, one marine league south of the port of San Diego, as called for in the treaty. It took six months to survey the line east 150 miles to Yuma, a job complicated by challenging terrain and the fact that members of the surveying crew kept quitting to join the parade of fortune seekers headed north to gold country.

The route east was fearsome. The brutal conditions where the border was carved across Imperial County impressed a subsequent boundary commissioner, John Russell Bartlett, who made the arduous trip as part of a border expedition in June 1852: "The weather was excessively hot to-day, the mercury standing at 105° Fahrenheit in the shade under the bushes. Took our departure, at 6 p.m. Each mile we advanced, grew more barren. The road continued through deep sand or loose gravel, reminding us that we had fairly entered upon the desert of which we had heard so much. On leaving this valley, all traces of grass disappear. A few stunted shrubs armed with thorns, strove hard for an existence; and the wonder is, that any vegetation life can flourish amid such barrenness. . . . The bleached bones and dried carcasses of oxen, mules, and sheep, began to mark our road, mementos of the sufferings of former parties."

As he pushed his wagon across the deep sand, Bartlett found himself mired in a bizarre diplomatic controversy that threatened to bring the two nations to war again. When negotiators hammered out the Treaty of Guadalupe Hidalgo, they established a boundary that would follow the Rio Grande west from the Gulf of Mexico until it hit the southern boundary of New Mexico. There, surveyors were to use as landmarks the city of El Paso del Norte and the Rio Grande itself.

Bartlett, a politically connected bookseller from Rhode Island who harbored fantasies of becoming a discoverer, landed the job of boundary commissioner in 1850, even though he had no practical experience or any real knowledge of diplomacy. Soon after taking the job, he and his Mexican counterpart discovered a serious problem: The map used by the diplomats to draw up the treaty was wrong. It placed El Paso too far north, by about 34 miles, and the Rio Grande too far east, by more than 130 miles. By following the erroneous map along with the letter of the treaty, the United States stood to lose out on a swath of land amounting to about six thousand square miles. More important, by placing the border too far north, the United States would surrender what many believed was the most promising route for a transcontinental railroad, an obsession in the capital of a nation feeling the tug of Manifest Destiny. Ill-advisedly, Bartlett took it upon himself to settle the matter. He and the Mexican commissioner, General Pedro García Condé, haggled over the matter for months before settling on a compromise that accepted the northern alignment.

But the move set off a political tempest in the U.S. Congress and sent the two countries heading toward new hostilities. Then the United States, in 1853, decided to buy the disputed strip as part of what is known today as the Gadsden Purchase. For $10 million, the United States got forty-five thousand square miles in modern-day New Mexico and Arizona, a region rich with minerals and one that could be used someday for a railroad. The purchase filled in the final outline of the contemporary U.S.-Mexico border. His blunder having been corrected, Bartlett, the bibliophile and would-be adventurer, was discredited and stripped of his federal funding. He gave up his post and returned home to Rhode Island, where he would later write a massive two-volume account of his adventures on the border.

It fell to Major William H. Emory to finish marking the international boundary, a dangerous assignment that put his surveyors in heavily loaded wagons and sent them into the midst of marauding Indians, migrating gold hunters and some of the cruelest terrain they had ever laid eyes on. "The heat, commencing to be excessive in May, becomes almost unendurable in the months of June, July, and August. Even in winter the sun is so hot, and the direct as well as reflected light upon the sand-plains so dazzling, that, excepting a couple of hours after daybreak and an hour before sunset, it is only possible to see objects through the best instrumental telescopes in the most distorted shapes—a thin white pole appearing as a tall column of the whitest fleece," writes one of Emory's aides, Lieutenant Nathaniel Michler, in describing the work in an area that today is Arizona.

"The winds blow up quickly and violently," Michler continues, "and it is useless to attempt to work with nice instruments. These dust-storms were our great drawbacks, as it was impossible to see many feet distant, and then only at the risk of being blinded. The gusts of wind which produce this unpleasant effect in winter are in summer like the simoons of the Sahara—they sweep over and scorch the land, burning like the hot blasts of a furnace."

It is into such surroundings that so many Mexican migrants would wander on their northward treks to the United States nearly 150 years later.

Though the border existed on paper and in a string of squared-off stone monuments, it would remain a wide-open and sparsely guarded area for decades after the treaties that created it. Texas Rangers and Arizona Rangers patrolled their stretches, while overall federal responsibilities for border enforcement and the passage of goods were carried out by mounted officers of U.S. Customs. Shortly after the turn of the century, the U.S. Bureau of Immigration was able to hire about seventy-five Mounted Watchmen—forerunners of the modern Border Patrol—to roam the Canadian and Mexican borders.

The Border Patrol was created by Congress in 1924, but the contemporary notion of a regulated border was all but unheard of. "There have been no natural barriers, the two nations being separated by an imaginary line, a barbed-wire fence, an easily forded river, an undergrowth of mesquite or chaparral," wrote J. Fred Rippy in 1926. "Citizens of both nations have passed back and forth with little difficulty or interruption, or have settled in neighboring states amidst natural surroundings which have not repelled them by their unfamiliar aspects. Bandits, filibusters, and Indians have raided freely back and forth. Smugglers have often plied their trade with ease and security. Robbers of stock sometimes have been able to operate on a large and profitable scale. Political insurgents and refugees have often sought and found safety across the international line."

Although there was scant enforcement, little was demanded. Mexican workers came and went on their way to jobs in American mines and to lay railroad tracks that were spreading quickly across the Southwest during the late 1800s. It was Chinese immigrants, not Mexicans, who were the main targets of U.S. efforts to mind the borders, following passage of the Chinese Exclusion Act in 1882. That law, written during a fit of anti-Asian sentiment springing from the West Coast, marked the first time the government had barred a specific ethnic group from its shores.

As a result of that law, authorities paid more attention to the nation's border with Canada and to its seaports. A focus on the porous Mexican frontier came later. "It may be reasonably anticipated that the next means to be resorted to by such aliens will be the Mexican boundary— a point of weakness in our defense from undesirable immigration that has already been discovered and utilized by the most resourceful of alien peoples—the Chinese," the immigration bureau stated in an annual report in 1903.

Meanwhile, movement by Mexicans into the United States was sporadic and negligible before World War I. Mexican workers came and got jobs as laborers and agricultural workers, often having been recruited by U.S. labor contractors who would set up shop next door to the immigration bureau offices. Then they returned home at the end of the farming season. "I don't know where they come from. They just keep coming, year after year," said one California grower quoted by the historian Carey McWilliams. "When the work is finished, I do not know where they go. That is the condition of our country."

North of the border, the migrants left in their wake a reputation for being durable, uncomplaining workers. American employers were happy to have them and no one in government seemed inclined to disagree. "Because of their strong attachment to their native land . . . and the possibility of their residence here being discontinued, few become citizens of the United States. The Mexican migrants are providing a fairly adequate supply of labor," noted the Dillingham Commission on Immigration in 1911. "While they are not easily assimilated, this is of no very great importance as long as most of them return to their native land. In the case of the Mexican, he is less desirable as a citizen than as a laborer."

Such nonchalance toward border crossers seems almost quaint today. In the interceding nine decades, much would change in Mexican immigration—and in the U.S. response to it. From World War I until the end of the twentieth century, migration from Mexico surged and receded according to the labor needs of American farmers and factory owners, and was influenced by a U.S. immigration policy that flung open the nation's door at some moments and slammed it shut at others. These U.S. policies would play a major role in shaping a tradition of back-and-forth travel by migrants—legal and illegal—that endures today.

It may come as a surprise, for example, that the original purpose of the U.S. immigration bureau—founded in 1864, it was the precursor of the modern INS—was to *attract* immigrant workers. A few decades later, stricter laws prevented employers from recruiting in Mexico, but immigration officials did little to prevent U.S. labor contractors from venturing south to hire railroad workers, for example.

Railroads were not alone in hiring Mexicans. Southwestern mines and agriculture also seemed to have a limitless appetite for Mexican workers. And by the early twentieth century, as historian George J. Sanchez has noted, Mexican policies that made life increasingly untenable for peasants left many with little alternative than to head north for jobs that paid a dollar a day. With lax enforcement on the U.S. border, "practically any alien desirous of entering the United States and possessed of ordinary intelligence and persistence could readily find means of so doing without fear of detection," reported one El Paso–based immigration inspector at the time.

Mexicans flocked north to flee the turbulence of the Mexican Revolution after 1910 and to answer U.S. labor shortages during World War I. They were for a time exempted from quota limits and other restrictions, including a head tax and a literacy requirement, that were imposed on other foreigners after the war. Mexican settlements filled up in places such as Los Angeles County, which became home to nearly 100,000 Mexican-born residents in 1930—an eightfold increase from just two decades earlier. California's Imperial County, hugging the border across from the city of Mexicali, boasted 28,000 Mexican residents that year, compared to just 1,461 in 1910. But the welcome mat was yanked away abruptly when the Depression deepened in the 1930s. As many as half a million Mexicans left amid an acute job shortage and a national mood change.

Mexican workers became popular again during World War II. As tens of thousands of able-bodied American men trooped off to combat, the same need for workers that drew large numbers of American women into U.S. factories for the first time created an unprecedented opening for laborers from south of the border. Under an unusual arrangement between the U.S. and Mexican governments, Mexicans were given permission to cross the border for temporary jobs as laborers, or braceros, a word rooted in *brazo*, Spanish for "arm." The bracero program, begun in 1942, was extended time and time again after the war. By the time it ended in 1964 amid wide concerns about employer abuses, it had provided official permits for five million laborers. The braceros kept the U.S. economy humming during and after the war. Earning just 50 cents an hour during the 1950s, they were favored by employers. One grower was reported to have said: "We used to own our slaves, now we rent them from the government."

But the program had important side effects. Once they worked in U.S. fields and on American railroads, many of the Mexican workers were hooked. The wages may have been cut-rate by American standards, but they represented more than workers could make in Mexico. Lots of braceros signed up more than once, returning year after year to citrus groves in California's Central Valley and apple orchards in Washington State. Rather than go back to rural towns deep inside Mexico's interior, they stayed at the border between their work stints in the United States.

It was no accident that during the 1950s Mexican border cities like Tijuana experienced the first spasms of growth that would accelerate during the following decades. Tijuana's population soared more than fifteenfold, from 22,000 in 1940 to 348,000 by 1967. Other Mexican border cities exploded nearly as fast. It also was a life-changing experience for the braceros. Even those who did not return north would remember their service for many years. (By 1999, many of the former laborers were trying to retrieve funds they said had been withheld improperly by the Mexican government for their work on U.S. soil decades earlier. They were very old men now, but many still held proudly on to their work papers, worn thin and feathery over the years. During a protest march along a Mexico City boulevard, several ticked off as well as they could the itineraries of their long-ago labors, a roll call of distant farm towns, with awkward American names, that had once needed help.)

In addition to the workers who came into the United States legally as braceros, many Mexicans slipped across the border for similar jobs without submitting to the formal application process. U.S. employers saved money by hiring these undocumented workers, thereby avoiding a $25 bond and $15 per-person contracting fee for braceros, and supplemented their bracero forces. The two groups regularly worked alongside each other in the fields.

Immigration authorities helped turn illegal entrants into official braceros through a process that became known as "wringing out wetbacks," the term for illegal immigrants commonly used at the time. Under an agreement by the two governments, undocumented workers arrested on U.S. soil were to be given preference over ordinary applicants as contract workers under the bracero program. This gave rise to an almost Kafkaesque process under which the Border Patrol "escorted them to the Mexican border, had them step to the Mexican side, and brought them back as legal braceros. In some cases, the Border Patrol 'paroled' illegal immigrants directly to employers," writes Kitty Calavita, an immigration expert who studied the bracero period.

The result of these forces was a massive wave of illegal immigrants during the ten-year period after World War II—a period dubbed "the wetback decade." Arrests of undocumented border crossers soared along the border, even though patrols remained thin. This surge in illegal crossings sent the door swinging shut again. On June 9, 1954, the U.S. government, fearing the wage-depressing effects of immigrant workers and harboring Cold War worries over possible terrorism, announced what would officially be known as Operation Wetback. It was a massive, military-style sweep led by immigration commissioner Joseph P. Swing, a retired general, and motivated as much by immediate Cold War political ends as by the quest for border control.

The campaign was a showy affair, involving federal, state and county officials, railroad police, the FBI and the military, and bore more than a few parallels to the Operation Gatekeeper effort that would be rolled out forty years later. When Swing, an army commander in California who had attended West Point with President Dwight D. Eisenhower, took over the INS early in 1954, the agency was seen by many as bumbling and ineffective. The future of the Border Patrol appeared to rest with the operation's success.

Roundups shot up to levels not seen since the Depression era, though many were indiscriminate and accompanied by widespread charges of abuse by officials. Slightly more than 1 million arrests were made in 1954. Deportations soared that year, capping in spectacular fashion a postwar period during which nearly 5 million undocumented Mexican immigrants were expelled. Then, just as suddenly, arrests fell—a sign, the officials said, that the border was under control. "The decline in the number of wetbacks found in the United States, even after concentrated efforts were pursued throughout the year, reveals that this is no longer, as in the past, a problem in border control," Swing said in 1955. "The border has been secured."

Swing's self-congratulations proved premature, as illegal crossings rose again during the 1960s, following the demise of the bracero program and a 1965 immigration law that imposed new quotas on entries from countries in the Western Hemisphere. Rising concern over illegal crossings spurred more federal legislation in the 1970s amid a wave of alarmist rhetoric from federal officials. (Writing about this "neo-restrictionism," scholar Joseph Nevins notes that Gerald Ford's attorney general, William Saxbe, was warning in 1974 that the social costs of undocumented migrants inside the United States amounted to "a severe national crisis.")

By the end of the decade, public opinion polls were registering a distinct chill in sentiment toward immigration, too. The theme of a border run amok even found its way into popular culture. The 1980 film *Borderline* features Charles Bronson as a San Diego border agent with a soft spot for the truckloads of migrants being sneaked across by their unscrupulous—and slightly warped—American smuggler, played by Ed Harris. The movie closes with something sounding like an appeal for help: "In 1979, more than one million illegal aliens were apprehended crossing the border into the United States." Despite the widespread worry, the INS, the agency primarily responsible for guarding the borders, remained pitifully understaffed and strapped for cash.

At the same time, a string of legislative efforts to stymie unlawful entries by punishing employers who knowingly hired undocumented workers faltered time and again until 1986, when Congress passed the Immigration Reform and Control Act, offering both carrot and stick. Immigrants who had been in the United States since 1982 could apply for amnesty, while employers who hired undocumented workers were for the first time subject to federal sanctions. The amnesty portion was put to full use, with more than 2 million Mexicans ultimately given legal status. That sent border arrests plunging for three years. But the employer sanctions were spottily enforced and served mainly to drive the hiring underground into the hands of so-called labor contractors, who were now responsible for ensuring that workers had legal documents. Though wages fell for these workers and the cost of hiring smugglers rose somewhat as a result, illegal crossings resumed anew by 1990, bringing an estimated 250,000 undocumented immigrants to U.S. soil yearly. This time, the outcry was ferocious, leading to the boldest border experiment yet.

Chapter Two
GATEKEEPER ARRIVES

If there was any place that crystallized concern over the government's apparent loss of control over its borders, it was the stretch between San Diego and Tijuana. There was no spot like it on the U.S.-Mexico border: two big cities, both relatively well-to-do by either nation's standards, both magnets for countrymen seeking their own versions of prosperity. They had grown from humble beginnings, initially part of the same vast ranch lands that owed settlement to various waves of Spanish missionaries. But the cities grew up separately, swelled by newcomers from other parts of their respective countries. The effect was to highlight the differences rather than similarities between the cities. In the process, San Diego and Tijuana reached adulthood as uneasy next-door neighbors.

San Diego grew up heavily Anglo and preferred to keep Tijuana at arm's length, except when it got a hankering to gamble or guzzle cheap tequila on Avenida Revolución. The American city never considered itself a true border town and, in the strict sense, it barely was. The city's core sits fifteen miles north of the border; its long arm touches Tijuana only gingerly, at the dense little Mexican-American enclave of San Ysidro. Modern San Diego's Republican elites didn't speak Spanish, and many longtime residents took pride in never having ventured over the border.

Tijuana chafed at the way it was often looked upon, but then reinforced its worst stereotypes as a Third World basket case with each disastrous flood or new outbreak of official corruption. It put on a self-consciously campy air for the American tourists it courted, but often ended up offended by how partying servicemen and frat boys carried on.

Like siblings stuck with each other for life, the two cities nonetheless leaned on each other. San Diegans flocked south daily to manage the ever-blossoming binational assembly plants known as *maquiladoras,* to purchase cut-rate medications or to grab a fresh lobster dinner farther south on the Baja coast. Tijuanans who possessed border-crossing permits poured north to shop, go to the dentist or catch the latest American blockbuster movie. Those who had papers authorizing them to work— and many who did not—commuted to jobs as janitors and waiters. Tijuana's privileged went back and forth to their seaside apartments in La Jolla and Coronado on the American side. The traffic jam was ceaseless at the San Ysidro port of entry; no entrance to America was busier. Night and day, a slow-moving river of cars coursed between Tijuana and San Diego, the lifeblood of a third, binational being that belonged to neither place entirely.

By 1990, the wild, darkened recesses on the outskirts of the San Ysidro crossing represented the worst of the border. The scene was surreal as the immigrants teemed along the filthy Tijuana River and in the canyons around Imperial Beach, from where they raced en masse through the border crossing and into oncoming freeway traffic. The Border Patrol closed four of the six lanes of Interstate 5 entering Mexico as the technique gained popularity. As a halfback might evade tacklers, the runners used the vehicles as shields against capture for hundreds of yards into U.S. territory, knowing that border agents would not give chase. They then made their way along the freeway divider to pickup spots. In response to these so-called banzai runs, California highway workers had to put up a fence and yellow caution signs depicting a family holding hands at full sprint.

In addition to the danger of being run over, there were plenty of other hazards, among them bandits and rapists who preyed on the comparatively helpless migrants, known colloquially as *pollos,* or chickens. A special police unit was assigned to patrol against such crimes on the San Diego side. Known as the Border Crime Prevention Unit, the squad was made up of volunteer officers who patrolled the crime-ridden canyons and mesas to head off robberies and rapes. It was modeled after a special team of daredevil undercover cops who dressed like migrants and worked the same canyons during the 1970s. (That short-lived squad is the subject of Joseph Wambaugh's 1984 book *Lines and Shadows*.) There was even talk of digging a five-foot-deep trench to keep cars from careening across in the area east of the San Ysidro crossing.

By 1990, a group of U.S. residents, fed up with the nightly spectacle, took to parking their cars along the line at dark with their headlights aimed south at the border in order to show their support for the beleaguered agents and to deter crossers. Led by Muriel Watson, the widow of a longtime Border Patrol agent, the group called itself Light Up the Border. The "light-ups," as the demonstrations were called, drew as many as two hundred motorists, ignited radio talk-show chatter and, in turn, attracted counter-protesters who saw the actions as hostile and provocative.

Tensions bubbled. In 1992 a nineteen-year-old San Ysidro resident, allegedly angered that a group of five immigrants had run through his backyard, chased the group down and shot one of the migrants dead with a pistol as the man was cornered in a cul-de-sac. Seldom had the border so resembled a dangerous and volatile free-for-all.

Although many California employers remained fond of the ready supply of cheap labor, resentment toward illegal immigrants was growing among residents around the state and elsewhere around the country. Once treated as a local problem, quite remarkably the border's enforcement had arrived as a national concern. Politicians and polemicists soon showed up with cameras in tow to fulminate against a border in disarray—and, by extension, to warn of a nation under attack. During his 1992 presidential campaign against George Bush, for example, Pat Buchanan ventured out to Smuggler Gulch, a favorite crossing point in the Imperial Beach section. Immigrants looked on from the Mexican side of the fence as Buchanan turned to reporters with his pitch: the government was failing to protect its own borders from an "illegal invasion" of at least a million people a year. If Buchanan's rhetoric seemed extreme, it is only because he was the first to utter it. Buchanan's anger about the border was soon adopted by all politicians, Republicans and Democrats alike.

It was an anger that resonated with Americans across the country. A

Time magazine poll in September 1993 found 73 percent were in favor of strict immigration limits. Nearly two out of three respondents said they believed most immigrants came into the United States illegally, though the magazine reported that, in reality, the vast majority of immigrants— more than one million a year—entered lawfully. The backlash was strongest in the big immigrant-magnet states, such as New York, Florida, Texas and, especially, California.

California had become the leading destination of the nationwide immigration tidal wave that began during the 1970s and continued into the 1990s, despite a souring economy. Immigration laws passed in 1965 and 1986 helped boost an influx from Asia and Latin America, and California felt the effects most directly. In 1960 the state was home to 1.3 million immigrants—about one in seven of the nation's foreign-born residents. By 1990, that ratio would grow to nearly one in three, representing about 6.5 million of the nation's 20 million foreign-born residents.

Many of them had been legalized under the 1986 immigration-reform law, and were primarily from Mexico. But many had not. By the early 1990s, studies estimated that more than 3 million undocumented immigrants lived in the United States, a third of them from Mexico. By 1995, estimates would put the number between 2.4 million and 4 million. The largest bloc nationwide—as many as 1.6 million—lived in California. A RAND study in 1997 asserted that the lion's share of undocumented immigrants in California had entered the country without papers, while elsewhere in the nation, illegal immigrants were as likely to have overstayed visas as to have entered unlawfully. The migrants were mostly men between the ages of nineteen and thirty-four, from a handful of states in Mexico, who by and large ended up in the same half dozen American states, and mostly in California and Texas. They usually had less than nine years of schooling. They tended to get hired as laborers or in service positions in restaurants and hotels; average weekly pay for Mexican-born migrants was $185 to $240 in the early 1990s, according to a binational study of migration overseen by the two governments in 1997.

The surge of immigration by the 1990s coincided with a growing indigenous angst in California. A series of military-base closings, economic recession and a shriveling of the defense industry that had paid

for so many of the tile-roofed tract homes carpeting southern California
had produced a populace jittery about the future and not very pleased
about the circumstances of the present. In a state that had been only too
happy to let undocumented immigrants pick its grapes, tend its children, mop its floors and clip its bougainvilleas, many residents now saw
a crisis demanding action.

California's concerns were echoed nationwide by writers like Peter
Brimelow, whose book *Alien Nation* blames overly liberal immigration
laws and failures to patrol the border for a tide of newcomers that threatened "even to destroy" the American nation. Polemicists and academ-
ics argued back and forth over whether undocumented immigrants
provided economic benefits to the United States or were costing tax-
payers in needed services, such as medical care. It was an unwinnable
debate; studies appeared showing that illegal immigrants contributed
millions to the public coffers at the same time border hospitals announced they were going broke under the weight of caring for those
without papers on U.S. soil.

Economic uncertainties, news stories about inner-city gangs running amok, worries about the financial toll of immigrants, the Los Angeles riots of 1992 and the 1993 bombing of the World Trade Center in New
York by Islamic extremists from abroad all softened the ground for a
full-fledged campaign against illegal immigrants. What sprouted in
1994 was Proposition 187, California's historic initiative to cut off certain public benefits to immigrants who lacked permission to be in the
United States.

Some supporters of the ballot measure described an apocalyptic sce-
nario that amounted to the very undoing of the Treaty of Guadalupe
Hidalgo. In a letter to the *New York Times,* a spokeswoman for the campaign described the stakes: "By flooding the state with 2 million illegal
aliens to date, and increasing that figure each of the following ten years,
Mexicans in California would number 15 million to 20 million by 2004.
During those ten years about 5 million to 8 million Californians would
have emigrated to other states. If these trends continued, a Mexico-
controlled California could vote to establish Spanish as the sole language of California, 10 million more English-speaking Californians could
flee, and there could be a statewide vote to leave the union and annex

California to Mexico." Not all supporters of Proposition 187 were motivated by such dire visions, but sponsors had struck a wellspring of public frustration.

Governor Pete Wilson clambered aboard the gathering movement in
hopes of breathing life into his reelection campaign. Even though Wilson had supported higher legal immigration while a U.S. senator in the
1980s, he now blamed the federal government's failure to control the
border for the state's crippling financial burden of providing services to
undocumented immigrants. In the midst of the 1994 campaign, he aired
a now-famous television commercial featuring grainy black-and-white
footage of immigrants darting amid cars across the border at San Ysidro.
The unnerving images were accompanied by an ominous voice-over.
"They keep coming," said the narrator. "Two million illegal immigrants
in California. The federal government won't stop them at the border, yet
requires us to pay billions to take care of them."

Wilson already had been anointed something of a political visionary
for seizing on the immigration issue. Fred Barnes, writing in the *New
Republic* during the fall of 1993, noted that it was Wilson's appeals for
the elimination of education, medical and welfare benefits for illegal
immigrants that produced his first jump in popularity in two years: Wilson's approval rating rose from 30 to 37 percent and disapproval fell
from 59 to 45 percent in a *Los Angeles Times* poll. "The Wilson effect,"
as Barnes called it, caught the attention of Republicans nationwide
by 1994.

It also did not go unnoticed in the White House. Bill Clinton, who
was elected two years before, in 1992, could see the warning lights
flashing around immigration and the border. The Democratic Party's
platform that year had spoken blandly about immigration, noting that
"Democrats support immigration policies that promote fairness, nondis-
crimination and family reunification, and that reflect our constitutional
freedoms of speech, association and travel." But now immigration was
seen as the sort of red-meat issue that could prove a boon to Republicans in the 1994 mid-term elections and inspire more divisive reactions
like Proposition 187, which the Clinton administration opposed. In July
1993, Clinton found his own swagger on the issue. He came out for
hiring six hundred new Border Patrol agents, in essence hijacking a

hobbyhorse of Duncan Hunter, a Republican congressman from the San Diego area who was known for favoring hard-line border policing. "Today we send a strong and clear message," Clinton declared. "We will make it tougher for illegal aliens to get into our country."

As California voters prepared to render judgment on Proposition 187 and on a new term for Wilson in 1994, the Clinton administration announced another step. This was the massive offensive to seal the leaking border, beginning in San Diego in October with Operation Gatekeeper and paid for with the help of a national anti-crime bill, passed in August 1994, that boosted funding for federal and local policing and prisons, among other things. The new border strategy was modeled on a bold—and largely unsanctioned—gambit taken by the chief of the Border Patrol in El Paso one year earlier. The chief, Silvestre Reyes, had arrived there in early 1993 to a border in serious disarray. The number of arrests was second only to the levels in San Diego. The Rio Grande was no real barrier to illegal crossings—any migrant incapable of crossing by himself had only to hire a *lanchero* to float him over.

Reyes's idea was radical for its time: he decided to station agents along the river's concrete bank densely enough together to dissuade crossers, many of whom went north daily for jobs on the U.S. side. This deterrence would also prevent the ugly spectacle of chasing migrants through the streets on the U.S. side. He dubbed his effort Operation Blockade. The novel strategy, launched in September 1993, hit like a bomb. Arrests plummeted immediately; the locals in El Paso loved it. Reporters from all over came running to the border city to trumpet the program's success. Reyes's superiors in Washington weren't pleased by his go-it-alone crusade, but they couldn't argue with its results. Reyes held his ground and was permitted to maintain the operation, renamed Hold the Line. Within months, the Clinton administration had embraced the strategy as its own and the mold for Gatekeeper was cast. (Reyes, a Democrat, was later elected to Congress from El Paso.)

It has been suggested that the Gatekeeper effort, launched just a month before the California elections, was an attempt to curb support for Proposition 187 by demonstrating the federal government's resolve in combating illegal immigration. If so, the tactic failed. Proposition 187 passed easily in November. It gained the support of two-thirds of white voters and about half of blacks and Asian Americans. It even won the approval of 23 percent of Latino voters. Aided by the immigration issue, Wilson gained a second term.

Gatekeeper was launched with dizzying swiftness. The main theater for America's new war on illegal immigration would be far from the impoverished villages in Mexico that migrants fled, and distant, too, from the crop fields, meat-cutting plants and factories in the United States where they streamed for jobs. The battle would be focused, for good or bad, almost entirely at the border.

Operation Gatekeeper debuted amid great fanfare, the symbol of the administration's determination to impose the rule of law along the border and to overcome, in the words of Alan Bersin, the U.S. attorney for San Diego and Imperial Counties, a "generation of neglect." Two hundred agents fanned out along the Tijuana River and spread out to the ocean at Imperial Beach. "We are tying everything together that we have been working on for the past eighteen months: personnel, fences, lighting, technology," proclaimed the chief of the Border Patrol in San Diego, Gustavo De La Viña. "We are starting to roll." The Border Patrol there received a $45 million infusion for the fight. It needed all this money; during the previous twelve months, San Diego agents had made 450,000 arrests of undocumented immigrants—accounting for nearly half of all border arrests nationwide.

The enforcement strategy devised by immigration officials, with the help of Pentagon specialists, rested on a concept the Border Patrol called "prevention through deterrence." It was a simple premise, based on the recommendations of a 1993 border study by a unit of Sandia National Laboratories, a government contractor that performs national security work. The plan envisioned, among other things, multiple layers of border fences. The nearly two-thousand-mile border was simply too vast to seal all at once; with only about four thousand agents nationwide in 1994, the defenses were too thin.

So planners focused on the most troublesome corridors, pouring in agents as a general might concentrate troops and fortifying the zones with floodlights, fences and an assortment of hardware, such as buried sensors, night-vision goggles and military-style infrared scopes capable of distinguishing human forms in the darkness. Even if agents couldn't catch all the crossers, the planners reasoned that so many migrants would be arrested that trying to jump the fence would no longer seem to be worth the trouble. As each of the busy urban corridors was brought under control, the less traveled zones would be plugged, one at a time, along the entire border.

In a stiffly worded document called "Border Patrol Strategic Plan 1994 and Beyond," the architects of the emerging crackdown labeled their goal as "restoring our Nation's confidence in the integrity of the border. A well-managed border will enhance national security and safeguard our immigration heritage." The planners noted that the job wouldn't be easy. In the border cities, those crossing unlawfully had ready access to roads, rail lines, airports and bus routes to the interior of the United States. False-document rings were growing in sophistication. More migrants were attempting to enter and get work authorization by asking for asylum. Increasing numbers of Chinese immigrants were showing up on the shores of Baja California. And, as always, the economic forces that sent Mexican migrants northward remained strong.

The document predicted that the recently enacted North American Free Trade Agreement, which slashes commercial barriers among Mexico, the United States and Canada, would help discourage illegal crossings by boosting the Mexican economy. But NAFTA remained a subject of considerable controversy on a number of fronts, including its effect on migration. While some saw it as a modernizing force sure to shrink the disparities between U.S. and Mexican societies, others believed that privatization, factories and more cross-border links would simply create a new set of reasons for people to head north. To prevent the latter outcome, the Border Patrol document called for tighter regulation over U.S. employers and the closing of loopholes by which undocumented immigrants gained asylum and work authorization in the United States.

The "strategy plan" was but a crude outline for an offensive that was revolutionary in its ambition and sweep. Conservatives and liberals had long believed that sealing the nation's southern border was impossible. Except for the Operation Wetback sweeps during the 1950s, the U.S. government had attempted nothing resembling a concerted effort to block illegal immigration at the border. Gatekeeper represented a high-stakes political gambit by the Clinton administration; it also came amid less than auspicious circumstances. Besides having to confront a decades-old migratory flow, U.S. officials would soon face a fresh surge of entries by Mexicans victimized by their nation's latest currency devaluation. Economic disruptions such as dips in Mexicans' buying power at home often led to immediate increased migration.

Soon after the October debut of Gatekeeper, Gustavo De La Viña was elevated to command of the Border Patrol nationwide and transferred to Washington, D.C. Although the San Diego operation was already under way, its precise shape and direction still remained to be ironed out. It would fall to De La Viña's successor—a lanky, forty-eight-year-old Texan named Johnny Williams—to make Operation Gatekeeper work. Williams took the reins in December 1994, just two months after the strategy was unveiled. As field general in this bold campaign, first as the San Diego Border Patrol chief and later as INS director for the western United States, Williams would come to be the strategy's public face. Over the next eight years he would serve as tactician, explainer and cheerleader. As the policy's byproducts came to include turmoil and tragedy, Williams was called upon, again and again, to soothe angry residents and to deflect charges that the government's enforcement scheme was killing migrants by the hundreds.

Though his South Texas twang and folksy delivery made Williams seem the antithesis of the Washington bureaucrat, he was no rube. He was politically shrewd, insistent and known at the agency as a hard-pushing workaholic. Williams was a border rat—a country kid who'd grown up next to the Rio Grande in Del Rio, Texas, to become a Border Patrol lifer. In the nearly three decades since he had joined the Border Patrol, Williams had been assigned to some of its loneliest outposts. Along the way, he developed ideas about the border-enforcement tactics that became central components of Operation Gatekeeper.

A bus driver's son, Williams served in the navy during the Vietnam War, floating on an aircraft carrier off the coast of Vietnam for three years as an airplane electrician. He signed up with the Border Patrol a couple of years after returning to Texas. The border agent's life appealed to the outdoorsman in Williams, who as a boy had hunted javelina, deer and rabbit in the countryside around rural Del Rio. The job had an alluring Rough Rider quality; an agent had to make it on his own out there on the line. An agent wore a six-shooter and, by necessity, operated at the end of a long set of reins. Unlike a lot of other law enforcement workers, border agents often worked far from the gaze of meddling supervisors. It demanded strict discipline, some creativity and a cowboy's self-reliance. Defending the nation's border added an extra, patriotic touch. Moreover, competition for agent slots was stiff. Williams swelled with a feeling of accomplishment when he was chosen in 1971.

His first post was farther down the Rio Grande in Laredo, where he worked for three years. It was a tiny operation in those days—just forty-two agents on the town's outskirts. He got skilled at tracking migrants' footprints and polished his Spanish by chatting up the people he'd arrested while they waited to be picked up for booking. He especially liked collecting the Mexicans' jokes. He took turns manning the downtown highway checkpoints that were aimed at catching those who had waded through the mucky waterway but had not yet made it to the interior. For Williams and his fellow agents, bragging rights went to those who made lots of arrests. Apprehensions gave an agent a feeling that his work mattered; they were the trophy at the end of a taxing and sometimes dangerous game. Catching a big load of marijuana provided an even larger thrill, especially because the stakes were higher since drug dealers came armed. Williams got shot at down there, and so did a lot of other agents.

Williams sympathized with the ordinary Mexicans he arrested each day. He'd grown up on the border, after all, and knew that most were decent folk who came north for the work. But smugglers were a different matter. From early in his career, Williams viewed the paid guides as parasitic, and his distaste only grew with each year he wore the Border Patrol's green uniform. It would reach outright loathing by the time Williams assumed the tie and blazer of an INS boss many years later, when smugglers began leading their charges into the cruel conditions of the mountains and deserts.

Williams moved in 1974 to a stint in Lordsburg, New Mexico, a lonely crossroads on Interstate 10. Seventy miles north of the border, the station covers a big empty tract making up the state's boot heel. For Williams and six other agents, the main job was to catch migrants on the highway. He took over the inspection checkpoint and developed a sharp eye for spotting fake documents. Williams would board a bus, make his way down the aisle checking papers and then return to the front, picking out the riders with cards he suspected were phony. "You, you, you, you and you," he'd say, as he moved back to the front. He was almost always right.

A four-year stint in Sierra Blanca, Texas, beginning in 1978, gave Williams his first chance to put his own stamp on a station—albeit one that was so small and isolated it was considered a hardship post by the Border Patrol. When Williams took over as patrol agent in charge, the outpost was moribund and nearly without significance. It sat in West Texas, some ninety miles from El Paso. Although the station occupies a strategic position on Interstate 10, Williams arrived to find its agents doing their job the old-fashioned way—by trolling the broad terrain for footprints—and paying almost zero attention to the highway itself. As Williams had learned in his last two assignments, without highway checkpoints, illegal crossers were home free once they made it past the first line of agents. He thought of it as not unlike a football team with a defensive line but no secondary.

So he set up a checkpoint, a miserable nine-foot trailer with an old stove for warmth, that was to be manned at all hours. If an agent gave chase, Williams, listening to the police radio at home, would jump into his vehicle and rush to the checkpoint to make sure it was covered. Agents soon got the point: the checkpoint was sacred. It was, Williams would say later, "the original X," a primitive version of the stationary tactic he would insist upon later as Border Patrol chief in San Diego. (And agents hated the first one, too.)

Williams's career climbed. He made stops in El Paso and Yuma, each time with more responsibility and the chance to innovate. In Yuma, he launched desert-rescue teams—agents assigned to patrol the stark backcountry and to apply first aid when needed. By 1990, he got his first big command, as chief of the Border Patrol's El Centro sector, which covers most of the hundred miles between the San Diego sector and Yuma. He began to think about strategy in fresh terms. He started experimenting, dividing the sectors into smaller pieces and focusing his agents on each in sequence, an incremental approach whose effectiveness he would measure by tracking arrests. It was, in miniature, what the U.S. government would attempt to do across the entire Mexican border. Williams also hoped to measure scientifically just how well the border was being guarded. Since it had not been done before, there were no good models. He had to make it up as he went along, consulting books on statistics and working out the best way to gauge the results whenever more agents were poured into a particular zone. He wanted numbers— numbers and evidence. It was an unusually wonkish approach for a seat-of-the-pants, frontier agency, and it was only one of the ways Williams was shaking things up.

By now, he had come to question one of the Border Patrol's most basic tenets: that arrests were good. Arrest rates for the Border Patrol were like vital signs. They justified budget requests, proved how hard the men and women in green were working. But Williams saw it differently. Arrests meant immigrants were getting into the country. A better approach, he reasoned, would be one in which the result of reinforcing a zone with more agents was to deter crossing attempts. In other words, the less action, the better. This notion dovetailed with the thinking contained in the new national Border Patrol strategy and would be at the heart of the Gatekeeper offensive, which still had plenty of doubters when Williams took over San Diego in late 1994.

It was a heady moment. Scores of new border agents flowed into San Diego, fresh from the agency's training academy in Glynco, Georgia, or on temporary loan from other border regions. The San Diego sector would see its contingent of agents more than double in size in just four years, from just under 1,000 in 1994 to 2,200 in 1998. As a further sign of the Clinton administration's determination to raise the profile of its border campaign, Alan D. Bersin, the top federal prosecutor for San Diego County, was named as Attorney General Janet Reno's point man for the boundary in October 1995—one year after the unveiling of Gatekeeper.

Bersin's role might have been special representative for Southwest border issues, but the press immediately applied a shorthand moniker: border czar.

If administration officials desired energy, political acumen and media savvy, they found it in the forty-eight-year-old Bersin, a hard-driving former defense lawyer and longtime Clinton friend. The two had met at Oxford University as Rhodes scholars during the 1960s and they kept up their friendship at Yale Law School. Part of Bersin's new assignment was to ride herd on the mishmash of federal agencies, from Customs and INS to the FBI and the Drug Enforcement Administration, that had responsibilities at the border. It was a tall order. The tangle of government jurisdictions, each with a separate chain of command and often fractured by geography, had over the years been beset by turf fights, inefficiency and a sense that the border was spiraling relentlessly into disorder. Bersin was to report straight to Reno while coordinating efforts to bring down drug trafficking and immigrant smuggling as well as improving the flow of legal cross-border traffic. He also was to represent the Justice Department in dealing with Mexico on ever-prickly border issues.

Bersin's new mandate was broad and largely symbolic, but his tenure as U.S. attorney since 1993 recommended his ability to handle the delicate mix of tasks. And he soon broke with a tradition of low-key predecessors in San Diego. He created task forces to combat drug smuggling and to investigate official corruption among U.S. border agencies. He was a master of public relations, cultivating relationships with key reporters and adept enough in Spanish to handle interviews with Mexican journalists. He became a frequent presence on Tijuana radio and television stations, and championed a vision of the local border as a shared region that he referred to as "San Tijuana."

As a prosecutor, Bersin naturally was tough on crime. But he took pains to distinguish between smugglers and criminals, on the one hand, and migratory job seekers, on the other. He said he had no interest in prosecuting the "economic migrants."

Along with Bersin's appointment, officials unveiled an immigration court at the Otay Mesa port of entry—the second crossing in San Diego—and introduced a high-tech fingerprinting system. That system, called IDENT, reads migrants' fingerprints electronically and stores them, along with a mug shot, in a computer database to help identify the person in case of subsequent arrest.

The border looked like a permanent construction zone. Crews and equipment on loan from the California National Guard were assigned to build fences as part of their exercises. The new barriers became such a prominent aspect of the border that a specialized vocabulary sprang up around them. The front line of defense was the landing-mat barrier built of corrugated steel panels, once used for making battlefield airstrips, donated by the military. The dark, rust-colored plates were welded into a nearly continuous line from the ocean to the foot of the mountains at Otay Mesa, fourteen miles to the east. The only gap was along a canyon too steep to traverse anyway.

Behind some sections of the landing mat went a bollard fence, a series of staggered, foot-thick concrete poles planted five inches apart—too close to each other for a person to squeeze through. A second variety of backup barrier was the so-called Sandia fence, made of shiny steel and dimpled like a cheese grater. It bent toward Mexico at the top to make climbing more difficult. The fence-building got a further push when a provision in the 1996 immigration-reform law required that the westernmost fourteen miles of border—the area fronting urban Tijuana—be protected by no fewer than three separate layers of fencing. (The second layer, including the portion proposed at Border Field State Park, remained uncompleted by 2003.)

The fence-building effort wasn't just limited to the cities, though. All along the southern California border, efforts were under way to plug spots where smugglers had found vulnerabilities. By the end of the decade, about sixty miles of such barriers would stand along southern California's border with Mexico, more than was fenced along the rest of the U.S.-Mexico boundary. The fences epitomized the government's new steadfastness in the face of illegal immigration, but they also served as a sort of baffle, diverting the flow of undocumented crossers into new corridors—and altering the border elsewhere as they did.

Chapter Three

THE END RUN

By early 1998, Operation Gatekeeper had been in place for more than three years; arrests in San Diego fell to modern lows from the astronomical rates at the beginning of the decade. It was clear then that the border story—at least the one that had spawned so much vituperation and political fervor—was turning. The chaotic scenes in San Diego described by Wambaugh seemed like so many war stories from a long-ago era.

Bersin and others dared speak publicly of having brought the rule of law to the San Diego border—Araceli Garcia and her fellow Border Patrol agents were doing their job. The Border Patrol's 1994 strategic blueprint, which called for focusing initially on the big urban crossings, was proving accurate in a number of regards. Massive enforcement had slowed unlawful entries in San Diego. Traffic fatalities were down, as was crime.

The plan had predicted, too, that smuggling patterns would shift away from those urban corridors and into "hostile terrain, less suited for crossing and more suited for enforcement." In other words, the migrants who still were undeterred from crossing would take routes where it was easier to catch them. The official planners got that part right. But what no one fully anticipated was the number of people who would flood these out-of-the-way zones, or for how long they would continue venturing into such "hostile terrain."

One of these places was Imperial County, a hundred miles east of San Diego. In early 1998 a news item described the discovery of 141 undocumented immigrants being sneaked inside the dump bodies of a trio of gravel-hauling trucks. There had been other, similar cases there in recent weeks: big-rigs with trailers packed with as many as 177 immigrants. These episodes suggested a new smuggling trend—one that could end in large-scale tragedy if a group of migrants were kept for too long or abandoned inside a trailer without fresh air, food or water. It had happened before. In 1987, eighteen undocumented immigrants died of heat and suffocation after being trapped in a rail boxcar in Sierra Blanca, Texas. (The case inspired a Mexican folk song called "El vagón de la muerte"—"The Boxcar of Death.")

The recent truck trend was just one facet of a new and abrupt increase in the number of migrants slipping across the border into Imperial County around the U.S. border city of Calexico. As the flow shifted to outflank the agents guarding San Diego, the new influx to Imperial County was a story in itself, hitting the farm communities like a force of nature.

It takes less than two hours to make the drive to Imperial County from San Diego along Interstate 8, the critical west-to-east artery for southernmost California. But it feels like a much greater distance. Climbing east into the mountains, you leave behind the high-rise office towers of San Diego's downtown and the surrounding bastions of a gleaming, high-tech economy. Ahead, on the other side of the mountains, lies a broad valley that represents California's agrarian past. Imperial County, home to 120,000 people, has changed dramatically since the era when boundary commissioner John Russell Bartlett journeyed over the same mountains and discovered a bone-dry valley that begged him to wonder how "any vegetable life can flourish amid such barrenness."

Indeed, the Imperial Valley is a study in stark contrasts. It remains the punishing desert at which Bartlett marveled. But drive on to its center and the unexpected sprouts from the parched expanse: a verdant heart of tremendously productive farmland. The scene is a quintessentially Californian, man-over-nature transformation, brought about by the construction of the All American Canal, which was completed in 1942. The concrete-lined waterway draws huge quantities of water from the Colorado River at the Arizona state line and then ferries it eighty-two miles west through desert sands to slake the thirst of Imperial County's $1 billion-a-year agricultural industry. "Food grows where water flows" says a highway sign on the way to the county seat of El Centro. And it's all grown here: alfalfa, asparagus, wheat, carrots, onions, cotton, beets. The names of the men who stubbornly willed farming communities from the area's harsh terrain are recalled in the names of towns like Heber and Holtville, and streets like Rockwood. While whites dominate the power structures of county government and farming, significant portions of the county, such as the border city of Calexico, are almost entirely Latino.

By April 1998, Calexico, a blue-collar town of 24,000, had become the scene of considerable turmoil thanks to spillover from the now-tightened border in San Diego. Lately, the midnight quiet had been splintered by Border Patrol helicopters spotlighting undocumented immigrants who were making a pedestrian highway of the irrigated rows below. The tiny downtown district was now the setting for a game of cat and mouse: would-be border crossers watched agents through the shabby border fence and dashed through gaps into neighborhoods on the U.S. side. The commotion was challenging the patience of residents here who generally were sympathetic to immigrants and who themselves could often trace roots to Mexico. During the month of March, arrests in Imperial County had soared to 30,111—way up from the same period a year earlier, and more than the annual total for 1994.

The Border Patrol answered the flood by shipping in dozens of reinforcements from San Diego, but it was clear smugglers now viewed this rural stretch of border as their best bet for getting through. "When the word gets out that the neighboring sector has fewer Border Patrol agents, they seem to take the path of least resistance," said the Border Patrol chief for the region, Thomas L. Wacker. "We seem to be that path, at least temporarily." Sitting in a Border Patrol impound lot were twelve semi trucks and three gravel-haulers, all of which had been seized recently by agents who discovered them carrying undocumented immigrants.

"Smugglers are our biggest nemesis," Wacker said, sitting at his desk in the Border Patrol's office in El Centro, up the road from Calexico.

"We've had a real time getting control. To what degree now we have control, I'm not really sure. What really worries us is that it gets hot here in the summer. We're very concerned about smugglers using trucks of that size in this heat. The probability of a catastrophe is pretty good if we don't break the backs of this kind of smuggling. For us, the semi is very new. We've gotten narcotics out of semis, but we've never had large numbers of people [in them]."

The dangers were already proving real. The migrants' steady trek eastward had begun to take its toll. In 1995 only one illegal immigrant had died in Imperial County due to heatstroke. That number had risen to seven in 1996 and to nineteen in 1997. Canal drownings claimed thirty-nine lives in those three years. The impending summer promised more trouble.

Agents here were also beginning to see the first signs of an established smuggling industry operating out of Mexicali. They'd started making busts at so-called drop houses—private homes or abandoned properties on the U.S. side serving as pickup spots for migrants who made it across the border. A few months earlier, agents had found eighty-eight people crammed into a house in nearby Brawley. It was a nice-looking house in an ordinary neighborhood, agents said, just across the street from a day-care center. Another house held ninety-two people, while agents found eighty-eight more migrants in three apartments of the same complex. Agent Salvador Wilson, head of a five-agent anti-smuggling team in the El Centro area, cited another sign of a growing professional smuggling trade: the prices were shooting up. By 1998, the fee for a guided trip across the line, which two years before had been $300 to $500, was now as much as $1,000.

Confronted by this mounting challenge, Border Patrol commanders were counting the days before they would get seventy-six new agents, soon to graduate from the patrol's academy, to beef up an overworked contingent of 379 agents. The agents guarded seventy-two miles of border and lately were making a thousand arrests a day, many of them in Calexico.

The effects of the increased migrant traffic were also apparent to people on the Mexican side of the border. One such person was Blanca Villaseñor, who ran a shelter for migrants in Mexicali that had become swamped with arrivals—those from the interior with plans to cross and others who had been caught by *la migra* on U.S. soil and expelled. She reported that about a thousand migrants were being deported to Mexicali daily, a number that jibed with Border Patrol figures. The migrants often were deported in the middle of the night and had no place to go since so many were hundreds of miles from their homes in the Mexican interior. So migrant shelters like Villaseñor's played an important role as lodging of last resort. They were often a good place to talk with migrants about their experiences.

The shelter—a no-frills building surrounding an open patio about a mile from the border fence—had become a temporary home to about thirty people. There were families, children and young men. Some were headed north. Others were returning south. Some hadn't figured out what to do next. Resignation collided with anticipation. Travel was described in terms of hopes more than actual plans. "Si Dios quiere," people would say. "God willing."

Among those housed there were Julio Callejas and his wife, Josefina Moyao, and their five-month-old baby, Julio César. They stood in the yard, hovering over the child, trying to decide whether to go back home to Guerrero, a state on Mexico's southwestern coast. Moyao had been deported from Stockton, a farming community in central California. Callejas crossed this stretch of border several months earlier as part of a group of twenty. He was on his way to Stockton, where the couple had lived for a year, when he got word of his wife's deportation and managed to track her down to the shelter here. The baby was born shortly after her deportation. The couple was now broke. Although Callejas had picked up some work in Mexicali during the past four months, he was far short of the $800 to $1,000 fee to hire a smuggler, known in Spanish as a *coyote,* to steer them across the border. They likely would return to their families in a tiny town in Guerrero, where Callejas figured he could work in construction, though for much less than he'd earn in the United States. Maybe they'd return north next year, he said. "We still want to go," his wife affirmed.

Also at the shelter but going in the opposite direction was a fourteen-year-old Honduran girl named Jenny Marilú Castellanos Zavala. She'd been there for a month, stalled on her way to Los Angeles. That's where her mother had lived, taking care of children, for eight years—more than half of Jenny's life. The girl said she could barely remember her mother, but had decided it was time to go join her. Equally determined was Wilfredo Cruz Hernández, a seventeen-year-old Mexican who was waiting for his two brothers in Michigan to send him cash to finish his journey north. He had arrived in Mexicali with 600 pesos, about $60. But he needed money to pay a guide for what he considered an essential service in such unfamiliar environs. "You don't know how to get past *la migra*. You don't know the roads," the boy said. He had slept on the street for eight days before finding the shelter. Wilfredo figured he'd be there for another two weeks. His sense of industry was paying off; already he had picked up work washing dishes at a Mexicali restaurant for the equivalent of $42 a week. If caught, Wilfredo vowed, "I'll try it again. I'll get another *coyote* and do it again. Until I make it."

It would take such willpower, and not a small amount of naïveté, to choose to slip across the border at Imperial County. True, the border agents were spread thin. But there were risks worse than getting caught by *la migra*. There were big empty distances to navigate. A person could make it past rattlesnakes and cactus and then end up in one of two ranges used by the military for bombing practice. Also perilous were the waters: the fast-moving All American Canal hugging the border on the U.S. side and the foul-smelling New River, which flows north from Mexicali into the United States. On the very day Wilfredo was describing his plans, four bodies were discovered, fully clothed, in separate sections of the canal and New River. Seventeen border crossers had drowned there so far in 1998.

Word of the latest deaths came after my return to the U.S. side in Calexico, where I had arranged to spend a work shift with Border Patrol agent Dan Murray, a freshly minted supervisor who had served in the agency for about ten years. Murray, a forty-two-year-old Wisconsin native, had been in Calexico for all his years of service. The Border Patrol, whose past heavy-handedness had made it the subject of civil rights complaints and of considerable hostility among the residents where it worked, had learned the hard way the value of good public relations. Agents now routinely took journalists along to view their work on the line. There were political motives for this openness. News reports about

the challenges of tending the border helped the agency win congres-
sional support for more funding. For the same reason, the military took
reporters up in fighter planes or out to sea on aircraft carriers. Riding
along here would provide a front-row seat to the nightly drama playing
out in places that remain far from the public view.

Darkness fell as Murray drove and narrated, waiting for the nighttime action to break out. He pointed out a newly constructed fence of
steel matting, similar to the one in San Diego, that had gone up on the
west edge of town. Nearby sat portable spotlights powered by genera-
tors. The same solid fence extended along the east side of Calexico, out
to where the town gave way to fields. In between, in the heart of the
city's downtown district, were only a beat-up chain-link fence and im-
provised sections of steel sheeting. The fence was a mess. There were
jagged holes and entire portions missing. Attempts to patch it were
quickly undone by smugglers and migrants, who reopened the gaps,
sometimes by the next morning. From homes in Calexico along the
street next to the fence, you could see right through to the border neighborhood in Mexicali. The Border Patrol had suggested erecting the solid
barrier downtown, too, but city leaders in Calexico balked. Critics said
such a fence would block the view from downtown into Mexicali and, in
the process, deal a symbolic blow to the sense of neighborliness shared
by the two communities. A wall was not the way they wished to relate to
their important neighbor to the south, not yet anyway.

Those close ties, of course, brought bad as well as good. Like other
border towns, Calexico had a long acquaintance with crime—smuggling,
petty theft, fugitives seeking a foreign haven and troublemakers of all
kinds. The Imperial Valley was well known as a corridor for moving
drugs north, and one of Bersin's early moves was to assign a task force
to target trafficking in the wide-open country there. Murray told us that
border agents working downtown also used to see young thieves from
Mexicali slip through the fence and "go back with a VCR." The fence
jumpers now were different, he said; they were long-haul travelers.
"Now they're just trying to get north."

On the outskirts of town, Murray pointed out an idle ranch, fallen
into disrepair, where thickets of oleander frequently used to provide a
hiding place for migrants who had just hopped over the border. The

bushes had been cleared now to eliminate the cover. It was nearly midnight when the evening tranquility began to give way. Another agent pulled alongside Murray's truck and the two talked through the open windows. "We're already taking a pretty good spanking," the second agent told Murray. One of the portable spotlights was out; the agent suspected it might have been sabotaged.

The radio soon came alive with what turned out to be almost nonstop reports of illegal crossings. In the radio chatter, the border crossers were referred to as "bodies," as in "I've got four bodies moving north." The area outside of town was a vast web of informal dirt roads and irrigation ditches, and agents in pursuit gave their locations in relation to landmarks such as the old golf course or such-and-such channel.

Just after midnight, one such report sent Murray speeding along Highway 98 to a field where a Border Patrol agent in a helicopter had spotted more "bodies." Two other agents pulled up to the field, too, and plunged into the knee-high alfalfa as the helicopter aimed a spotlight from above, lending a ghostly glow. In moments, sprouting with the suddenness of cartoon plants, seven men popped up from the rows. They didn't try to run. Instead, they trudged toward the agents and handed themselves over with a resigned shrug. (Agents cautioned that you never knew who might turn violent, but in witnessing the arrests of scores of migrants during my four-year border tenure, not once did anyone run away or put up even minimal resistance. More often, they joked about their unhappy luck. Nor did I see any agents act abusively toward an undocumented immigrant, but then only a fool would do so in front of a reporter.)

The men were loaded into a Border Patrol van that would transport them for booking at the Calexico station. One of the migrants, who gave his name only as Alejandro, said he was headed for Los Angeles. He'd been on the road from Hidalgo, in central Mexico, for fifteen days, he said. Then he joined the others in the van.

A similar group of ten people was soon spotted, again by helicopter, in a field of wheat that fringed a settlement of tract homes on the edge of town. It was a disturbing clash of images—the enclave of suburban order and the noisy chase scenes taking place just outside its stucco walls. Murray drove to where yet another agent was parked, manning a night-vision scope. That agent tracked a group of six people as they walked along a field. The people showed up as black figures on the black-and-white viewing screen. In this way, an agent was able to scan a broad area up to a mile away, then direct colleagues to the migrants.

Soon after, we were speeding down a dirt road near the Alamo River, a rather grand name for what was, in essence, an overgrown drainage ditch. Agents had followed a group of people into the thick rushes. There, several men lay clustered in the underbrush, sweaty and smeared with fetid mud. An agent wearing a radio headset barked instructions as a second agent plunged deeper, turning up more migrants. There were twenty-one altogether. Several coughed from the dust that had been kicked up. Most were covered in brambles and caked in mud. They toted small knapsacks back to the roadside and waited for the agents to take them away.

As they sat on the ground, one of the men said the group had set out from Mexicali at about 6 p.m., some seven hours earlier. It was the fourth time in two months he had been caught trying to cross from Mexicali. "Bad luck," he said. He identified himself as José Salvador Rocha Ramírez. He was thirty-seven, but looked a decade older. He wore a white Reebok cap, muddy jeans, a beige windbreaker and leather work boots.

Rocha said he had left a wife and six children back in the central state of Guanajuato, one of the major "sending states" that provide the bulk of Mexican migrants. Throughout much of the twentieth century, a third or more of Mexican migrants came from three such states, including Guanajuato, north of Mexico City. The other two were Jalisco and Michoacán, along Mexico's western flank. Once made up primarily of rural peasants, the immigrant flow now carried more city dwellers—a reflection, scholars asserted, of Mexico's growing urbanization and the disruptions caused by fast economic changes.

After a three-day bus trip, Rocha shared a hotel room with nine others in Mexicali before making the crossing. They were aiming to make it to the highway. Rocha was headed for Los Angeles, where his brother had been working as a truck driver for fifteen years. His skin was the dark-caramel color of someone who labors outdoors. He worked in the fields back home, making twenty pesos, about two dollars, a day. A car wreck had left him with a troublesome rib that made such work painful. For Rocha, the United States represented a fresh opportunity.

Booking the migrants took little time. They were led single file into the Border Patrol station processing area, where agents behind a counter entered the arrestees' biographical data into the computers. The immigrants were asked their names, hometowns, birth dates and parents' names. Agents assumed that many of the answers would be made up because smugglers coached the migrants to give fake names to avoid more serious charges if they were arrested again. But unless a person goes through formal deportation proceedings, he can be caught repeatedly and simply handed back over the border without having to worry about federal prosecution.

That is where the new IDENT system comes in. The arrestee places his finger on an electronic pad, which reads the fingerprint and enters it into the INS computer system. The idea is to use the fingerprint to identify the person as a repeat crosser even if he gives a false name. The computerized file also includes a photograph. Migrants are asked to sign a form saying that they agree to be kicked out of the country without a hearing. This process is called "voluntary removal" and is what happens in almost every one of the tens of thousands of immigrant arrests made at the border each month. Agents referred to it shorthand, saying that a particular immigrant was "VR'ed."

That night, each migrant was handed a packet of cheese crackers and a plastic bottle of juice, then led into one of several large cells. The cells held up to fifty people each for several hours until the migrants could be bused back to the border. In Cell 11, about forty men lay about on the floor, some sleeping, others staring off.

Every several hours agents loaded a new bus with immigrants to be removed. They would be driven the few miles to the border and ushered back to Mexico through a gate next to the formal port of entry. A Mexican immigration official took down their names as they passed. It was nearing 4 a.m. when we stopped by the gate to watch a group of forty-five men step off the Border Patrol bus and shuffle back into Mexico after their abbreviated journey to the United States. In this absurd revolving-door game, agents could expect that many, if not most, of these migrants would try again the next day. "I'll be back!" one of the men announced defiantly.

Then, turning to me, he seemed to come up with a better idea. "Take me to Los Angeles," he said.

The burst of illegal entries had put Calexico in an awkward position. Longtime merchants were watching in horror as migrants came racing into their downtown shops to escape Border Patrol agents. Alma Ellis, whose family had run a clothing store near the fence on 1st Street for decades, described the disorder that sometimes spilled right into the shop. Ellis was born and raised in Calexico. Her father began selling clothes by horse and buggy before World War I. He later established a permanent store and called it La Tienda del Pueblo—The People's Store. The shop, now called Sam Ellis Store, has been on its current site for more than fifty years. Never had the family seen anything like what was playing out recently. "You stand right over here and you can watch them come over the fence and then between the Border Patrol agents there," Alma said. "It's a game of cat and mouse. They come in here and hide right under the racks." One time a man came in wearing two full sets of clothes, one over the other; he ran into the store, peeled off the outside layer and strolled out of the store with a new appearance, she said.

Suddenly the Border Patrol was enjoying newfound popularity. Some locals who had formerly viewed the agency as aloof and arrogant now counted themselves among its supporters. Residents kept the agency's phone number close at hand or had even memorized it. Hildy Carrillo-Rivera, the outspoken editor of Calexico's weekly newspaper, had come full circle from earlier days when she would hardly speak to her brother, a border agent in Texas. In an editorial, she once chastised agents for being too aggressive in pursuing immigrants. But then she accompanied a patrol one night. After seeing groups of forty and fifty would-be crossers dodging Border Patrol officers, she said, "I was converted." For their part, Border Patrol officials were trying the small-town approach, holding public meetings to explain their ideas and listen to community opinion. Over burritos at one chamber of commerce lunch, for example, they explained that they were now leaning toward an alternative fence design for downtown to preserve the open view to Mexico.

Still, as the objections to the border wall showed, many people were uneasy over the new militancy along the border. Laura Rodriguez, for one, said she was sick of the Border Patrol trucks that raced up and down her residential street, treating it like "a racetrack." She and her husband had moved in five years before, during a vastly different time. Now she was weary of all the lights and the constant thumping of helicopters at all hours above the field next to her house. "If we had known it would be like this, we wouldn't have bought a house here," Rodriguez said. Just then a border agent drove past and Rodriguez, clutching a broom, scowled. "I don't like them," she said.

It is a complicated place. Sitting smack on the international line, Calexico seems more an appendage of Mexicali than a foreign counterpart. It is a classic border town in the way San Diego is not, bound snugly to Mexicali by family ties, business and culture. Families straddle the border and many residents who live on one side trace roots to the other. In fact, Mexicali's soon-to-be-elected mayor, car dealer Eugenio Elorduy Walther, was born in Calexico. His U.S. ties and flawless English also would make him a favorite among businesspeople north of the border when he later was elected governor of Baja California.

Calexico merchants were quick to point out that commerce would wither away if not for Mexicali, whose 600,000 inhabitants and scores of *maquiladora* assembly plants made it the commercial powerhouse of the two. Throughout Calexico's weather-worn little downtown, the clothing stores, currency exchanges and pawnshops advertised in Spanish. Ranchera music blared from an electronics store. You could buy gas with pesos and order a *torta* at the donut shop. Shoppers from Mexicali came by the thousands each day, flashing their border-crossing permits and streaming on foot through the port of entry. Imperial County's big farms were dependent, too. You could measure the significance of Mexican labor by heading downtown before dawn any morning. Hundreds of farm workers from Mexicali with papers to work on the U.S. side poured across onto Calexico's street corners, waiting for rides to the fields. In the early-morning darkness, the downtown sidewalks bustled with the energy of the middle of a business day.

The completeness with which Calexico weaved two cultures was also evident in the schools. At Calexico High School the schoolyard chatter about the prom or the Bulldogs baseball team was a borderland fusion of Spanish and English. Teachers, many of them products of Calexico public schools, faced the usual challenges of rural poverty while also overcoming language deficiencies among the students, 98 percent of whom were Latino. Nearly a fourth of the district's students were the sons and daughters of migrant farm workers. The average Calexico family made less than $12,000 a year. Unemployment generally ran above 25 percent. Yet small-town pluck and the devotion of teachers like Juan Orduña, a latter-day Jaime Escalante figure who routinely offered extra math tutoring on weekends, had helped Calexico establish an enviable record of keeping kids in school and sending them on to more schooling. Sit in on an AP English class and you'll hear a discussion about Blake that is sprinkled with *español*.

The immigrant roots of many of Calexico's residents made them, as a rule, fairly sympathetic toward the aspirations of the new ranks of illegal border crossers. That compassion tempered their exasperation, but it did not extinguish it. Ellis, the department store owner, put it this way: "I feel sorry for them in a way. I say all they're trying to do is find a better place to live and raise a family. But I don't know why it has to be us."

When tragedy came to Imperial County in mid-August, it did not arrive in the trailer of a big-rig truck or railcar, but in the sparse, wide-open desert nearly thirty miles north of Calexico and the border itself. The initial report was sketchy: at least half a dozen immigrants had been found dead at the eastern edge of the Anza Borrego State Park, a huge arid preserve with stunningly hot weather that time of year.

The migrants—five men, a woman and a teenaged boy—apparently had been left behind in the 115-degree heat by their smugglers not far from a huge and polluted agricultural drainage lake called Salton Sea. They were severely decomposed and had likely been dead a week or ten days. One man, from the Mexican state of Michoacán, had a voter's identification card; the others would have to be identified by dental records, if they had any.

The migrants had sought refuge under a grove of salt cedar trees and, in their desperation to cool off, had peeled off most of their clothing. One of the men had stripped down to his boxer shorts. The victims had no water containers or luggage and had worn jeans, short-sleeve shirts, sneakers and cowboy boots—hardly the gear required for a desert trek. Border Patrol officials surmised they had been taken that far by vehicle and told by their smugglers to wait. The area made for a handy smuggling route because it skirted a Border Patrol checkpoint on rural Highway 86 a few miles to the east. This was the largest group to die along the Southwest border in recent years, an INS spokesman reported. "One or two people may die, but not a whole group," the official said. As heat-death cases went, this incident was also unusual for occurring in the open desert, rather than inside an enclosure, such as a trailer.

Among the dead was Julio Gallegos, twenty-three, who had crossed illegally before and, at the time of his death, had a wife waiting for him in Los Angeles, where the two had met and wed. They had not gotten around to getting his documents in order, so when he returned from a visit to Mexico to see his ailing father, Gallegos hired a smuggler to sneak him back to Los Angeles, where he lived in a Mexican-American neighborhood called Boyle Heights and worked packing frozen Chinese food. He was traveling with a seventeen-year-old niece and a nephew. Only the girl's body was found immediately. It was thought that the group might have started with as many as twenty-three people. A body discovered a day earlier was believed to have been someone from the group, and officials would later make the same conclusion about a person found dead the following week. At the time of Gallegos's death, his wife was pregnant with their second child. The dead also included Fernando Salguero Lachino, a forty-eight-year-old farm worker from Michoacán. He left behind six children, none older than twelve.

The following day, the Imperial County coroner's office said the victims might have been dead as long as five weeks. The INS announced a $5,000 reward for help in apprehending the smugglers believed to have left the group in the desert. It was the first time the government had offered an incentive in a smuggling case, a sign of growing concern about fatalities. Johnny Williams, by now the INS regional director, presided at a press conference announcing the reward. He characterized the offer as a "starting point" meant to "step up the heat" on the suspected smugglers. He said investigators already were working decent leads based on evidence they found on the bodies. Williams had met with the Mexican consul a day earlier and was promised the full cooperation of Mexico's government in the probe.

Williams was no stranger to the desert, of course. His ascension through the Border Patrol had taken him to Yuma and through Imperial County. Anyone who would steer the unsuspecting migrants—whom Williams pronounced "innocents"—into such terrain represented the height of callousness, he said. "It's a terrible death, an excruciating death, and one nobody should have to endure."

The fatalities also signaled a new and macabre seasonal cycle along the border. It was Imperial County's worst year so far for migrant deaths, with ninety known fatalities (though there would be more three years later, in 2001). Summers were turning deadly. An unintended consequence of Operation Gatekeeper had been to make a killing ground of the desert here. During winter it would be the mountains of San Diego.

Chapter Four

"WE WERE NOT PREPARED"

On both sides of the mountain pass the early-spring storm took the form of a dull, leaden drizzle. It was early evening in April 1999 as I returned to San Diego after a day of reporting in Imperial County. I was traveling on Interstate 8, a dramatic westbound drive, climbing abruptly from the desert flats across a rugged range of boulders and chaparral before tumbling again, past horse ranches and meadows into a suburban landscape of car dealerships and Home Depot stores leading to San Diego. The drizzle thickened into a light snow on the upward climb, then worsened into a driving blur atop the Tecate Divide, at just over four thousand feet. Visibility was almost zero. The cars, which normally zoomed along at 75 miles per hour on this stretch, slowed to a parking-lot crawl. Traffic narrowed to a single lane. With eyes glued on the taillights of the car just ahead, we all eased our way down, like hikers grasping hands along a tricky trail.

Safe in the heated comfort of our vehicles, we were unaware of the sorry drama unfolding in the darkened canyons just south of the highway. In a wildland area covering twenty miles down to the Mexican border, the drenching snow and frigid winds had suddenly overtaken more than three dozen immigrants who were dressed only in light jackets and sneakers and were left defenseless. By morning, eight were dead—the worst winter disaster on this part of the border in anyone's memory. Two more migrants who had barely set out were found dead in the hill country on the Mexican side, about thirty miles east of Tecate, a quaint town best known for its eponymous beer.

The migrants had crossed in separate groups two days earlier through the steep and rocky ravines that furrow the borderland as it climbs into the mountainous Cleveland National Forest on the U.S. side. Traversing the twenty miles from the border to the freeway is especially challenging. This is the topography of cowboy movies. Canyon walls are sheer in places and car-sized boulders stand out from hillsides like jewels on a crown. The mountains inside the national forest, such as Mount Laguna, reach above seven thousand feet and are favorite spots for hikers and weekend car campers from San Diego. The forest vegetation—chaparral, sage and live oak, among other plants and trees—are thick and hard to penetrate. Summer heat can be withering and winter frost can drop without warning. The whole mix adds up to a journey that is, according to one government report, "slow, difficult and dangerous." It might have taken immigrants in the early 1990s just a few hours to skirt the Border Patrol by foot near the San Ysidro border crossing. But it could take two or three days to trudge through what is known as "East County," where the terrain is so rugged that fire commanders wouldn't send firefighters into it.

In spite of these obstacles, the backcountry, as locals describe it, had become a favorite place for smuggling people across the border since Operation Gatekeeper tightened the vise around San Ysidro and Imperial Beach. The increased traffic manifested itself in ugly ways in the 427,000-acre national forest, where by 1995 rangers were coping with piles of discarded trash in the woods and outbreaks of wildfires sparked from the warming fires of hiking border crossers. San Diego County officials soon set up a special border agency fire council made up of nineteen separate local, state and federal agencies to deal with the fire dangers. They set up emergency-response protocols and mapped trouble areas.

Natural perils began to take their toll, too, as rangers and border agents now found themselves racing to rescue groups of migrants with increasing regularity. Sometimes it would be a case of a leg broken during a fall from the rocks. Other times it would be heat exhaustion; even Border Patrol agents had succumbed to the heat in the area. Often, it was the cold.

Though the conditions could be difficult, deaths due to environmen-

tal factors were virtually unheard of before 1995, when growing numbers of migrants began entering places like Tecate and Jacumba and
then hiking north. In 1994 the Mexican consulate in San Diego counted
just one exposure death in San Diego County. That figure climbed to
four the following year and then jumped to twenty-seven in 1996. Exposure deaths involving migrants hit twenty-nine in 1997 and then fell
slightly to twenty-seven fatalities in 1998. Nelson Dean, a longtime
ranger and supervisor in the Descanso district, which became the busiest
crossing route, later recounted that the migrant deaths were "the single
most dramatic issue I've had to deal with." In most of those years the
majority of the deaths occurred in the national forest. Most were due to
cold. The fire council took action, distributing drinking water in some of
the most dangerous spots and producing a video in Spanish to tell television viewers about the physical dangers. Rangers and border agents
also began stepped-up patrols on commonly used back roads when
storms were predicted. The measures helped, and deaths on national
forest grounds accounted for fewer than half of the exposure deaths in
San Diego in 1998.

The problem was not merely the extremes of below-zero. Rather, it
was the migrants' lengthy exposure to temperatures just low enough to
render useless the light clothing that had been perfectly suitable in
their home regions. Few headed into the hills expecting a hike of several days; often they were told by their guides that it would be only a
short walk before they would be picked up. "They may be hoofing it out
there in the hills for two or three days, and then they get caught in these
storm events," Dean explained. "They get wet in the lower elevations
and then climb up and get into the colder and snowy conditions. Then
they just get into trouble. . . . It doesn't take much."

Hypothermia doesn't fell its victims instantly. The combination of
wet clothing and chill air lowers the body's temperature through a process known as convection, as happens when a coffee drinker blows
across the top of a steaming mug. The colder the air, or the stronger the
wind, the greater the risk of a loss in temperature from its normal level
of 98.6 degrees. While exercise helps keep the inner body warm, sustained exertion, through hiking or long-distance running, for example,
can siphon off body heat. The insulating value of most clothing drops
sixfold once wet. Experiments have found that in order to counter the

effects of wet clothes, a person has to expend as much oxygen as if running a ten-minute mile. As a person's temperature begins to drop, the body fights back by cranking up its metabolic fires within: it shivers involuntarily. Shivering creates body heat, as much as five times the amount produced by a person at rest.

As the body's temperature falls below 95 degrees, the shivering campaign begins to fail. Soon the person starts getting tired, losing dexterity. Clumsy hands may make it awkward even to unzip a pack or tie a shoe. Between 95 and 90 degrees the shaking becomes violent, making it difficult to speak clearly or to walk without stumbling. Below that level, hypothermia becomes severe. As the body temperature drops below 88 degrees, the shivering gives way to stiff muscles and numbness. Thinking is confused; the person grows careless.

At below 86 degrees the pulse and breathing slow and a kind of stupor sets in. Muscles stiffen. The pulse and heartbeat become erratic. By 82 degrees, the heart is susceptible to fibrillation, the chaotic contractions that often are what cause death in cases of hypothermia. If the body temperature descends below 78.8, it's rare for anyone to remain conscious. There is almost no chance of survival once the body's temperature falls below 75 degrees.

For would-be rescuers along the border, preventing the loss of life is made more difficult by the simple fact that people who have sneaked across the border illegally don't want to be spotted. That means they often are reluctant to summon help even when they are close enough to civilization to be able to do so. Indeed, Dean's rangers found people who "literally died along highways that are well traveled." And in winter, chances of being rescued—or discovered—plunge with the mercury because there are fewer people available to help. Temperatures sank into the twenties during the unusual 1999 storm—a freak event that dropped a foot of snow at elevations as low as two thousand feet. Although the natural perils were ever present here, it would have been difficult to imagine such a severe storm occurring in April.

It was about 1:30 a.m. when seven of the shivering migrants managed to slog their way to an emergency call box on the freeway. Exhausted and soaked to the bone, they reported to authorities that others were behind them in the wild, shrubby valleys to the south—and in even worse condition. The report, coming in the midst of the sudden cold and precipitation, quickly triggered a middle-of-the-night search-and-rescue operation by twenty-eight Border Patrol agents, members of a specially trained unit called Border Search, Trauma and Rescue, or BORSTAR. By 3:30 a.m., five more trekkers were located alive in canyons south of the freeway. They reported still others missing. An hour later, a spotter aboard a U.S. Coast Guard helicopter that had joined the search saw another person and airlifted the victim out. At 8:30 a.m., Coast Guard searchers found twelve more people farther south.

By mid-morning, the rescue effort had grown to include searchers from the San Diego Sheriff's Department, the U.S. Forest Service and California Highway Patrol, as well as civilian mountaineers. In foot-deep snow, the searchers, using dogs, began locating migrants in three rugged arroyos in the national forest, more than twelve miles north of the border. The migrants reported having been lost for more than two days, without food and with only stream water to drink. Some migrants said they had been abandoned by the *coyotes* they had hired to sneak them across the border.

By noon, the rescue teams had ushered the majority of the migrants, more than thirty, to safety. Most were men, but there were some women, and two sisters aged five and seven. They somehow had survived night-time temperatures in the twenties, wearing only sodden T-shirts and flimsy sneakers. The operation unfolded from a parking lot near the alpine town of Descanso that had been converted into a command center for the searchers and a station for transferring survivors. Six helicopters churned the frigid air as rescuers scanned the snow for signs of people and then flew them back to the command post. Ambulances whisked the victims, wrapped in dry blankets, to hospitals at the base of the mountains. One twenty-nine-year-old man who was airlifted to the command post appeared to be barely conscious as he was given first aid and placed in an ambulance. He was swaddled in a wool blanket. Left behind were his soaked clothing and the trash bag that had been his only added protection through the harrowing night.

At Sharp Grossmont Hospital in the San Diego suburb of La Mesa, one of the survivors, Pablo Huerta, arrived with a body temperature of 90 degrees. In an interview in his hospital room, he recounted to a *Los Angeles Times* reporter that none of the border crossers had expected to face such conditions when they set out from near Tecate. "We were not prepared," Huerta, forty-four, said tearfully from his bed. "We were not expecting to encounter snow and ice." He said that he was betrayed not only by the elements, but also by the smuggler who had abandoned him and his twenty-five-year-old son, Antonio, during the most arduous part of their journey.

Huerta, a father of fourteen, said the pair paid a total of $1,800 to a man who was supposed to shepherd them all the way to a farm somewhere north of Los Angeles. "Instead, the man just took us to the border, took our money and then pointed north and said, 'You go in that direction,'" Huerta recalled, looking dazed. Huerta and his son wandered in the mountains and soon came upon a separate group of immigrants who said that they, too, had been abandoned by their smugglers. They banded together. "We knew that we wanted to go north, everybody was going north," Huerta said. "But none of us knew how to get there."

The situation grew bleaker as rain and then snow began to fall. Huerta wore only jeans, a sweatshirt and tennis shoes. Antonio had only a light jacket for extra protection. Both were rescued: the younger Huerta had been taken to another hospital. But the father still knew nothing of the son's fate. "Do you know where my son is?" he asked, weeping softly. "Do you know how my son is?"

Back at the canyons, searchers trudging in the slush had rescued more than thirty-five migrants. Some were alone, others huddled in groups of up to a dozen. They were clustered in three areas—some about one and a half miles south of the intersection of Interstate 8 and California 79, in an area known as Nelson Canyon; others about seven miles east of there, near a mountain road called Sunrise Highway; and the rest near the rural town of Campo. The dead, all victims of exposure, were found in two areas of Nelson Canyon and near Sunrise Highway. They ranged in age from around fifteen to thirty-one. Border agents elsewhere in the region began scouring their zones, too, in case there were other stricken groups.

. . .

News of the disaster sent telephones ringing in the offices of the California Rural Legal Assistance Foundation, sixty miles away in the coastal city of Oceanside. The branch of the statewide legal-aid group had long been known as an advocate for the Mexican migrant workers cultivating the sprawling fields of tomatoes and strawberries in northern San Diego County. Among its efforts had been to denounce abuses of the civil rights of the migrant workers, a crusade that put it and a handful of other border activist groups into occasional conflict with the Border Patrol and INS over alleged beatings and other transgressions by agents. But change was now in the air; just as the U.S. border crackdown was altering life along the border, it also began to shift the battle lines between activists and federal enforcement agencies.

Activists had previously focused on specific allegations of excessive force and questionable shootings by individual border agents, but now they began taking aim at the enforcement policy itself. This strategy was advanced most persistently by Claudia Smith, a Guatemalan-born lawyer and the foundation's point person on border matters. The urbane, fifty-one-year-old Smith had never set out to be a watchdog of the Border Patrol, nor of border-control policies. She was a labor lawyer— a banner-waving, button-wearing child of 1960s street activism and a *veterana* of the long-running battle on behalf of farm workers in California. She had grown up in a well-to-do family in Guatemala City; her businessman father did well enough to send his kids to the American school in Guatemala City and then to the United States for college.

Smith was about to graduate from George Washington University in Washington, D.C., when the persuasive power of a speech by Cesar Chavez at the National Cathedral about the nationwide grape boycott changed her life. Instead of going to graduate school, she signed up as a VISTA volunteer and traveled west to California, working with teenagers in San Ysidro. She then enrolled in law school at the University of San Diego. She joined California Rural Legal Assistance in the 1970s while a law student, and after earning her degree and signing up with CRLA as a lawyer, she accepted a post in Delano.

Smith soon was immersed in the rough-and-tumble of organizing laborers in the state's farming centers, like Delano and Salinas. She set up the CRLA's office in San Diego in the late 1980s as tensions stirred the agricultural belt in the northern half of the county. Many once-undocumented workers now held papers making them legal immigrants, thanks to the 1986 amnesty. Emboldened, they emerged from their encampments and were unafraid to live and seek work where they chose. That didn't sit well with a lot of residents in North County; Smith soon found herself filing lawsuits over housing issues and municipal attempts to stop curbside hiring, in addition to the usual dustups with the growers who hired workers but didn't always pay up.

There seemed no end to the legal struggles cropping up around migrant laborers. Many were indigenous Zapotecs and Mixtecs from southern Mexico who had made their way to San Diego despite the fact that they knew little English and often didn't even speak Spanish. Smith led a project to organize the indigenous workers. She relied on Indian translators since English and Spanish were useless in the fields. Smith's little downtown office near the beach in Oceanside became a do-it-all service center for migrants. She'd be filing a brief in federal court one minute, teaching a client how to dial a telephone number the next. She lost count of how many people she taught to sign their own name.

Some of her work necessarily involved immigration. There were cases in which migrants had been caught in Border Patrol neighborhood sweeps or wanted to report an agent's misconduct. So, like everyone else, she had paid attention to news reports in 1994 of an emerging crackdown along the border. What worried her was the possibility of abuses against migrants now that agents would be arresting and jailing more people. She decided to monitor the program closely. The very week the strategy was put in place in October, Smith dashed to the Mexican side of the border at Tijuana, stopping migrants as they were returned by U.S. agents and interviewing them about the conditions in which they had been held on the U.S. side.

During the next several years she would do the same at other border crossings, waiting around with her clipboard, sometimes all night, for the next batch of dejected immigrants to be expelled. Based on her surveys, Smith fired off letter after letter to immigration authorities, complaining about accounts of overcrowded and frigid holding cells, about the way Border Patrol agents crammed migrants into their trucks for transfer to the station house and about the fact that agents didn't routinely carry water. The letters, bearing copious footnotes that would become her trademark, were the chief weapons in her skirmishes with immigration officials on behalf of migrants in custody. While other activists summoned the TV cameras for their diatribes, Smith waged a lawyerly campaign. She wrangled assurances from officials that they would improve detention conditions and carry water. Her file cabinets brimmed with the spent casings of her war with the INS—copies of the reams of letters she had launched and responding salvos from immigration officials in Washington and San Diego. (Years later Smith still held on to one broadside against her, sent anonymously, that satirized to stinging perfection her scholarly writing style and fondness for footnotes.)

Smith's focus on detention conditions gave way eventually to what she saw as a far more serious problem. The shifting tide of migrants toward the countryside looked to her more and more like a direct consequence of Gatekeeper. She'd been seeing the reports and interviewing migrants as they were expelled back into Mexico in distant spots like Tecate and Mexicali. The faces grew more despondent, she noticed, perhaps because the stakes had grown higher. It was harder to talk to them—the *coyotes* always wanted to hurry them away. Her turning point came in 1997. Two deaths—of a woman who perished in the Tecate Mountains and a fourteen-year-old boy who succumbed in Imperial County near the Arizona line—tripped in her a sense of moral wrong. She interviewed the deceased woman's husband in Tijuana and came away haunted.

As the death toll mounted, Smith's self-appointed mission shifted. In prior years she had criticized the INS for not feeding detainees or keeping them in unheated cells, but she had never questioned the government's right to arrest them if that's how they saw fit to enforce the border. Now she saw the dangerous border conditions as an entirely predictable result of the border policy itself. It was on Gatekeeper that Smith now trained her considerable capacity for the uphill fight. Smith's argument, outlined in statements to the news media, in her meticulously footnoted letters to authorities and in conversations with anyone who would listen, was that the design of Operation Gatekeeper itself represented a violation of the human rights of illegal border crossers. Instead of being kicked or beaten, she argued, the migrants now faced a more grave threat—death—because the U.S. government had crafted a strategy that diverted them from San Diego into dangerous, out-of-the-way routes through the mountains and deserts. Smith became the first border activist in the United States to push such an argument with vigor, but she would be joined by others.

Roberto Martinez, a longtime Chicano activist in San Diego, was one of the first. For nearly three decades, Martinez had jousted with the Border Patrol over improper detentions and use of excessive force. He had come to the same conclusion as Smith—that the most compelling civil rights issue on the border was no longer whether a particular agent had overstepped his authority, but whether the nation's entire border policy was wrong.

A mild-mannered former engineer, Martinez had helped to create a community of human rights advocates along the border when he began defending Latinos in San Diego during the 1970s. As head of the U.S.-Mexico border project for the Quakers, Martinez seemed to have spent a lifetime marching, handing out leaflets, calling press conferences and issuing denunciations of the Border Patrol. Working out of a shopworn office on the ragged fringes of San Diego's renovated downtown quarter, Martinez had made himself into a professional burr under the Border Patrol's saddle. He spoke softly. With his Hush Puppies and a somber expression that always seemed to be leaning toward worry, Martinez looked like someone more at home with a slide rule than a bullhorn. But when it came to the rights of migrants in San Diego, he was indefatigable. Veteran border agents turned up their lips in disgust when his name was mentioned. They said his allegations of abuse had been so numerous, and often based on evidence so thin, that he could no longer be taken seriously. They believed he was too quick to trust the allegations made by migrants—that he failed to see that even a false claim might allow an undocumented immigrant to remain in the country while it was being investigated. Some agents suspected Martinez was on the payroll of the Mexican government. The agents' union in San Diego once even tried to dig up evidence to prove this claim, but couldn't come up with anything.

Meanwhile, Martinez doggedly kept on. He issued an annual report on rights abuses. In between, he'd call reporters from both sides of the border to his cramped offices to detail his latest allegation of injustice at the hands of the Border Patrol. The reporters wrote stories when there was enough information that could be verified. Often they left with little to use. There were times, though, when Martinez was vindicated. Regardless, for him, there was always a new incident, another press conference.

A small movement targeting the border policy was also taking shape in Tijuana, where church activists pointed blame at the U.S. government and, with equal energy, at Mexican officials who they said were responsible for the conditions at home that drove so many peasants and city dwellers to abandon their own country. Just a few months before the winter tragedy, Smith and the Tijuana activists had gathered on the Mexican side of the border fence to commemorate Day of the Dead, the autumn holiday when Mexican families honor their deceased loved ones by visiting gravesites and making altars. Along the graffiti-spattered border fence running in front of Tijuana's busy airport, the activists planted a mile-long row of 340 white crosses. Most bore the names, ages and home states of illegal immigrants who had died since 1994. In cases where no name was known, the wooden crosses were marked simply *No identificado,* "Unidentified." Rafael Romo, Tijuana's Roman Catholic bishop, blessed both the crosses and an altar heaped with sweet bread and candles, flowers and fruit to honor deceased migrants, who represented nearly every one of Mexico's thirty-one states. Said Lourdes Arias, who worked at a migrant aid center in Tijuana, "We want them to know that we haven't forgotten them, that they go on living."

A few days later the Mexican Senate passed a resolution zeroing in on Gatekeeper and the American government: "The anti-immigrant strategy implemented by the U.S. government to seal its border becomes more aggressive every day, raising the cost in human lives of those who attempt to obtain better living conditions," the resolution stated. It noted that "migrants must make their way through heavy vegetation, deep and rocky canyons, and high mountains that make the crossing difficult, slow, and dangerous. Add to this the lack of food and water and the bad climate . . . and the high number of deaths that the undocumented suffer is explainable."

Integral to the activists' emerging cause was a kind of grim score-keeping. As the INS trumpeted the success of its San Diego project in terms of fewer apprehensions and reduced crime rates, the foes pulled out their own statistical cudgel: body counts. Smith regularly sent out updates tallying deaths along the California border with Mexico. She compiled her figures mainly from the Mexican consulate in San Diego, then organized them into detailed charts showing causes of death, locations of the incidents and even the home states of the deceased, when they could be ascertained. The activists posted two large banners—along a busy truck route in Tijuana and on Interstate 5 south of downtown San Diego—decrying the deaths and bearing the newest death count, which was updated weekly.

The Border Patrol had not tracked fatalities in any systematic way, but as migrant deaths became a source of increasing public concern, the agency started keeping its own count in 1998. Smith used Mexican government figures, which tended to be higher because they included the deaths of migrants who perished before getting across the border. The Border Patrol counted only those who died on U.S. soil. The agency gathered annual totals according to the U.S. government's fiscal year, which runs from October 1 to September 30. The activists counted by calendar year. Trading mathematical cannon fire, the two sides touted numbers and argued with increasing intensity over their meaning as the debate over border enforcement focused more and more on safety.

When the Descanso tragedy struck, Smith was ready with the number of those dead so far during the three-month-old new year: twenty-seven. Her voice seemed to be caught in an internal struggle between the cool analysis of the lawyer and the seething indignation of the rights advocate. "These were entirely foreseeable consequences," she said, "of a strategy that maximizes the risks to migrants crossing the border." It was the same assertion that her foundation, joined by the ACLU chapter representing San Diego and Imperial Counties, had made just two months earlier in a petition to the Inter-American Commission on Human Rights, a branch of the Organization of American States.

That petition had marked a novel use of international human rights law, which for the most part had been wielded against repressive governments around the world. Rights-monitoring groups, such as Human Rights Watch, had turned their attention to the U.S. border, issuing reports in previous years on alleged abuses by border agents, in keeping with border activists' traditional focus on use-of-force issues and agent misconduct. But the OAS petition filed by the two southern California groups charged that the United States had overstepped its right to protect its border.

The petition claimed that the U.S. government border policies "knowingly and ineluctably led to the deaths of an ever increasing number of immigrants seeking to enter the United States to obtain jobs or family reunification." It said: "Operation Gatekeeper has steered this flow of immigrants into the harshest, most unforgiving and most dangerous terrain on the California-Mexico border. The United States has purposefully done this knowing that the policy would dramatically increase the number of illegal border crossers who die and without taking adequate steps to prevent these deaths."

The complaint charged that any government policies that served to undermine the basic rights of others amounted to violations of the terms of the OAS charter and the American Declaration of the Rights and Duties of Man, both of which the United States had signed. By enforcing its own border in this way, the petitioners argued, the United States was hardly better than a thuggish dictatorship. Worse still, the groups charged, the policy wasn't even working to keep immigrants out. It was merely moving them. The fifty-page petition asked the commission to recommend that the United States take steps to prevent further fatalities and pay damages "to the victims of the human rights violations caused by Operation Gatekeeper, including the survivors of those who have died as a result of the enforcement strategy."

For their part, INS officials dismissed assertions that the border policy was designed to place anyone in danger. One had to understand the overall strategy, they insisted. Phase One of the Border Patrol's 1994 strategic plan, issued just before the launch of Gatekeeper, called for closing the migrant corridors that had accounted for the most illegal entries and that provided undocumented immigrants with the quickest access to rides—taxis, buses, trolleys, private cars. That meant San Diego and El Paso. Next in line for attention, under Phase Two of the strategic plan, were routes through central Arizona and South Texas. The enforcement offensive south of Tucson, dubbed Operation Safeguard, was launched there just weeks after Gatekeeper was rolled out in San Diego, though it was not carried out in earnest for three years. Subsequent phases would cover the remainder of the border, once the worst spots had been sealed. The plan described the strategy as requiring "multi-year implementation," but did not specify how many years it would take.

By 1999, pieces were being dropped into place along the full length of the border. Operation Rio Grande, for example, targeted the zone in South Texas by pouring more than 460 new Border Patrol agents into areas around McAllen, Brownsville and Laredo. Arrests were already dropping in those two sectors, and U.S. officials hoped for similar results as the border was hardened west toward the established beachhead in El Paso and into New Mexico. (The push along the Rio Grande in South Texas ran into opposition from environmentalists, who feared that installing fences and high-powered lights along the river endangered wild ocelots and jaguarundi, nocturnal cats that prowl the thick, thorny bushes along the wildlife corridor there.)

If immigrants had continued to cross in high-risk areas, the U.S. officials argued, it was the fault of smugglers who led them there in spite of the well-known dangers. INS officials argued that by imposing order along the line and cleaning up the canyons in San Diego where immigrants once had been vulnerable to being robbed and raped, authorities had reduced some kinds of harm. As an example, Border Patrol officials reported that there were only three homicides involving migrants in 1998, down from nineteen in 1993. Fatalities due to being hit by a car dropped from nineteen to two during the same period. Thirty to forty people died annually in Imperial County during the 1980s—a figure roughly in line with the thirty-nine tallied by the agency there in 1997. (As we will see, deaths would soon increase to more than twice that level, and remain high through 2002.)

Officials asserted that, lamentable as was even a single death, migrants always had died crossing the border. Robert Gilbert, a former San Diego Border Patrol agent assigned to the INS's regional headquarters in Laguna Niguel, summed up the agency's stance in a telephone conversation at the time the OAS petition was filed: "Death on the border is unfortunate, but it's nothing new," he said. "It's not caused by the Border Patrol. It's not caused by Gatekeeper."

He had a point. The border's long history of danger was indisputable. The conditions that had plagued the nation's front step before the crackdown in San Diego would have been intolerable in any city in America. But it was also true that U.S. officials knew that by squeezing one section of the border, they invariably would force a bulge somewhere else—and that it wouldn't necessarily be pretty. "Illegal entry trends react quickly to border control initiatives," said the Border Patrol's 1994 national blueprint. It continued: "The prediction is that with traditional entry and smuggling routes disrupted, illegal traffic will be deterred, or forced over more hostile terrain, less suited for crossing and more suited for enforcement." A separate paper written by the agency's San Diego sector noted, "Methodically closing corridors of preference, channelling illegal entrants to areas where physical interdiction is more easily accomplished, and making better use of available technology are the foundation of the Sector's strategy." It went on: "Given adequate resources, the border within San Diego Sector's area of responsibility can be controlled in a safe, humane manner."

The mountain disaster lent fresh energy to the government's effort to point to smugglers as the problem. Just as Johnny Williams had lashed out at smugglers following the Imperial County desert tragedy the previous August, U.S. officials were quick to lay blame for this new episode at the feet of the *coyotes* who had led unknowing migrants into harm's way. The day-long search was still under way when Border Patrol agent Mario Villarreal told reporters that three of the rescued men had been identified by survivors as paid guides. They would be prosecuted by federal authorities, he said. A fourth smuggler would later be identified. Sheriff's rescuers found the eighth body shortly before dark. The search was called off that night, twenty-five hours after the first migrants were found. Thirty-six people were saved; eight were hospitalized. Among the survivors were four who agreed to serve as material witnesses for the government in pressing smuggling cases against the accused smugglers.

The suspects, Mexican nationals, were indicted April 14 by a federal grand jury in San Diego, less than two weeks after the incident. Three of the suspects were charged with smuggling five of the migrants into the Cleveland National Forest. One of those customers, Sebastian Díaz Avila, a twenty-eight-year-old father of four from Mexico, was among the eight who died. Díaz had been traveling with his nephew Francisco, but became too weak to go on walking. Francisco made the excruciating choice to continue without his uncle. He peeled off his jacket, handed it to Sebastian Díaz and trudged on through the snow. He was later rescued by the Border Patrol. The fourth suspect was charged in connection with the death of a separate migrant, José René Benítez Tadillo, whose age was thought by authorities to be somewhere between fifteen and seventeen.

The men were charged under a provision of federal law that targets cases of immigrant smuggling resulting in death. The charge carried with it a possible maximum punishment of life in prison. The men also were charged with smuggling for financial gain, bearing a possible ten-year prison term. The cases would give federal prosecutors a chance to make good on their vows to come down hard on smugglers. They had made a start: the number of immigrant-smuggling cases prosecuted in San Diego had shot up tenfold since Gatekeeper began in 1994. But it didn't seem to deter the *coyotes;* smuggling seemed to pick up each year.

On that snowy April day, as the helicopters thumped in the air overhead, ambivalence also swirled about Descanso. In the fireplace warmth of a general store, for example, owner John Elliott wrestled with mixed emotions about the tragedy. That jumble of sentiments had become familiar to a lot of the country dwellers in these parts, which tended to attract exiles from the city and other independent-minded folks who preferred to live and let live. Since the border crackdown forty miles west in San Diego, immigrants increasingly were turning up in the sage-scented backcountry here. Sometimes they'd trespass onto horse farms, angering the owners. Other times, residents would let them drink from a garden hose. The migrants often stopped at Elliott's store, just north of Interstate 8, to buy food or warm themselves by the fire.

If the migrants who were now being plucked from the snow had made it into the store, they would have encountered a warming scene: inside the door was a table stacked with homemade apple pies baked in the orchard-dotted mountain town of Julian. Behind the counter, Elliott was sorting out his feelings about the border crossers. "I don't want to turn them in," he said. "But they still don't belong here. And then you have these tragedies." The new border reality made even emotions exceedingly complicated.

Chapter Five

THE GREEN LINE

Anyone who has entered the United States by air, seaport or through any of its fifty-five land crossings has probably encountered the white-shirted inspectors of the U.S. Immigration and Naturalization Service.* The inspectors are charged with enforcing immigration laws at the official ports of entry. They ask about citizenship and check visas, stamp passports and look out for signs of smuggling—imperfectly faked documents, the nervous glance of a driver whose car trunk is stuffed with people. The inspections are tedious and generally orderly.

But guarding the vast border zones between the official entrances falls to the green-uniformed ranks of the Border Patrol. It's a job unique in American law enforcement in both setting and demands; the terrain is often wild, the conditions solitary. No law enforcement agency in America arrests more people than the Border Patrol, which in recent years grew accustomed to logging more than a million apprehensions on the Southwest border alone. Academy training includes the usual law-enforcement fare—law and weapons training—but also incorporates classes that few police officers elsewhere are likely to see, such as tracking human footprints. Border Patrol agents also must master Spanish, which many say is the most difficult requirement for those who didn't grow up bilingual.

By 1999, the agency was marking its seventy-fifth birthday. It was a

---

* The INS was absorbed into the Department of Homeland Security in March 2003 and its functions redistributed among several divisions; border inspection fell under the Bureau of Customs and Border Protection.

fitting time to celebrate such a landmark. The Border Patrol was riding a wave unlike any in its history. In a reversal of the normal budget-begging that goes on in Washington, politicians were tripping over themselves to expand it. The 1996 immigration law had ordered the INS to hire 1,000 new agents annually for five years, in hopes of achieving a force of 10,000. The biggest problem was whether the agency could find candidates fast enough to comply. By 1999, the Border Patrol had some 8,000 agents arrayed along the Southwest border—more than double its contingent of 3,670 in 1994.

The growth spurt had dramatically altered the face of the Border Patrol. The stereotype of the old Border Patrol had always been that of a posse of Anglo enforcers, but recent years saw a growing contingent of Latino agents. The expansion accelerated that presence, turning the Border Patrol into the most Latin of any U.S. agency. There were now nearly 3,000 Latino agents, accounting for about 40 percent of the force—a significant jump even from the mid-1980s, when Latino agents made up a fourth of the Border Patrol. Like agent Araceli Garcia in Imperial Beach, many were themselves the children of Mexican immigrants who came into the United States illegally.

Agents named Martinez and Rodriguez were now routinely arresting people with the same surnames. At times they endured on-the-job insults from migrants suggesting a kind of ethnic treason. The work also placed some Latino agents in the uncomfortable position of justifying their job to family members who viewed border agents as cruel and abusive. For most, their ethnic roots made no difference; they were there to uphold the law. If anything, they had become doubly certain of the rightness of any job that would keep smugglers from preying on unsuspecting migrants. "The way I see it," a Mexican-American agent in San Diego told the *Wall Street Journal*, "you carry the badge in one hand, and in the other hand, you carry your heart." During our shift together, Garcia approached her job as any cop would. The best busts, she said, were those involving migrants with criminal records. Garcia said she sympathized with many of the Mexicans she arrested, whom she referred to as "illegal migrants," as opposed to "aliens," the traditional designation. But she worried that they had no idea what they were getting into by heading north for jobs. "I do feel bad. But you know what? Everybody thinks it's easy to get a job out here, but it's not."

Twenty-five years before, when her parents crossed without papers, prospects for a decent job in America didn't depend so much on advanced education, computers and the like. But things had changed. Indeed, scholars were pointing to evidence of a growing gap between the schooling levels of the new arrivals and the needs of a high-tech economy in places like California. RAND researchers noted that 60 percent of California's immigrant population arrived with only the most basic education and skills, while newly created jobs were going mostly to people with at least some college training. The low-end jobs filled by immigrants were already stagnating, they said.

From her perch on the line, Garcia saw broader, more nuanced effects from a tighter border: Many migrants think that they come north and in "two days you have a job," she said. "It's not like that anymore, unfortunately." She wondered if the exodus of migrants let Mexico's government off the hook. "If we stopped all the illegal migrants from coming here, would they wait and demand that their government pay attention to them? Would they have a place they could be proud of?" Garcia added: "I can relate a lot with them. But I try to explain, it's not like when my parents came through. It's a big difference from then and now."

The same was true of the Border Patrol, where the tools of the job were now much different from when the agency was established by Congress in 1924 as part of the Bureau of Immigration. At its founding, the agency had 450 agents, and was successor to a small contingent of so-called Mounted Guards, based in El Paso, that roamed as far as California. The Mounted Guards were so consumed with catching excluded Chinese migrants that they were often referred to as "Chinese inspectors." With the passage of fresh immigration restrictions in 1917 and 1924, the new Border Patrol gained a wider charge: in addition to guarding the Mexican and Canadian borders, the agency was assigned responsibility in 1925 for patrolling America's coastline, amid concern over smuggling from the Caribbean through Florida and the Gulf Coast.

Guarding the land borders was a daunting task, not least because

Prohibition had complicated matters, turning the gaping frontier into a battleground against bootleggers from Mexico who were eager to turn Americans' appetite for liquor into tidy profits for themselves. New inspectors were drawn from the ranks of the Mounted Guards, along with Texas Rangers and sheriff's deputies. Immigration officials also found a rich source of potential agents among railroad mail clerks. The best candidates were seasoned horsemen, preferably with military experience. A civil service job posting at the time described the work of line-riding as being "closely comparable in nature and requirements to the duties of a soldier under actual field conditions." Riding on horseback along the vast border zones, which in the case of the Mexican frontier meant navigating rough and mountainous terrain, promised to be "arduous and frequently dangerous," the posting noted. "Assignments of duty," it continued, "may at times involve contact with smugglers and other criminal characters." A help-wanted notice in a Douglas, Arizona, newspaper put it this way: "The patrol, which is a branch of the immigration service will accept no man unless he is strong and fearless. He must have experience in cowboy work, tracking and general border occupations."

The job paid $1,680 a year. The government provided the badge and revolver, but it was up to the inspector to supply his own horse and saddle. With so few officers to go around, patrol areas were huge and lonely and the hours were long, with just one day off every month. Moreover, the warnings about job dangers proved warranted. In the first two years, five inspectors were slain in gunfights, all but one of them against liquor smugglers. During a decade of Prohibition, officers assigned to the El Paso district engaged in a gun battle every seventeen days on average, according to one historical account. Adding to the perils, the earliest inspectors had to make do without uniforms, leaving them only their badges to distinguish them as officers of the law.

The early inspectors were tough, crafty and unapologetic in their use of force. One story holds that a Texas-based inspector who survived a shootout with a mescal smuggler had to fill out a report after the confrontation. In the space marked "Disposition of Prisoner," the federal inspector wrote, "Mean as hell—I had to kill the son of a bitch." The account, perhaps apocryphal, has all the favored seasonings of Border Patrol lore—the menacing bandit, the hard-bitten agent, the salty pride in frontier justice dispensed. Not surprisingly, a federal civilian review panel that began to scrutinize the inspectors' practices during the 1930s met with derision among veteran agents, who saw it as a bunch of effete interlopers.

In the 1930s, the Bureaus of Immigration and Naturalization were combined and then, in 1940, moved from the Labor Department to Justice, creating the Immigration and Naturalization Service. The Border Patrol had begun to modernize. A training academy opened in El Paso, providing a one- to three-month course in the basics of criminal law, Spanish, firearms, tracking and jujitsu. Agents came to rely increasingly on cars, trucks, boats and radios to do their jobs. But the arsenal still remained a far cry from the high-tech gear of today. Instead of mounted low-light cameras, border guards in El Paso watched from a steel tower that afforded a view over the border into Mexico. Observers climbed into a hut teetering seventy-five feet off the ground. The little house measured only forty inches square and, as one chronicler pronounced at the time, was "no place for a fat man."

By World War II, the patrol had 856 agents who, on average, made a total of 45,000 arrests yearly. During the war, the Border Patrol drew responsibility for guarding several of the internment camps that had been set up by the U.S. government to incarcerate Japanese immigrants and other foreigners designated as "enemy aliens." The agency also was assigned to watch Axis diplomats and help guard the coastlines against enemy submarines. An outbreak of anthrax among Mexican cattle in the late 1940s added another job to the Border Patrol's portfolio—agents were to be on the lookout for diseased cows ambling over the border, and to shoot them.

The war and its aftermath witnessed a huge increase in the number of undocumented Mexicans, many of whom were drawn north alongside the tens of thousands of legal bracero laborers. From 1948 to 1953, Border Patrol agents made 2 million arrests, for a yearly average of 400,000—nearly ten times the volume before the war. A program to airlift migrants back to their homes in the Mexican interior lasted only a year before it ran out of money. A similar "boatlift" begun in 1954 to shuttle migrants from Port Isabel, Texas, to the Mexican port of Veracruz petered out after two years.

It was this postwar wave that led the Eisenhower administration to launch Operation Wetback, aimed at driving undocumented Mexicans from U.S. soil. Many older U.S. citizens of Mexican descent recall this as an especially dark period in the government's treatment of Latinos because the arrests often swept up those who were in the country legally. For many Mexican Americans, the mistreatment would have a radicalizing effect, leaving a lingering mistrust of *la migra.* For example, Roberto Martinez, born and raised in San Diego, was a teenager at the time. He recalled being stopped regularly by border agents and police who suspected him of being in the country illegally. Martinez would pull out his school identification to prove who he was, explaining himself all the while in his native English. (He learned Spanish thirty years later as an adult.) His experience wasn't unique; "it was a terrible time for Chicanos in California," he said.

By the 1960s and 1970s, the border was the scene of a growing smuggling trend, as shipments of drugs were being sneaked into the country in greater volumes, bundled into hidden nooks of cars and trucks or tucked into the knapsacks of hikers. For border agents accustomed to watching for usually harmless illegal immigrants, the development added a menacing new dimension to the job. The danger came fully into focus in the southern California countryside in June 1967, when a pair of border agents, Theodore Newton and George Azrak, met the fate that agents and cops envision only in their darkest moments.

Late on the night of June 16, the two agents set up an inspection checkpoint on State Highway 79, a rural stretch on San Diego County's northern fringe about seventy-five miles from the Mexican border. By morning, no one at the Border Patrol's Temecula office had heard from the officers, who had not responded to two radio calls during the night. A search of the checkpoint site turned up no sign of the pair. Soon after, one of the agents' vehicles, a Jeep, was found in an open field about a mile away. A frenzied search guided by the FBI led to the second vehicle, a sedan, two days later. The car had been covered with brush in an attempt to hide it. It sat just fifty feet from a ramshackle cabin in a place called Bailey Ranch, a remote spot about eight miles from where the pair of agents had been working.

Inside the shack, the federal agents' search ended. Newton and Azrak lay sprawled, their arms reaching toward each other inside the shelf of an old stove and then handcuffed, wrist to wrist. They had been shot dead. Newton was struck by bullets three times in the head, Azrak twice in the head and once in the chest. They were the first border agents slain in the line of duty in fifteen years. Authorities would ultimately solve the crime: the two were kidnapped and slain after stopping a car carrying eight hundred pounds of marijuana. Four men, two in the smuggling car and two following in a pickup truck, overpowered the officers. The four men, all of them convicts, were later captured. Two pleaded guilty to the slayings and the other two, brothers, admitted their role as accomplices.

Newton and Azrak are remembered today in a Border Patrol award given to agents exhibiting unusual courage—and in warnings that are hammered, mantralike, into all new border agents. Go out on the job with any agent and you'll get an earful about how fast tedium can turn into serious trouble. It's a rare agent who has not been pelted with rocks. Windshields get smashed, kneecaps wrecked. Sometimes it's worse. During the late 1990s, someone on the Tijuana side of the border took to shooting a gun over the fence, though no U.S. agents were hit. In June 1998, a Border Patrol agent named Alexander Kirpnick was shot to death in the hills near Nogales, Arizona, after he and his partner stopped five suspected marijuana smugglers. The very conditions that make up the agent's existence—working alone, often in deserted spots far from the nearest witness, and chasing down groups of people who are in violation of the law simply by being on U.S. soil—create a recipe for workplace danger unusual in American law enforcement.

But those same conditions can be a breeding ground for abuses by agents: beatings of migrants, improper shootings, rapes, poor treatment of detainees, theft and cover-up. The isolation in which many Border Patrol agents operate gives them wide latitude, and for some, the temptations are too much. In May 1999, just as the Border Patrol was marking its seventy-fifth anniversary with a reception and retrospective video, an off-duty agent from El Centro took his pellet gun to the All American Canal and fired upon a rubber raft carrying illegal immigrants north across the waterway. The raft capsized. Two immigrants had to swim to safety in currents that could have killed them. A third was said to have been thrown out, but no body was ever found in the canal.

Also in May 1999, Blanca Bernal, a young Mexican woman in Arizona, was pursuing a civil lawsuit against the U.S. government, claiming it was negligent in supervising a Nogales-based agent she said had raped her after arrest. The case stemmed from a 1993 incident in which the agent arrested the woman, then twenty-one, as she sneaked under the fence in Nogales. The victim said the agent took her to the outskirts of town, where, she alleged, he tore off her clothes and raped her on the tailgate of his Ford Bronco. State authorities filed a rape charge. The agent, Larry D. Selders, pleaded guilty to a reduced charge of "transportation of a female other than his wife for immoral purposes" and to a lesser federal charge that he had violated the woman's civil rights. The government was ordered to pay $753,045 to Bernal. The judgment reflected the government's failure to supervise Selders, but the case uncovered worse lapses: Border Patrol officials had been notified of allegations of two previous sexual attacks by Selders, including a 1989 case involving the wife of a fellow agent. The verdict buoyed rights activists and led the *Arizona Daily Star,* which pays careful attention to the border, to pronounce that a "weighty message" was conveyed: "Federal officers now have less chance of getting away with abusing their authority in the tumultuous border region."

This was hardly the first time alleged abuse has been brought to light. For years, the agency had been the target of a wide range of abuse allegations by groups like Roberto Martinez's. Sometimes those allegations held up; during the 1990s agents were prosecuted along nearly every region of the border for crimes ranging from murder to embezzlement. In a 1995 report, the group Human Rights Watch claimed that border agents "are committing serious human rights violations, including unjustified shootings, rape, and beatings, while enjoying virtual impunity for their actions." The report cited the Selders case, among others. A border-state advisory committee to the U.S. Commission on Civil Rights found the high volume of complaints a cause for concern.

Widespread allegations of abuse eventually prompted the INS to establish a citizens advisory panel in 1994 to figure out ways to reduce the reports of abuse across the entire immigration service, especially the

Border Patrol. The panel's suggestions, issued in 1997, recommended more civilian scrutiny of the INS, a better process for receiving and handling complaints about alleged rights violations and improved training for its agents. The INS adopted most of the recommendations. Informal advisory boards began sprouting along the two-thousand-mile border, though they lacked the teeth sought by rights advocates.

Meanwhile, allegations persisted as the Border Patrol grew in size. The INS Office of Internal Audit, a group of investigators who were the equivalent of a police department's internal-affairs division, reviewed 3,718 complaints against INS personnel in 1998, more than twice the caseload in 1995, according to the *San Diego Union-Tribune*. That represents more than one complaint for every four employees; the INS is made up of 13,500 inspectors and Border Patrol agents. A little over a third of the complaints were warranted, the newspaper said. Investigators also looked into complaints by undocumented immigrants and other detainees, and substantiated roughly one in eight of those. Few, however, resulted in punishment. In sum, the findings gave rights activists like Roberto Martinez little to cheer about. Among the most controversial allegations were those involving shootings by agents, but use of force was almost always found to be justified. The INS investigators looked into 27 shootings resulting in death or serious injury in 1998—out of 104 shootings overall—and found only two instances in which agents violated INS policies. The agents in those cases were suspended.

An Amnesty International report focusing on the border in 1998 found "credible evidence" of a wide range of mistreatment by U.S. agents, from beatings and sexual abuse of suspected undocumented immigrants to withholding food, water and medical care during extended periods. "The allegations of ill-treatment Amnesty International collected include people being struck with batons, fists and feet, often as punishment for attempting to run away from Border Patrol agents," the group said. The group also found the process for reporting complaints confusing. Some Border Patrol stations did not even stock complaint forms in Spanish.

But not all the criticism directed at the Border Patrol was fair. As the public face of federal immigration control, the agency was always a lightning rod for zealous opponents and a handy target for poorly substantiated or even trumped-up charges. And considering that it made a million and a half arrests yearly, only a tiny proportion of encounters result in problems, its defenders said. Agents conceded there are some abuses. But they also were quick to point out, like cops everywhere, that there are good ones and a handful of bad ones who stain the image of the rest.

Public relations was becoming an increasing concern. For decades, the Border Patrol had operated on the nation's geographic fringe as a forgotten army, and it paid little attention to local political niceties. By the late 1990s, though, the agency was being pushed to improve its ties to residents in the communities where it was working in greater numbers. In late 1998 the San Diego office set up a six-week "citizens academy" to acquaint residents with the Gatekeeper strategy, along with the agency's basic functions and rules. The purpose was not to recruit agents but to reduce tensions with U.S. border residents by making them more familiar with the Border Patrol's workings, the same way a fire station might hold an open house. A dozen or more residents sat around a table one night a week listening to agents lecture about Border Patrol history, Gatekeeper and some of the intricacies of immigration law, and got tours of the port of entry and of the line where the agents worked.

The sessions were polite and businesslike. Still, a couple of people attending the sessions the following year described past hostile run-ins with agents. One was a twenty-year-old Latina college student named Cynthia Diaz, who recounted having been stopped on the streets of San Ysidro and asked about her citizenship status. It was the sort of encounter that had made many Latinos resentful toward the Border Patrol over the years. The episode angered Diaz, she recalled, but she was keeping an open mind about the agency—a sign the public-relations efforts were working. She decided to attend the academy because she was now contemplating joining the Border Patrol, as were some other college-age attendees.

As in the case of the civilian academy, it was with community relations in mind that Border Patrol officials accepted blame at the end of 1999 when residents in rural eastern San Diego County—near where the winter rescue took place—noisily complained of harassment by agents looking for illegal immigrants in the countryside. They said agents were constantly stopping their cars for searches and disrupting ranch life by leaving gates unlocked as they made their rounds. The Border Patrol later responded by handing out brochures and holding a new round of classes to improve relations with locals.

In addition to infuriating some rural residents, the border buildup was leading rights activists to complain that deploying so many new and untested agents had increased the chances for trouble. Indeed, Martinez was now complaining on a regular basis that the Border Patrol was hurriedly handing guns and badges to agents who lacked training and had not been screened sufficiently to make sure they had never committed crimes or suffered psychological problems. Even the labor union representing border agents warned that the flood of newly minted agents was diluting the quality of the force and bringing suspect recruits on board through the program of "expedited hiring."

Worries grew with news of several cases, including the firing of two Texas agents who got hired despite having criminal records—one for burglary, the other for immigrant smuggling—and the arrest of an agent in Arizona on charges of murder and drug dealing. (The INS noted that the Arizona agent had a spotless record when he was hired and only became a suspect in the murder later.) In 1998 a San Diego agent hired two years earlier was indicted after he was caught with six hundred pounds of marijuana stuffed into duffels in his Border Patrol van. INS officials insisted that their hiring had been careful, but they tightened the review and also began to sound nervous over the greenness of their corps of border agents.

By late 1999, the Clinton administration's passion to hire new agents had begun to cool, in part over concern that there were now too many rookies. In response to charges that the administration was dragging its feet in recruitment, officials pointed out that 40 percent of the eight thousand agents had less than two years' experience. Sixty percent, they added, had less than five years' experience. In any case, INS recruiters, like many police agencies elsewhere in America, were having trouble finding new hires. At the same time, existing border agents were leaving for better-paying work with the FBI, Drug Enforcement Administration or police agencies.

So the Border Patrol faced a delicate balancing act. Many in Congress were keeping up the pressure to add a thousand new agents a year, even as activists decried the rapid expansion. And the demands of continuing the campaign to seal the border were growing increasingly apparent as the immigrants pushed determinedly into new areas. To the usual rigors of guarding the frontier was added the growing responsibility for saving lives and stemming smuggling along the most fearsome segments of the border.

The fight against smugglers wasn't a new one. Sneaking people across the Southwest border for money goes back to the late nineteenth century, when the smugglers and the illegal immigrants were most likely to be Chinese. When crossing restrictions were extended to Mexicans in the twentieth century, smuggling Mexican workers was a natural development. Although people smuggling shared some parallels with drug trafficking, it never carried the same notoriety or romance. The swagger and impunity of gunslinging Mexican drug traffickers had helped turn them into larger-than-life heroes as a new genre of folk songs, known as *narco-corridos,* soared in popularity during the 1990s. There was even a patron saint of drug traffickers, Jesús Malverde. Mexicans had a soft spot for the outlaw who stuck it in the gringo's eye, going back to the lost war against the United States.

When it came to smuggling immigrants, there was a more democratic impulse at work. For years, many ordinary Mexicans who wouldn't have gone near drugs—nor transported them across an international boundary—had helped relatives, neighbors or even perfect strangers sneak across the border. The transborder passage was the subject of any number of Mexican immigration films—a highly developed genre that already boasted close to a hundred feature-length movies. While many had unhappy endings for the immigrants portrayed, the films were a sure sign of the significance across Mexican popular culture of the emigrant experience. "There's a tradition of viewing these *coyotes* as Robin Hood–type characters, outsmarting the gringos," according to University of Pennsylvania migration expert Douglas Massey.

Although smuggling is a federal crime in Mexico, crossing the U.S.

border in violation of American law isn't: Mexicans have a constitutional right to leave their country as they see fit. If it is over a fence or through the mountains, so be it. Even in the most rural spots deep within Mexico, almost everybody knows someone who has made the crossing or who still lives in the United States. In many towns the fruits of a stint working in the United States are prominent in the form of the booty brought back or purchased from abroad: new stucco homes, satellite television antennas, shiny pickups. While for many years the Mexican government took a dim view of emigrants, shunning or even disparaging them for their disloyalty, Mexico was deeply dependent on those who flocked north. The 18 million Mexicans living in the United States wired back to their families more than $7 billion a year in remittances—one of Mexico's three top sources of national income, along with oil and tourism. The ability to leave also helped relieve the frustrations and resentments that might have ignited social unrest against Mexico's long-ruling Institutional Revolutionary Party (PRI), which was finally defeated in 2000 after seventy-one years.

Thanks in part to the bracero program, and subsequent cross-border travels, the trails north were well paved. In many towns, there was someone, often a respected elder, who helped arrange the journey north, even to a specific employer. In years past, it had been a straightforward matter of taking a rattletrap bus for two days to get to the border and then leaping the fence, or paying a local teenager a few bucks to show you how to get past the border guards. In Mexican border cities like Tijuana, local residents who held full-time jobs during the week moonlighted as weekend guides for extra spending money. In El Paso, the small-time *lancheros* made a living floating immigrants across the Rio Grande on truck inner tubes.

By the end of the 1990s, the easy informality of these mom-and-pop enterprises was fast giving way to an immigrant-smuggling industry that increasingly bore the worrisome markings of its cousin, the multi-billion-dollar narcotics trade. Weekend guides who once charged $50 to $100 to lead migrants over the former tattered fence in San Diego had been run out of business by the crackdown there. As the difficulty of crossing grew, the prices that smugglers could charge rose higher. The organized smuggling groups increasingly came to resemble crime syndicates, loosely structured but often ruthless organizations vying for a slice of a dizzyingly profitable business. A *coyote* trade that once relied on gumption and quick feet now stacked its arsenal with cellular telephones, global-positioning navigational aids and computer technology. High-tech equipment also helped in the production of phony visas, which enabled those without valid papers to pass through official ports of entry instead of risking the overland crossing.

With the human-smuggling industry at $7 billion to $8 billion, the know-how of the *coyote* was now at a premium. As seventeen-year-old Wilfredo Cruz had noted at the migrant shelter in Mexicali, the task of crossing now was too difficult to attempt without a *coyote*. In fact, he held a view of smugglers that was quite different from their portrayal by U.S. officials as heartless mercenaries. Cruz saw the guides as kind of an insurance policy, in part because they typically wouldn't get paid in full until they had successfully escorted their charges across the border. "The *coyote* gives us more security because the *coyote* takes responsibility," he said.

Like Cruz, fewer and fewer migrants were willing to make the trip unguided. Border scholar Peter Andreas has noted that in 1970 only 8.4 percent—about one in twelve—of undocumented migrants arrested by the Border Patrol in the Southwest attempted their entry by using a smuggler. By the late 1990s, officials said, more than 90 percent of border crossers were believed to have paid someone to guide them. Multiply the rate of $800 to $1,000 by five to ten people a day—or several hundred or thousands of people over the course of a year—and you get some idea of the profitability of Mexican immigrant smuggling and its allure in a nation where the minimum wage is $4 a day.

Not everyone gets rich, of course. It takes several people to smuggle immigrants over the border: the person who runs the operation; the street helper who trolls the border-city bus stations and hotels for clients; and the guides who can make more than a U.S. schoolteacher by accompanying the migrants over the border.

On the U.S. side, there are drivers, or *raiteros*, who pick up the groups of migrants at preassigned spots along rural highways and take them to drop houses, where they remain, sometimes as semi-hostages, until relatives or some other sponsor inside the United States pays the smugglers. Only then are the migrants delivered to their destination. It is a hard-hearted business in which the travelers often are handled more as cargo than as people. U.S. authorities have noted several cases in which violence erupted among smuggling gangs after one group "stole" immigrants from another and then sold the migrants to a buyer, usually a relative or employer.

With profits rising, immigrant smuggling was also increasingly attractive because traditionally the penalties had been mild compared with those imposed in drug-trafficking cases, and prosecutions were quite rare. In the few cases that made their way into federal court, the resulting prison sentences tended to be light—two years or less. This was partly because enforcement tools were flimsy. For years, U.S. authorities lacked many of the weapons, such as wiretap authority and the power to seize the assets of smugglers, that they wielded against drug syndicates. In recognition of the immigrant smugglers' growing sophistication and clout, Congress in 1997 granted the INS authority to tap telephone and e-mail conversations. Investigators could penetrate the smuggling rings from afar, a big improvement over having to rely on informants or undercover agents, who often were unable to pierce deeply into the core of a smuggling gang. A later law also gave agents the power to confiscate assets and provided for stiffer mandatory minimum prison sentences.

As the cops got tougher, the smugglers got smarter, improvising quickly to frustrate new government initiatives. They melded with other organizations to create new ways of ferrying immigrants to the United States across many countries. They'd throw away cell phones every few days and buy new ones to prevent having calls traced. The smugglers invested in their own night-vision gear and sent surveillance vehicles north of the border to scout checkpoints. Like nations in an arms race, the two sides kept upping the ante, always looking for an edge.

The war on smuggling was not a fully binational one. Even amid the border crackdown in the late 1990s, U.S. officials were getting only tepid support from Mexico's government in smuggling investigations. Sometimes, however, especially in cases where American authorities had hoped to extradite a suspect from Mexico, the response was outright resistance. That posture constantly frustrated American investigators, who estimated there were anywhere from fifteen to twenty-four major smuggling organizations operating in both countries. With little overhead, they were highly fluid groups, capable of moving quickly from one border location to another. There also was criminal cross-fertilization, in which drugs and migrants had become interchangeable cargo. "You'll see a lot of alien smugglers who used to be drug smugglers, or they'll be doing both," a top INS anti-smuggling official said. "In many ways they mirror drug-trafficking organizations. And I would argue that they're just as dangerous."

Along the Southwest border, few immigrant-smuggling syndicates achieved the sprawling reach of a Tijuana band led by a set of brothers named Peralta. During the 1990s the gang was said by federal authorities to have brought thousands of immigrants into the United States from Mexico. Many of them originated from outside Mexico—places like Egypt and Central America—and were assembled into groups at a central Mexican ranch before being shuttled to the border at Tijuana and slipped across in a van. One Tijuana human rights activist and researcher reported that the group took in $250,000 by smuggling up to a thousand immigrants a week. American agents cited witnesses who reported seeing assembled groups of as many as six hundred immigrants.

The Peralta clan, whose workers were drawn from their home state of Guanajuato in central Mexico, made use of top-end cellular phones and a fleet of vehicles. They paid Tijuana cops bribes to ignore the safe houses that they kept there, and rented more homes and hotel rooms on the U.S. side of the border in California for transshipment. The group's network extended to Los Angeles and El Centro. The Peraltas' reputation spread so widely that they were sung about in two *corridos* that glamorized them as wily and tough.

During a seven-year investigation during the 1990s, U.S. agents discovered the full extent of the gang's reach: U.S. Customs inspector Guy Henry Kmett was found to have been helping the gang by allowing their vans crammed with immigrants to slip through his lane at the busy San Ysidro entry. In the words of one customs official, Kmett became the Peralta group's "keys to the kingdom." By the end of the decade, the probe had led to the arrests of more than fifty people, including a top-ranking aide responsible for renting safe houses in Los Angeles. One Peralta brother, Mario, was kidnapped and slain in Mexico. But true to their folk-legend status, two others, Vicente and José Ismael, remained free, despite being indicted in 1999.

There was ample irony to be found in the growth and professionalization of the immigrant-smuggling industry, for if there was any primary catalyst for the increased profits and sophistication of the enterprise in recent years, it was the U.S. government's border crackdown. Immigration officials conceded that shifting enforcement had sweetened the smugglers' market. In fact, the 1994 blueprint predicted a rise in smuggling fees as one sign of the effectiveness of the planned enforcement offensive. Ultimately, it was hoped, the cost would become prohibitive and migrants would have another reason to stay home. But as the rates doubled and tripled, there remained little evidence that a few hundred dollars, whether it was scraped together back in the home village or loaned by relatives who were already living and working in the United States, was keeping anyone away from the border.

By October 1999, as federal criminal proceedings moved forward against the four accused smugglers involved in the snowstorm disaster, Gatekeeper was turning five years old. It was an ideal time to assess the success of America's most ambitious effort to secure its troublesome Southwest border. But it was nearly impossible to find a reliable yardstick with which to do so. Statistics were essential to making policy, but also subject to a staggering range of often conflicting interpretations. You can't count what you can't see. And much of what goes on along the border is not meant to be seen.

A few things were crystal clear. For one, Gatekeeper had created an entirely new border at San Diego. Anyone returning after an absence of several years would have been flabbergasted at the difference. The dark rust fences carving the countryside for miles on either side of the principal official entry at San Ysidro now etched a rigid boundary. The hot intensity of the border lights, visible for miles as you approached the border by freeway, seemed to embody the fervor with which officials had chosen to make this a test case.

Where there had been 1,272 agents patrolling the sixty-six-mile strip, now there were 2,200. Perhaps most significantly, the number of people arrested for unlawful entry here had fallen to levels not seen since Richard Nixon was president. Apprehensions in the San Diego sector now totaled 182,267—the lowest since 1973 and a breathtaking drop from the 524,231 arrests made during Gatekeeper's first year. Among the nine Border Patrol sectors spanning the Southwest border, the San Diego division now ranked behind those based in El Centro and Tucson in the number of arrests. Five years earlier, it had accounted for nearly every other apprehension made along the entire Mexican border.

The new figures were cause for celebration among INS officials and politicians who had joined the call earlier in the decade for a more aggressive stance toward illegal crossings. It also was vindication for an enforcement drive in San Diego that by now alone was costing more than $200 million a year. "Operation Gatekeeper has really been an unprecedented success," Democratic senator Dianne Feinstein said when asked for an assessment. "What it tells me is it's a myth that the border can't be enforced. It can be enforced."

Down in beleaguered Imperial Beach, city leaders and Chamber of Commerce boosters dared to imagine a full-scale urban revival and, at last, property values that would be in line with a beachfront location. It had been a promising year. In late 1998 officials opened a huge sewage-treatment plant meant to clean up overflow waste washing north across the border from Tijuana through the Tijuana River. The pollution pouring into the ocean at the river's outlet had forced countless beach closings at a good surfing stretch between Imperial Beach and Border Field State Park. Between the decades-long pollution problem and the illegal immigrants, efforts to market Imperial Beach to outsiders had often seemed like a cruel joke. Now hope seemed appropriate. There was already a tussle between the Clinton administration and others to take credit for the turnaround. Duncan Hunter, the Republican congressman from suburban El Cajon who had sponsored legislation demanding more border agents and fences, groused: "I build fences and put Border Patrol in the budget and they do all the press conferences."

But for all the triumphant talk that the arrest numbers were inspiring, they proved upon closer inspection to carry a decidedly mixed message. During the five-year period that saw the precipitous fall in arrests at San Diego, apprehensions across the rest of the border increased by an even greater margin. It appeared that migrants indeed were avoiding San Diego, but that the problem had merely been palmed off on other parts of the border. Arrests were still high in El Centro (225,279) but down slightly. But farther east in Arizona, it suddenly became clear who was now taking the brunt. The Tucson sector, covering eastern and central Arizona, had 470,449 arrests, about a fifth higher than the year before, while Yuma, covering the western corner, had 93,388, nearly one-fourth more. Overall, arrests across the entire border had increased to 1.5 million, some 20 percent higher than during the first year of Gatekeeper in California.

The criticisms being lodged by activists weren't simply moral ones. They cited the arrest numbers to broaden their attack on pragmatic grounds, arguing that the border was no tighter than before the U.S. government had increased its annual spending on the Border Patrol from $374 million to nearly $1 billion. One noted immigration expert was already pronouncing the beginning of the policy's end. He said it had reached a point of diminishing returns: each gain was being offset by other migrants who remained committed to making the trip. The agents' union complained that by assigning agents to guard specific spots on the border—the famous X's that officials called "visual-deterrent positions"—the Border Patrol was abdicating its job of catching undocumented migrants farther north, at highway checkpoints and on farms and at other workplaces.

INS officials steadfastly defended the border program, saying it was too soon to judge the success or failure of a strategy that itself was designed to move fluidly along the border. "You can't just put in place all along the border what it would take to gain control in certain places. You have to do it in steps," said Robert L. Bach, the agency's executive associate commissioner for policy and planning. "It's not failure and it's not uncertainty. It's a planned work in progress." Bach and other officials said that adding agents and technology to block illegal crossings in key locations had brought calm to a handful of former trouble zones, but more time was needed if the formula was to be replicated in other spots.

The debate over the policy's efficacy, however, pivoted on a highly questionable gauge: the arrest numbers themselves. Apprehensions—

traditionally the chief means by which government policymakers, journalists and analysts sought to measure how leaky the border is—are a
highly imperfect gauge. For one thing, they measure each arrest, even if
the same person is caught again and again, as is often the case. More
important, the numbers don't show who got through, since the successful crosser doesn't get arrested. So unlike in a typical American neighborhood or city, where reported crimes include those that are solved and
unsolved, the border has only arrests for judging the effectiveness of
law enforcement. And that leads to a war over interpretation.

On a political level, the INS had cited high arrest figures to show
that it was swamped and in need of help or, contrarily, to show that it
was effective. For example, immigration officials said there might be
good news in the figures showing that there had been increased apprehensions borderwide after five years of Gatekeeper. It was possible,
they said, that agents were catching a higher percentage of migrants
than in past years. In other words, both higher and lower arrest totals
could mean fewer people were now getting through the defenses. But
the INS could not prove this. The new computerized fingerprinting system was supposed to help by identifying repeat crossers, but by late
1999, it remained hobbled by too many glitches to make for reliable
yearly comparisons.

The federal General Accounting Office was ordered by Congress to
make periodic reports on the state of border enforcement as part of the
Illegal Immigration Reform and Immigrant Responsibility Act of 1996,
the same law that ordered triple layers of fences in San Diego and mandated the hiring of five thousand new border agents in five years. In its
first review in 1997, the GAO had criticized the INS for lacking any
meaningful process for measuring its effectiveness at the border. It also
found that the immigration service and its Justice Department parent
had no plans for determining if indeed the strategy was preventing
would-be border jumpers from trying to cross. Two years later those
flaws had not been corrected.

In its 1999 update the GAO noted that the IDENT electronic-
fingerprint system was still of little help in measuring repeat efforts to
cross the border. In part, the problem was that not all migrants were being entered into the computer database after their arrest. The rate var-

ied from station to station. In some places, 90 percent of the arrestees were logged electronically; in others, only 17 percent. While it was clear that arrests had dropped in San Diego and risen elsewhere, the auditors threw their hands up when it came to drawing any important judgments on the strategy. Sounding a note of frustration, the GAO reviewers wrote: "Available information on the interim results does not provide answers to the most fundamental questions surrounding INS's enforcement efforts along the Southwest border. That is, given the billions of dollars that INS has invested in implementing the strategy, how effective has the strategy been in preventing and deterring aliens from illegally crossing the border?"

At Gatekeeper's fifth anniversary, then, the only certain thing was that it would take more time for the results of the grand border experiment to reveal themselves fully. Claudia Smith and the other activists weren't waiting: On the Mexican side of the border fence from Border Field State Park, they had begun affixing vinyl sheets with the names of deceased migrants. Their goal was to get the media focused on the issue of border fatalities and to remind the public that those dying along the way were more than cold numbers.

Chapter Six

"DO SOMETHING!"

As the debate over human rights heated up in San Diego, tensions of a different sort were snapping in the grassy countryside around Douglas, Arizona, some four hundred miles to the east. The sustained pressure of tightened border controls—Operation Gatekeeper in San Diego and Imperial Counties in California and Hold the Line in Texas—had begun to funnel a massive wave of undocumented immigrants into mesquite-specked ranch lands here by 1999. Almost overnight, rural Cochise County was the busiest point in the country for illegal crossings. Accompanying the phenomenon was a wrenching debate that raised a troubling question: how far were cattle ranchers and residents willing to go to stanch the flow? Already, some ranchers were threatening to take matters into their own hands. To many worried locals, the dry air carried more than a whiff of potential violence in a region that was no stranger to tumult.

Arizona's southeastern corner is spare in its physical charms, with broad, sloping valleys hemmed by low, khaki-toned mountain chains. But the area brims with lore—some of it true, some of it not, much of it occupying a hazy category in between. It is a region intimately tied to the border, with an Old West past featuring gunslingers and mining fortunes, labor strife and hopes raised and smashed. Some scholars believe it was near modern-day Douglas that the Spanish explorer Francisco Vázquez de Coronado and an expeditionary party entered Arizona in 1540 during his bid to find the Seven Cities of Cíbola—a land that, according to the intriguing tales that circulated, was awash in gold. The

Spaniards failed, though they followed tantalizing tips as far north as Kansas. But more than three hundred years later, discoveries of silver and gold sixty-five miles from Douglas gave birth to Tombstone, the iconic Wild West boomtown. Not far from the town of Douglas, Geronimo, the tough Apache warrior, surrendered in 1886 after years of raids on both sides of the border. Later, during the Mexican Revolution, twenty thousand U.S. troops dispatched by General "Black Jack" Pershing to protect Douglas enjoyed front-row seats when Pancho Villa, the Mexican revolutionary leader, launched his attack for control of Agua Prieta, across the border in Mexico. Residents on the U.S. side climbed onto the roof of the stately Gadsden Hotel in downtown Douglas to watch the fighting rage.

Douglas was not alone among border towns with a troubled and blood-flecked history. Cattle rustlers often sought refuge by crossing the border, Indian raiders bedeviled border denizens for years and smuggling flourished all along the southern flank of what would later become the state of Arizona. Brawls spilled across the international divide, prompting a nineteenth-century Mexican diplomat to propose keeping the peace by building a steel border fence between Naco, Arizona, sitting twenty-five miles west of Douglas, and its Mexican counterpart, also named Naco. (The idea was rejected by Mexico's president.) As the Mexican Revolution raged south of the border between 1910 and 1920, stray bullets zinged into the United States in Naco and Nogales, often injuring bystanders.

Douglas was originally used as a staging area for cattle roundups in the late 1800s. It owed its growth during the twentieth century to copper, as mining transformed the economies of southern Arizona and the Mexican state of Sonora. Mining also helped forge remarkably strong cross-border ties between the two areas. Douglas, little more than a crude encampment after its founding in 1901, was named after Dr. James Douglas, a Canadian metallurgist who turned the Phelps Dodge Mercantile Company into a mining powerhouse in Arizona. Copper extracted from the company's Copper Queen mine twenty-two miles away in Bisbee was hauled to Douglas, which had a sufficient water supply to support two smelters, one of which would close in the 1930s. Through most of the century, Phelps Dodge, locally known simply as "PD," was the town's benefactor and its raison d'être. Douglas provided the water and the workers; PD provided work that in modern years paid up to $15 an hour, though all the best jobs tended to go to Anglos. Douglas never got rich, but it knew where its next paycheck was coming from. That certainty ended in the late 1980s when, under order of the U.S. Environmental Protection Agency, the remaining smelter was shut down.

The closure was a body blow to the town, sparking an exodus of well-paid Phelps Dodge employees. The economic withdrawal shuttered many turn-of-the-century brick buildings in downtown Douglas and left the city heavily dependent on shoppers from across the border in Agua Prieta for economic sustenance. The two cities had long been tightly bound across the border, though not always in legal ways. Prohibition had drawn the alcohol-deprived to the border, putting cash into the pockets of bootleggers on both sides. In modern times, Agua Prieta made headlines when officials discovered a sophisticated drug-smuggling tunnel being built under the border. On the Mexican end, the entrance was disguised beneath a pool table hoisted by a hydraulic lift.

Now in 1999 a different problem was making itself felt. Arizona was experiencing the arrival of the immigration bulge created by the continuing clampdowns that had also swelled the ranks of migrants trying to make it over the border in Imperial County, California. Traditionally, the favored crossing spot along Arizona's 360-mile border was Nogales. Now, as the U.S. government's border-enforcement push evolved, agents were being added there. As a result, the flow was soon zeroing in on Douglas, eighty-five miles to the east, near the state's boundary with New Mexico. Adding to Douglas's attractiveness as a crossing point, the town of fifteen thousand residents sat on a route that was more direct than San Diego for many migrants heading from the Mexican interior.

By April, the town was setting regional records for migrant arrests and was home to increasingly bizarre scenes amid the scrubby plains an hour's drive from the OK Corral. Some ranchers had taken to rounding up immigrants on their land. It was no longer unusual to see lines of sixty or more border crossers, including small children, trooping among the shrubs and yucca, even in daylight. Two weeks before my arrival, six hundred people crossed en masse until U.S. Border Patrol agents arrived and rounded up nearly a third of the group. The rest fled back south across the border. One Border Patrol official likened the strange scene to "the beginning of a 10K run."

Meanwhile, the border community was in full uproar. To many of the residents of rural Cochise County, the steady parade of migrants had been a cruel onslaught, though foreseeable. It had taken nearly four years for the effects of Gatekeeper and Hold the Line to make themselves felt here. By 1998, around the same time the San Diego crackdown was squeezing thousands of migrants into the desert lands of Imperial County, the first ripples were appearing in the ranches around Douglas. By now, the results were undeniable. Formerly isolated grazing lands were now littered with plastic water jugs and soiled diapers left in the migrants' wake. Feed grass lay trampled in many places and ranch dogs barked so insistently at night that it had been months since owners last slept peacefully. Many now refused to leave their properties unattended.

One of those folks was Larry Vance Jr., who lived on twenty acres about a mile from the border that was now so frequently traversed that border agents were using it as a landmark for tracking immigrants. Vance, a forty-three-year-old utility repairman with a drooping gunslinger's mustache, met me in his Dodge pickup. In darkness, we rode along Highway 80 and other country roads while Vance described the chaos that had descended around the home where he had spent the previous twenty-five years. His brother lived next door. His parents occupied a third house on the property. Vance said he'd been burglarized three times and had migrants show up at his front door, asking to use the telephone. One afternoon a month earlier, while relaxing on his porch with a cold beer, he called the Border Patrol after hearing gunshots ring out in the surrounding shrubs. No one was arrested.

You don't live next to the border for as long as the Vance family had without encountering border crossers. For years, the Vances had grown accustomed to seeing laborers hike over from Agua Prieta to work in the local fields and ranches, then go home. Vance's own father was born in Mexico and had come to Arizona as a seven-year-old boy, joining an uncle to work the crops around Tempe. The elder Vance became a U.S. citizen and later served as an Arizona state trooper. But to Larry Vance, this new tide of migrants augured ominous change, exemplified by the gunshots he heard punctuating the prickly countryside. There were hardened smugglers plying their trade now and doubtless other opportunists, too—thieves and rapists drawn to prey on hundreds of helpless migrants. Vance couldn't help thinking of wildlife shows, of herds of migrating wildebeest and caribou being pursued relentlessly by predators. He feared it was only a matter of time before trouble erupted. His house sat very close to the action. "We don't know anything about these people. We don't know them from Adam," he told me as we drove. "It's naïve to think nothing's going to happen."

We passed the site of the old copper smelter—now a flat-topped mountain of black slag—and a lime-processing plant. Vance said he had gone months without a full night's sleep. "You can't imagine what it's like to go eight or ten months without being woken up half a dozen times a night," he said. "This border is so open, it's a goddamn joke." He stopped along the side of the road at one point and honked his truck horn—a signal commonly used by smugglers' drivers to call out immigrants hiding in the bushes at their designated pickup point. On this night, no one came out. Vance sounded angry and nervous about the future of an area his family had called home for so many years. He had four dogs to deter intruders. "I don't like having to have vicious dogs," he said. "It's like this." He patted a handgun on the truck seat next to him. "It's a hefty situation."

Vance had never been much into politics. A registered Republican, he belonged to the National Rifle Association, but that was about the extent of his activism until now. During the past several months, he and other residents had watched with dismay as the 275 Border Patrol agents stationed in the area found themselves overrun. Those living near the border swapped disturbing stories of a growing number of burglaries and other crimes. In March, Vance and some like-minded residents formed a group called the Cochise County Concerned Citizens. Among their first public moves was to ask Arizona governor Jane Hull to dispatch National Guard troops to bolster the local Border Patrol contingent. "As longtime residents of Cochise County, we have always experienced a trickle, and on occasion, a stream, of illegal aliens; however we are presently in the middle of a true flood," Vance wrote in a letter to the governor on behalf of the group.

But Hull already had rejected the idea, saying she opposed "militarization" of the border. Nonetheless, the idea had sparked a debate around town. Using military troops to guard the border had long been a touchy matter. While soldiers had been helping to build fences along southern California's border with Mexico for nearly a decade, the military's involvement on the Southwest border had been limited mainly to surveillance work on anti-drug patrols, under a program called Joint Task Force 6. Even that practice had come to an ignominious end in 1997, when marines on patrol in rural South Texas fatally shot an eighteen-year-old high school student as he tended goats. Employing troops in domestic police work had been barred since passage of the Posse Comitatus Act in 1878 during Reconstruction. But the Douglas ranchers said the flood of immigrants represented exactly the type of emergency for which the National Guard had been designed.

Still, even beleaguered local government officials and many residents said such a step would be too drastic. "The last thing we want is untrained people patrolling the border with weapons against people with babies in their arms," said Mayor Ray Borane. The debate over the National Guard fanned the growing tension and frustration. One rancher in the neighboring town of Sierra Vista worried aloud that "someone is going to die because of all the frustration down here." Already, nearly two dozen ranchers had signed a proclamation warning, "If the government refuses to provide this security, then the only recourse is to provide it for ourselves."

One ranch owner, Roger Barnett, had made good on that warning. Armed with a pistol and wearing a camouflage jacket and badge labeled "Ranch Patrol," he and two brothers made headlines after rounding up twenty-seven immigrants on his sprawling property and holding them until Border Patrol agents arrived. The immigrants were returned to Mexico, but authorities said they were investigating whether Barnett had broken any laws by acting in the role of a lawman. At that time, Cochise County sheriff's officials were looking into a separate incident in the nearby town of Hereford involving an immigrant. The migrant, who said she had become separated from her party, claimed that a ranch owner fired shots after she showed up at his house for help. For his part, the rancher said there were six migrants and that he fired warning shots in the other direction after they refused to leave during the early-morning darkness.

Barnett, a fifty-six-year-old former deputy sheriff, agreed to escort me around his twenty-two-thousand-acre Cross Rail Ranch. He said he wanted to show the effects of what he called an "invasion" by undocumented immigrants and to explain his actions, which had evoked cries of vigilantism and added one more volatile ingredient to the conditions around Douglas. Barnett was a weekend rancher—and a fairly new one at that. His real vocation was running a towing and propane business in Sierra Vista. He'd always been drawn to ranching. His grandfather worked on a ranch and the life appealed to Barnett, then a child. In recent years he'd kept his eyes peeled for a good deal on a ranch. One appeared in 1995. The ranch sat off Highway 80, sandwiched between the Pedregosa Mountains to the north and the Perilla range to the south, about ten miles from the Mexican border. Barnett bought about a third of the acreage; the rest, state-owned land, he leased. He and his wife, Barbara, spent weekends on the property, and by early 1999, Barnett had about 250 head of cattle grazing on the land. It was quiet for the first two years, and the couple got used to seeing wild pigs, deer and other wildlife.

But soon Barnett began to notice changes on the ranch outside Douglas. Previously it had been rare to spot trash on the flanks of the mountains except for the odd windblown plastic bag. Now Barnett was seeing more of it—not just bags, but plastic jugs, paper and other refuse that had been dropped, not carried by wind. The animals got scarcer. There were more human footprints despite thirty-six miles of barbed-wire fence and No Trespassing signs that ringed the property. The problem grew worse. Barnett and his brother Donald, who also was a former deputy, settled on a solution: they would patrol the land themselves.

Their first capture came after following tracks to a windmill, where they found seven men resting. The brothers, who were armed at the time, rounded up the group and drove them to the highway. Barnett later surmised that the men were drug runners. As time went on, he and his brother took to employing binoculars and night-vision goggles, hiding out in the bushes where they thought bundles of marijuana were likely to be dropped. They also detained groups of migrants. It wasn't hard to find them. Often, the groups trooped in single file across the ranch in plain view. Other times, it took a bit of tracking, a technique Barnett had learned from a former border agent. Barnett said he was told by Border Patrol commanders to advise them when he had detained a group so that agents could come and pick the immigrants up. He said he had rounded up several groups, some with as many as forty-eight people, and handed them over to the Border Patrol without incident until word got out about his doings following the detention of the group of twenty-seven. The story would get wide play, especially in Mexico, where he was portrayed roundly as a vigilante and a racist. On the U.S. side, the episode prompted officials to counsel civilians not to take the law into their own hands. Meanwhile, rights activists excoriated the ranchers, deploring their actions as crude Old West justice. A Tucson newspaper editorial cited Barnett's deeds as evidence of the deteriorating mess around Douglas, calling it "a dangerous situation that must be defused."

On the afternoon that I met Barnett at his ranch, he wore no badge, though there was a 9mm pistol stuck into the back pocket of his jeans and a baseball cap, with an NRA logo, on his head. Barnett's rugged face and penetrating, pea green eyes suggested a man who was quite willing to back his words with action. A book of Spanish phrases was on the dashboard of his pickup. A few miles outside of town, we eased through the fence on foot, picking our way along terrain littered with water jugs, soda bottles, discarded clothing and food wrappers. In places, it more closely resembled the site of a previous night's rock concert than a grazing ground for cattle. There were pants, soda bottles, towels and sneakers. In one dry wash, about five miles north of the border, were twenty-two spent water jugs, along with abandoned shirts and socks.

Amid one pile of trash, Barnett reached down and picked up a scrap of paper. It was a discarded boarding pass from an Aeroméxico flight. He was clearly disgusted. To Barnett, the detritus represented a violation. His feed grass had been flattened by humans. He'd had to install spigots on the cattle watering tanks so that people would stop tearing up rubber water hoses to get a drink. But some of the eight-thousand-gallon tanks had been left bone-dry when the spigots were left open.

"I'm not against them. It's just the multitude coming across. There has to be some relief," he said, his voice low and even. The previous weekend, Barnett said, his brother had pulled over to the roadside to check the ranch fence. When the brother returned, Barnett said, "they were climbing into his truck."

Barnett said he never drew his pistol in detaining the twenty-seven migrants and merely was protecting the land against trespassers. That day his two brothers had been following footprints while Barnett, perched on a mountaintop, scanned the countryside using binoculars. He spotted some members of the group and guided his brothers to their hiding spot by radio. Barnett came down from the mountain and joined his brothers in walking the immigrants to the road and into the arms of the Border Patrol. To his way of thinking, he was merely doing his civic duty by "assisting" a Border Patrol that to him appeared impotent before the oncoming tide. Barnett brushed aside the charge of vigilantism. "A vigilante goes a lot further than I did," he said. "I didn't play vigilante. I didn't go out and beat anybody up."

Charges of vigilantism weren't unknown around Douglas. Memories of an incident twenty-five years earlier, known as the Hanigan case, had resurfaced in Douglas since Barnett's freelance roundups. It was August 1976, when three Mexican men—Bernabé Herrera Mata, Manuel García Loya and Eleazar Ruelas Zavala—slipped across the border near Douglas in hopes of getting to the highway and farther north to jobs. All three had worked on the U.S. side before and so were no strangers to the trek across the border in Arizona. This time, though, they made the mistake of choosing as their route a border-side ranch owned by the Hanigan family, which also operated Dairy Queen outlets in the area. The account the young men carried back with them to Mexico, wounded and terrified, was one of stunning brutality. The attackers were identified by the authorities as George Hanigan, sixty-seven, a Republican stalwart well known for his Goldwater-style conservatism, and his two adult sons, Pat and Tom.

According to the stricken migrants, the three ranchers seized them and accused García of having previously stolen firearms (a charge he denied). They then hauled the Mexicans to an isolated arroyo. There, they bound them with rope, stripped off the migrants' clothes, which they burned in a campfire, and took turns torturing the men. The Americans dragged them by the ropes, hacked at the migrants' hair with a knife, touched a red-hot poker to their bare skin, even passed a sharp blade near Herrera's scrotum, threatening to castrate him. Finally, one by one, the Mexicans were released and told to run. As the migrants raced unclothed through the shrubs, the vigilantes fired shotgun blasts, striking Herrera and García with bird shot as they fled. All three made it back to Mexican soil and were treated at a hospital in Agua Prieta.

As Tom Miller chronicles in his 1981 book, *On the Border*, the incident crystallized anti-Mexican anger among Douglas ranchers while reminding Mexican Americans of the uneasy realities "of growing up in a polarized town." Like the ranchers of 1999, the Hanigans had grown concerned over growing reports of thefts; Pat Hanigan's mobile home had been ransacked during a burglary a month earlier. "They would make it known that from that day forward Hanigan property was off-limits," Miller writes. Like the latter-day Barnett brothers, the Hanigan boys began patrolling the family's ranch land.

Then the Hanigan case began its long and twisted course through the American judicial system. The injured migrants identified photographs of the Hanigans; Ruelas accompanied U.S. authorities back into Douglas and recognized the Hanigan ranch house. Sheriff investigators retrieved shotguns, ropes and other evidence. The three Hanigan men were indicted by a Cochise County grand jury on an assortment of charges relating to the torture incident, including assault with a deadly weapon, kidnapping, armed robbery and related conspiracy counts. George Hanigan would die several months later, right before his scheduled trial in state court. His sons fared better. After two weeks of testimony, during which the Hanigan defense lawyers pried at apparent inconsistencies in the victims' accounts, the all-Anglo jury acquitted the brothers on all counts. An outcry ensued. The Mexican consul said the decision amounted to declaring "open hunting season on every illegal alien." Advocates for Mexican migrants joined with other rights groups in pressing the U.S. Justice Department to file charges against the pair in federal court. Even congressmen weighed in.

The campaign paid off. In 1979 the government found an unusual way out of its dilemma: it charged the brothers with having violated a federal law barring interference with commerce, which in this case was the attempt by the three victims to go to work north of the border. This time the evidence was better—a fingerprint on Tom Hanigan's truck matched the thumb of victim Ruelas. It was "the first clear independent physical evidence linking the Hanigans with the three Mexicans," Miller writes. And Pamela Hanigan, the ex-wife of Pat, testified about the brothers' "wetback hunting trips." The jury snagged, unable to reach agreement. But a retrial, this time before two juries, finally produced verdicts: Pat Hanigan was found guilty, Tom acquitted. The split verdicts made little sense to many folks on either side and served instead to harden opinion along conflicting poles. Now, many years later, ill feelings about the case remained in Douglas. The ranchers' newest antics threatened to bring them to the surface again.

As Barnett and I were driving away, he thought he spotted someone in the bushes along the rural two-lane blacktop. He pulled his pickup over to the dusty shoulder and hopped out. He had indeed seen someone—there, barely visible, was a group of immigrants. But this time, rather than making the arrest, Barnett called the Border Patrol on the walkie-talkie he carried. Agents arrived moments later, rounding up nineteen people, including two women and two boys who looked to be under ten years old. The group had taken shelter in the bushes from the afternoon heat, already severe in late April. Barnett watched the arrests, then got in his truck and wheeled off back to town.

The sudden flow of immigrants was more than an inconvenience for a handful of landholders—it had created a civic crisis for Douglas. Mayor Borane labeled the situation "uncontrollable" and threatened to sue the U.S. government as a way of spotlighting the disruption. The previous month had seen a record number of arrests along much of Arizona's southern border, led by Douglas with 27,225. The monthly total here was now double that of a year earlier. More startling, the number of arrests in and around Douglas was about equal to apprehension figures for the San Diego region, which had been the border's most permeable spot for as long as anyone could remember. "This thing is on a crescendo. It's escalating every day," Borane said during an interview in his city hall office. Half a block away, Pan American Avenue carried traffic to and from the border crossing a half-mile away. Among the vehicles were a growing number of Border Patrol trucks.

Borane, a wiry, sixty-year-old former teacher and school superintendent in Douglas, had served as Arizona's deputy school superintendent in Phoenix and later assistant to the president at Northern Arizona University in Flagstaff before returning home to run for mayor in 1996. He won a second two-year term in 1998. The $300-a-month job offered little in prestige to a man who had rubbed elbows for years with the state's top politicians, but Borane, a lifelong Democrat, saw it as a chance to boost the fortunes of his down-at-the-heels hometown.

Douglas needed all the help it could get. In addition to high unemployment, which at times exceeded 20 percent, and general economic anemia (nearly two-thirds of its residents lived in poverty), Douglas had managed to earn a reputation as a den of graft. A federal prosecutor labeled it "seriously corrupt" in 1996, thanks in good measure to investigations into whether U.S. border agents were in any way linked to drug traffickers on the Mexican side.

As mayor, Borane's goals were modest: to get a local branch of the community college, to build a new highway link that would put Douglas more directly into the flow of growing trade with Mexico and to draw more tourists. He had not planned to be swallowed up by a tense national debate over immigration while watching his beloved hometown convulse around him.

Borane sat in a unique position. He was raised in Douglas astride two worlds, Anglo and Mexican. He had grown up "semi-Anglo" in a Spanish-speaking barrio so poor it was known as *la hilacha,* Spanish for "the threadbare one." His father traced roots to Lebanon, and his mother to Lebanon as well as the state of Sonora, just across the border. The family spoke English and Spanish in the home, and Borane, despite blue eyes and fair skin that gave little outward clue of his shared heritage, was able as an adult to slip effortlessly between both longtime Anglo residents and the majority-Latino populace of Douglas. He also enjoyed close ties with officials across the border in Agua Prieta and found himself on the Mexican side almost daily, something that would have been unheard of for San Diego mayors.

By 1997, Borane had started noticing a strange phenomenon during his drives across the border. The streets were growing so crowded with men awaiting passage to the U.S. side that a careless driver ran the risk of striking someone. To Borane, the normally tame scene now resembled "the streets of Calcutta." Growing chaotic, too, were the streets and sidewalks to the north around downtown Douglas. Nights were now alive with groups of migrants racing along sidewalks and through back alleys. Smugglers had even taken to leading immigrants through the maze of storm drain tunnels beneath the city streets, popping to the surface through manholes. One of the favorite manholes was near a hotel used for smuggling.

On the east side of town, where Borane lived, he spotted people hiding in a vacant lot across the street. Thirsty migrants drank from his garden hose. One night he answered a knock on his door. There stood two young girls, accompanied by ten to fifteen other people shivering in the cold outside. "We're freezing—can you let us in?" one of the girls asked in English. Borane declined. Instead, he handed them two jackets and blankets before closing the door. He asked himself later with some regret whether he should have given them shelter in his garage. He wondered when some of these people would get themselves into serious trouble.

An answer of sorts came that summer in the form of a midnight telephone call. A sudden monsoon rain had sent a torrent of water rushing through the subterranean drainage network. A woman who had been caught inside was found dead. Her body was washed into a ten-foot ditch that skirted the border. Borane hurried down to the border to watch the recovery. The woman had not been alone. The water receded overnight and through the next day and evening, revealing a horrifying scene. Three more bodies were located, one by one. Then four more appeared in the muck, having been deposited by the rushing water in a sickening stack. Spectators lined the border fence as the authorities dragged the corpses out. In another part of town, six survivors from the group had been able to pop open a manhole cover by pounding on it with a wrench.

To Borane, the incident revealed a grotesque contradiction in U.S. immigration policy. Here were people, he thought, who had died in pursuit of jobs that Arizona's farms, hotels and construction sites desperately needed filled. Something had to change. Borane, who had carefully watched his every word during a long career in the jumpy confines of the educational bureaucracy, would be cautious no more. From his post as part-time mayor of an obscure and sagging border town, Borane launched his plea for help. He was angry at the federal policymakers who had designed a border strategy that treated tiny Douglas, in Borane's words, as "a Moroccan outpost." By early 1999, he began to call loudly for an overhaul of immigration policy, urging the adoption of a new guest-worker program similar to the bracero arrangement that had ended a generation earlier.

In March, Borane fired off a letter to President Clinton begging relief from "the deplorable and exacerbating situation in our communities stemming from the incessant, ever-increasing flow of undocumented aliens." The migrants, he wrote, "have simply overrun our community. Douglas is regularly in the media. The result has been negative exposure that has resulted in tremendous difficulties in business recruitment and retention efforts." The United States, Borane said, was mired in a losing battle. It was time to admit the obvious: Mexican workers would come as long as U.S. jobs beckoned and their own nation's economy remained backward. A new guest-worker program, Borane said, should guarantee decent wages and conditions and safeguard workers' rights. American employers, from hoteliers to farm owners, needed the workers. "The problem will not go away by throwing money at it. It will not go away by sticking our heads in the ground as we pass the chambermaid cleaning our room or the agricultural worker picking our fruit. We need to make it legal for the many aliens who are now working illegally and the many that are coming to fill these jobs," Borane wrote. "Our situation is grave," he warned in closing.

Borane did not mention what some in Douglas had come to see as the more corrosive potential results of the crisis: the loss of the town's binational character. Once mostly Anglo, but in recent years a predominantly Latino city, Douglas had always kept its door opened to residents of Agua Prieta, and vice versa. No fewer than six radio stations on both sides of the border broadcast Mexican music into the Douglas air; a reader eager for Mexican news could now choose among five Mexican newspapers that circulated on the American side. Especially since the shutdown of the Phelps Dodge smelter, many believed Douglas would crumble and its biggest stores would founder if not for Mexican customers. In the past, before there was any fence to speak of, Agua Prieta residents simply ambled over the border through open fields to visit American relatives or to shop. Douglas's enduring Mexican ties were still apparent at the Safeway supermarket and Wal-Mart store, which faced south toward the border. On a given night, most of the cars in the parking lot sported Mexican license plates, just as outside the big-box stores in Calexico and El Centro, back in California.

The possible toll on this deep connection between the two places also gnawed at Father Robert E. Carney Jr., who was ministering to two parishes in Douglas, where he lived, and Pirtleville, just north of Douglas. As the passions surrounding Douglas's immigration woes heated, Carney became a leading voice—sometimes the only one—against more border enforcement here. A New Jersey native, he had moved to Douglas only four years earlier, after a stint in Casa Grande, south of Phoenix. He started shaking things up at St. Luke's, the main English-speaking Roman Catholic parish in Douglas, by sprinkling his Mass with Spanish words and making his liberal views on immigration clear.

Carney, at fifty-five, was also a relative newcomer to the priesthood. He'd been ordained eight years earlier, completing a made-for-TV turnaround from a life that had once been devoted mainly to consuming all the booze and speed he could get his hands on. Rock bottom came in 1980 in St. Louis when Carney, then a skid row bartender so lost that he had taken to stealing from the friend he worked for, decided that he could live that way no longer. He sat down one day ready to consume a bottle of vodka and a pile of drugs. But at that moment Carney recalled being pulled away from the brink by an unexpected force, a warm, swaddling sensation that he interpreted as the embrace of God. Carney rose from the poison-laden table, got himself clean and sober—a task that took several years—and, at the suggestion of a priest who befriended him, eventually went to seminary in Wisconsin. He picked up Spanish working for a spell in San Antonio and during a stint in Guatemala.

Carney was deeply committed to the powerless, showing a preference for the poor that the Catholic Church had embraced as doctrine during the 1960s. That doctrine had prompted many Catholic priests and nuns into social activism as a central part of their religious obligation. Hospitality toward the stranger, a recurrent theme of the Bible, was, to Carney, a central measure of humanity, along with feeding the hungry and clothing the naked. These were not matters of personal political agenda. In God's eyes, Carney believed, kindly treatment of the outsider was a crucial test of one's moral comportment on earth.

By the time he arrived in Douglas in 1995, Carney had seen the earliest trickle of immigrants being pushed into Arizona by the border-enforcement drives that were just under way elsewhere. In visiting agricultural camps in central Arizona to perform baptisms and marriages, he encountered laborers who once had found it easy to cross into California and continue north to chase the crops to Oregon and Washington. Stymied there now, more of the migrants were making their way into central Arizona and staying put, working in the cotton fields and feedlots. At the two parishes where he now presided in the Douglas area, Carney adopted an open-door policy toward the border crossers, many of whom he could hear scurrying in the alleys past his quarters in the middle of the night. Couples and small groups would show up at the doors of his two churches, drawn by word of mouth and by the familiarity that most Mexicans have with the Catholic Church. Carney fed them and allowed them to shower and rest before moving on. When I first met Carney in a coffee shop at the Gadsden Hotel in downtown Douglas, he was vague about the help he was providing, leery of attracting unwanted attention. Later, though, he would urge clergy and religious laypeople to take a more militant role in defending undocumented migrants.

As the flow of immigrants through downtown Douglas increased, the Border Patrol erected a twelve-foot fence in May 1998. Carney staged his own one-man protest. As officials unveiled the barrier, Carney stood nearby holding a sign: "Instead of celebrating walls, build bridges." Parishioners, some of whom already felt alienated by the introduction of Spanish during the Sunday services, had begun to leave St. Luke's for other parishes. Carney wore a T-shirt that said: "Paz con Justicia" (Peace with Justice). His voice sounded sad.

Carney fretted that stricter border controls threatened to drive a wedge between the two cities. "It's almost like a piece of your body's cut off," he said, leaning across the table. "What I see happening if we keep using the force-and-violence answer—the next step is that we have a no-man's-land here. Then the next step is land mines. It's getting out of control. We have to respond in a different way. We must. The way we respond here in Douglas is going to be key to the way the North responds. If they see [us] build a higher fence or get more guns or call out the National Guard, that instills a deeper fear and that's how they will respond," Carney said. "Maybe it's more of a test of the individual," he continued. "Local people, if they're suspicious of people walking down the street, will call the Border Patrol. Others will see strangers using the hose on their property to get water and won't respond the same way. It's terribly complex."

That complexity and the community's bubbling rage were made clear a few days later during a town hall–style meeting with federal officials. The local congressman, Jim Kolbe, had summoned Johnny Williams from the INS office in southern California, along with representatives from the U.S. attorney's office in Phoenix and the Border Patrol in Tucson. Kolbe had a problem on his hands and he was ready to get an earful. His constituents, who had always enjoyed a commercial bonanza in shoppers from across the border when Mexico's economy was good, now were suffering the flip side of their border location. There was an overpowering feeling that Cochise County was paying the price for tight border control in California—a place for which Arizonans never held warm feelings. The meeting was an attempt to figure out how to cope with the rechanneled immigration flow. Douglas was now a test case. "How to handle this is going to be symptomatic for the rest of the border," a Kolbe aide said before the session.

Williams joined the other officials at the meeting, which took place in Bisbee. He and the INS were coming under increasing heat, first from human rights activists and now from ordinary residents, who felt like the victims of a chain reaction triggered far away. Williams arrived, certain that the strategy he helped engineer was working. What was needed, he was sure, was time—time to train new agents and to ship them in to plug the latest leaks. Nonetheless, he wanted to let the ranchers vent their anger and to improve the INS's showing there, which had been less than stellar. For example, callers were unable to get through to the Border Patrol station by telephone to report undocumented border crossers on their properties. During his long Border Patrol career, Williams had faced similarly sensitive situations. Even as a green agent in Lordsburg, New Mexico, during the 1970s, he had been called upon to soothe ranchers and pig farmers whose properties were raided by gung-ho border agents.

He seemed to be a magnet for delicate errands, whether cleaning up a troubled personnel division in El Paso or addressing beatings and other misconduct by agents while deputy chief in Yuma. Later, as the new chief of the El Centro sector in the early 1990s, Williams set himself to repairing frayed relations with community members who had grown outraged over what they saw as the impunity of agents—the result of border shooting incidents and reckless driving by agents. His experience had taught him that it was better to sit down and talk with critics than to hide behind a wall of officialdom. Long before community policing would become a vogue, and then a standard, for law enforcement agencies, Williams was a believer in its basic precepts. While posted as the station chief at Sierra Blanca in rural Texas later, Williams even joined the school board, helping to run a tiny district of only 156 pupils. It was one thing to draw up position papers and complex, multi-year enforcement blueprints in the air-conditioned comfort of a government office, and another thing entirely to have to endure the calamity that had been unleashed on a community. Even with all this insight, however, Williams's considerable political acumen would be put to the test at the meeting in Bisbee.

It was a scorching Saturday afternoon as 150 or so residents filed into the school auditorium, down the road from the old Copper Queen mine that was now a tourist stop. Many wore the cowboy hats, boots and dungarees that constitute the uniform of the cattle ranchers here. This was not a crowd in the mood to suffer bureaucratic doublespeak—not while immigrants were traipsing across their land in the middle of the night and the threat of violence hung in the dusty air. The government officials sat in their suits at a long table on the stage, looking like popgun targets at the county fair.

Kolbe introduced the meeting by conceding that a problem as complex as this would require some time to fix. Mayor Borane was first from the audience to rise and talk. He spoke with his usual crisp diction, seeming calm and reasoned. He said the community lacked the resources to cope with "international problems" and urged resurrection of the guest-worker program to answer what he called an "insatiable hunger" for Mexican labor. The guest-worker idea was seen as discredited in many quarters. Some critics viewed it as exploitative, others as unnecessary. A joint study on immigration by the United States and Mexico in 1997 concluded that such a program would be unlikely to solve the problem of unsanctioned crossings and could leave workers unprotected from exploitation by unscrupulous employers. The study concluded that it could end up worsening the illegal immigration situation by creating more routes for undocumented immigrants, rather than fewer.

The idea of guest workers was also a touchy subject here in the Bisbee auditorium. Hard-liners in the audience, like Barnett and Vance, listened to Borane and rolled their eyes. To them, inviting more Mexican workers north was a stupid notion—promoted by an unabashed liberal, no less—that would only accelerate illegal entries. The answer, they were sure, was in further tightening, not loosening, the barriers to Mexican labor. Barnett believed American workers would fill these job openings if U.S. employers simply paid them a fair wage, a position shared by many on the political left as well.

Borane sensed that what he was saying was not going over well with many of his constituents and longtime acquaintances around town. But by this point, he had begun to worry that his town sat atop a powder keg and might fall prey to outright violence. He had not condemned Barnett's quasi-military activities except to say that he wished the rancher would stop. Borane feared Mexican smugglers might seek to harm Barnett by somehow infiltrating the ranchers' group and doing violence. He fretted, too, about the flood of angry Mexican protesters who would cross the border and take to Douglas's streets if harm were to come to a helpless immigrant on U.S. soil. Borane's town, he worried, was one rash action away from an international incident. At the meeting, he warned the officials to move fast, declaring, "We're nearing a boiling point."

He was right. A Bisbee man named George Solewin, in plaid shirt and boots, asserted that it was time to take the millions spent on foreign aid in Europe and spend it on border enforcement here instead. "It's time to close the border until the bureaucrats and politicians can get this thing worked out," he said. The crowd applauded. Other residents rose, one by one, to describe the lines of border jumpers moving across their properties each night. They spoke of broken fences. Dogs barking. Fear.

"Do something!" shouted Tom Bohmfalk, of the neighboring town of McNeal. Clutching his cowboy hat, Bohmfalk said he had awakened two days earlier to find a group of intruders trying to break into his car. "If I am threatened anymore at my house," he intoned, "I will defend myself."

Others made similar vows, their frustration rising from the rows of seats. One man who owned twenty-four acres in Hereford suggested that authorities teach civilian residents how to help agents make arrests. He also suggested spending federal emergency-aid funds to clean up the trashed ranches. Williams listened, then spoke. First, he promised to publish an 800 number to enable residents to call the Border Patrol immediately. He also said that more telephone lines would be installed at the Douglas station to accommodate the higher volume of calls. On the way, too, he said, were more agents. Another four hundred were due to arrive in Arizona by year's end, most of them to the Tucson-based zone that includes Douglas. He described the addition of the IDENT electronic fingerprint system at Arizona stations and outlined a new operation to snare illegal immigrants who were making use of the Phoenix airport. Smuggling fees in Arizona now had zoomed to anywhere from $1,000 to $2,500—a sure sign that human trafficking had arrived in Arizona with full force, Williams told the group. The U.S. attorney, Jose de Jesus Rivera, promised to use an iron hand against smugglers. "If you cut off the head, a lot of problems will stop," he said. But the federal prosecutor and Cochise County attorney Chris Roll urged residents against taking the law into their own hands. It "only complicates" matters, Rivera said.

That assessment comforted no one here. Charlie Miller, a fourth-generation rancher in Bisbee, said he'd had thirteen cattle killed by trespassers, who ate what they needed and left the rest of the carcasses to rot in the heat. Others muttered their own gripes, and soon the meeting dissolved into a sour din of shouted questions and angry catcalls: "What are we supposed to do as ranchers when we see ten, twenty, thirty people come across our property?" demanded rancher Fred Giacoletti. "Are we supposed to go inside and cower?"

Kolbe's reply was limp but inarguably accurate: "There aren't easy answers to these things."

After the meeting Williams conceded that the INS had done a poor job of community relations here. But he insisted the overall border plan was working—the crackdown was robbing the smugglers of the easiest, urban access. "It's exactly the plan, not that we want the aliens to inundate Arizona," Williams said. "It's really an enforcement operation in progress. It's not instant pudding."

Meanwhile, the consternation in Douglas was shared on the Mexican side. Ray Borane offered to introduce me to his counterpart across the border in Agua Prieta. Borane thought nothing of making the cross-border trip at the spur of the moment—a sign of how close and casual the ties were between the two towns. Only as we were pulling away from his city hall office did he remember he was carrying a .22-caliber handgun in the truck. Taking it across the border would be illegal in Mexico. He stopped, left the weapon behind in city hall and then spirited us off for the ten-minute drive to downtown Agua Prieta.

On the Mexican side, local officials had been watching with horror as the transient population soared amid more and more acts of violence linked to feuding immigrant smugglers. Murders were multiplying. Just recently a municipal police officer had been killed after breaking up one such showdown over turf between rival traffickers. The mayor, Vicente Terán Uribe, had his hands full. If the problems were bad in Douglas, he said, they were much worse here in Agua Prieta, whose name means "black water" and comes from a stream that crosses the border. A rancher himself, Terán said he sympathized with angry property owners in Douglas, though he had been disturbed at the reports of roundups by civilians.

Terán said his city was struggling to accommodate a "floating population" of migrants. Arriving from two directions—from their homes in southern Mexico or repatriated from the United States after being arrested by U.S. border agents—this pool of rootless souls now was adding up to 100,000 people per month. It was an astounding figure, especially considering that the city's permanent population was only 120,000. The city had sought relief from the population boom by buying bus tickets for discouraged migrants who would give up and head home. Funds, though, were limited; many city streets remained unpaved. "Not many people go back," Terán said. "We can't help everyone."

The effects of the recent flood of newcomers—and an accompanying economic boomlet—were immediately visible in the blocks nearest the border crossing in downtown Agua Prieta. Dozens of men waited in clusters in and around the quaint central plaza. More than a dozen new restaurants and four hotels had popped up to accommodate the busloads of fresh arrivals, and some clever residents were hurrying to cash in by converting spare rooms and even offices into guest quarters. But, Terán noted somewhat sourly, the unwelcome development boom owed more to U.S. government border-enforcement strategy than to the wishes of city leaders. "It's the Americans who are making this such an industry," he said. Meanwhile, Terán continued, the disruption had hurt the town's traditional tourism trade. The Americans who normally traveled down from Arizona and parts farther north weren't showing up to spend money in the restaurants and curio shops in the same numbers. Terán believed it might take a guest-worker program such as the one being promoted by his friend Borane to restore peace. It seemed, Terán said, like a good way to render the budding web of people smugglers unnecessary and to make the passage safer for migrants.

Short of some kind of miracle, Douglas boosters said resilience was the best hope for the twin border cities in the face of an immigration wave far beyond their control. But even the most sanguine already saw a dusty landscape of hurt, from the migrants who had been driven by desperation to the ranchers now driven to distraction. Among those lamenting the changes was Ginny Jordan, who was Mexican-American and formerly directed the chamber of commerce in Douglas. Her father was now a member of the city council's Latino majority. Ginny had grown up in Douglas, and saw a simple beauty in border living that was getting overshadowed by the hype over the immigrants and the ranchers. Older Douglas residents were now afraid to cross into Agua Prieta. Strains of prejudice were now worming into radio call-in shows. She was disturbed to hear even Latino residents referring derisively to "wet-backs." And all the media attention was leaving the ranchers with a bum rap, she said, citing the renewed talk about the Hanigan case.

"Everybody is a victim here—everybody is," Jordan said, sitting in her home on the outskirts of town. "There are so many victims. But everybody wants to see the perpetrator. Who *is* the perpetrator?"

The ranchers' controversy continued to flare for months, into 2000. Tensions were fast approaching the level of an international incident. U.S. Senator Jon Kyl, an Arizona Republican, had warned that "people could get hurt." He accused the Clinton administration of abandoning the border and urged the hiring of more agents to make up for turnover and recent recruitment shortfalls. Meanwhile, the Barnetts made more headlines. In the year since Douglas first caught notice, they had continued their practice of rounding up illegal immigrants, despite word that Jose Rivera, the U.S. attorney, had opened a file with the Barnetts' name on it. If anything, the brothers were more determined that what they were doing was right and necessary. Roger Barnett was regularly fielding inquiries from reporters now, and he and his brother had even invited crews to film them while on their unofficial patrols. By 2000, the Barnetts' activities also attracted growing scrutiny in Mexico, where officials and commentators alike were reacting with escalating dismay. Mexican federal officials began tracking instances in which U.S. ranchers in Arizona and Texas had detained undocumented immigrants. Not surprisingly, Barnett's name was well represented on the list.

Cochise County Sheriff Larry A. Dever placed blame for the worsening debacle squarely on the doorstep of the federal government's overall border-control strategy. In an angry four-page statement issued in April 2000, he said his rural county had descended into a mess that his fifty-two deputies were powerless to make right: "Our fences are cut, our water sources damaged or destroyed, our lands are littered with tons of garbage, clothing, and human waste. We can't just drop our kids off at the school bus stop. Our highways are rendered dangerous by inexperienced drivers in unsafe vehicles, and hundreds of trespasses against our homes, our properties, and upon our cherished way of life occur daily." The sheriff charged that the INS policy of blockading the border in San Diego and El Paso had been designed deliberately to steer migrants to sparsely settled zones where political protest would be muted—just as Ray Borane had grown to believe. "It was done on purpose, with a belief that there would be less impact on fewer people, and therefore a lesser outcry. WRONG! Those who plotted this strategy did not anticipate the resolve they would awaken in the people who call this place home," Dever said.

Then, a day later, the stew reached an even faster boil, thanks to an anonymous flyer that heightened everyone's fears about the potential for vigilantism. Someone in Douglas had distributed a letter-sized flyer inviting Arizona's wintertime vacationers to join a "Neighborhood Ranch Patrol." According to the haphazardly punctuated flyer, participants would park their recreational vehicles on border ranches to help property owners guard against illegal border crossers. "This vacation is for the Winter visitor that wants to help an American Rancher keep his land protected while enjoying the southwestern desert at the same time," said the flyer, which featured a picture of a cruise ship. "No great big sailing ships on the desert. Just the great outdoors and good 'OLE western individualism 'spirit of private property' and enjoyment of the great outdoors. . . . Be a part of the American Way Team." The two-page leaflet suggested that participants be deputized with arrest powers to allow them to "legally arrest the lawbreaker." The flyer was unsigned but carried two e-mail addresses, which began with "A_Freeman2000" and "RUAfreeman." The leaflet was sent anonymously, bearing a Douglas postmark but no other distinguishing clues. No one knew quite what to make of the thing. Was it someone's idea of a joke? Was it for real? If so, many thought, Douglas faced the prospect of trouble that was potentially far worse than the Hanigan incident.

Ray Borane received one of the flyers at his city hall office. He first thought it was a gag. Then he wondered. Even if it was not serious, he thought, it threatened to produce the nightmare he'd envisioned: hordes of yahoos showing up in his city to hunt migrants for sport. "People are going to think it's open season here, and they can go down to Douglas, Arizona, for the winter and have fun chasing human beings," he told a reporter.

For his part, Barnett denied having anything to do with the flyer. But he said he'd already been contacted by people offering to stand guard on his ranch. He said he had rounded up some three thousand illegal border crossers on his land, most of them since I'd last visited. "Hopefully the federal government will get something done. We're American citizens down here."

The alarm felt by Borane was widely shared, especially in Mexico. News of the flyers was prominently reported south of the border, often with headlines shrilly suggesting that a "migrant hunt" was under way amid the dry creeks of southeastern Arizona. The matter of the Arizona ranchers had begun to anger officials at the highest levels of the Mexican government. A few days after the flyer was publicized, Mexico's Foreign Ministry issued its list of transgressions by U.S. ranchers. The ministry counted twenty-four incidents during the previous twelve months in which Cochise County ranchers had detained Mexican migrants "at gunpoint and with threats." The Barnett family had carried out thirteen of the roundups, according to the Mexican government. The latest had come only days earlier in May, when the Barnetts, with an ABC News camera crew in tow, detained nine immigrants who were sleeping on the ranch. While the tape ran, the ranchers' dogs awakened the migrants, who were placed in custody and handed over to the Border Patrol. The incident drew an angry reaction from Mexican diplomats, who already had begun to pressure U.S. officials to stop such behavior. The head of the Mexican government's human rights commission asked the United Nations to investigate possible abuses. Nothing had been done. Mexico's foreign minister, Rosario Green, was vowing to put the matter on the table during upcoming annual talks with U.S. diplomats. "The issue of the Mexicans and the Arizona ranchers is seen, without a doubt, as a red alert that could generate a relatively tense situation," she warned.

Green's comments came a day after a twenty-year-old Mexican migrant named Miguel Angel Palafox Arreguín reported to Mexican authorities that he had been fired upon and wounded in the neck by two black-clad American ranchers on horseback near Sasabe, Arizona. Palafox made the allegations after returning wounded across the border to Mexico. Authorities on both sides were stumped as to who the alleged shooters were. If his story was true, Palafox would have been the third migrant injured in gunfire at the Arizona border in a matter of months. That same day, another Mexican migrant, Eusebio de Haro Espinosa, twenty-three years old, was shot to death in Texas after he and a fellow border crosser stopped on a rancher's property, apparently, authorities said, looking for a drink of water. He was the third to die in such an encounter along the Southwest border that year. Mexico announced it was hiring an American law firm to gather evidence and bring cases against ranchers engaged in vigilantism.

Fear percolated, too, among Arizonans. The chairman of the county's governing board of supervisors, Mike Palmer, added his voice: "I don't want to regress into a vigilante state like the 1880s and have human life taken over the protection of private property. It's almost getting to that level." The board threw itself into crafting an appeal for federal help. On May 15 it issued a grave-sounding resolution saying the county was "under siege to a level that constitutes an invasion by undocumented aliens." Noting that fifty thousand such migrants were now being arrested monthly across Cochise County, the supervisors argued that a federal problem—immigration—had now become a costly local one due to the expenses of increased law enforcement, courts and hospital care. The resolution concluded by calling on Governor Hull to send the National Guard. In pleading for troops, the county's ruling politicians were echoing the calls of the ranchers made a year earlier.

In Washington, the INS announced it was sending 250 more immigration officers to the Arizona border, beefing up its Tucson-based force of 1,356 agents. Most of the new ones were headed to Cochise County. The contingent of agents assigned to answer ranch calls was being beefed up from twenty-four to thirty-four. To help agents on the ground, the INS also was readying a host of hardware: remote surveillance cameras capable of seeing in nighttime darkness, infrared night scopes, fences and high-intensity lights along two miles of the border at Douglas. This was all in addition to the nine miles of fencing that already stretched between Douglas and Mexico, despite Father Carney's protests.

Even Attorney General Janet Reno felt prompted to address the passions stoked by the ranchers' actions. Acknowledging Mexico's consternation, Reno said U.S. authorities knew of no violations of U.S. law so far, but were watching closely. "We are working to address the root cause of the problem—the increasing incidence of illegal immigration and smuggling through the area," Reno said in a statement. "I recognize the concerns of the Arizona residents who feel overwhelmed by the flow of illegal migrant traffic," she added, "but I urge them not to try and take the law into their own hands. It is important that local residents contact the Border Patrol rather than risk their own safety by confronting persons whom they suspect to be illegal migrants or smugglers."

Government officials weren't the only outsiders with their eyes on Cochise County. The cause of the ranchers had become an overnight rallying cry of California groups with a long history of antipathy toward illegal immigrants. The head of a southern California–based group called Voices of Citizens Together, which warned that illegal immigration presaged an imminent Mexican takeover of the Southwest, organized a rally in support of the ranchers, and especially of Roger Barnett, in Sierra Vista. The meeting drew a couple hundred folks, including some Cochise County officials. Among them was Dever, who urged attendees to "stay 100 percent within the law so I can always be firmly on your side." Also present was Barbara Coe, who had been a central figure in the Proposition 187 ballot measure dealing with illegal immigration in California in 1994. The immigration crisis of the early 1990s, it seemed, had come full circle. Douglas was the new San Diego. Even Pat Buchanan made the trip to Douglas. Larry Vance took him to see the border where migrants were crossing illegally. When Buchanan gave a speech at the Cochise College auditorium, a lone protester stood outside. It was Father Carney, carrying a hand-lettered sign with a quote from Martin Luther King Jr.: "Injustice anywhere is a threat to justice everywhere." Yet among those who filed past to hear Buchanan were some of his parishioners.

At the meeting in Sierra Vista, Coe represented the California Coalition for Immigration Reform, which not long before had made headlines by erecting signs along freeways greeting motorists in California. "Welcome to California. The Illegal Immigration State. Don't let this happen to your state," said one sign near the desert town of Blythe, close to the Arizona border. "Demand Illegal Aliens Be Deported. The job you save may be your own," urged another, in central California. In her remarks in Sierra Vista, Coe lauded Barnett and said it was the government's failure that forced him and other ranchers to guard the border and themselves against "the illegal alien savages who kill their livestock and slit their watchdogs' throats."

The meeting also drew some unwanted attendees. Organizers booted two Phoenix men who were affiliated with David Duke's racist organization after Ku Klux Klan flyers began turning up on car windshields outside the hotel where the rally was taking place. Dever seemed nervous about the prospect that the county could become a cause célèbre for meddlers from outside. "I fear there are people around us that want to take advantage of us," he told the group. "I have a fear that there are people with other agendas. I don't know that they're bad agendas, but they may be a little bit bigger than we are."

By summer 2000, a group headed by a former army infantryman named Jack Foote had sprung up to help Barnett and the other ranchers. That fall, the group, called Ranch Rescue, recruited volunteers from around the country and dispatched a delegation to Cochise County. There, according to the group's website, volunteers withstood torrential rains and resulting mud in order to repair damaged ranch fences and to erect highway signs decrying the illegal immigration problem. "Stop the Invasion," urged one of the signs. "If This Were Scottsdale the National Guard Would Be Here," said another, referring to the more tony part of Arizona.

The Ranch Rescue group caught the notice of observers inside the Justice Department. An internal "officer safety bulletin," citing information received by the INS's intelligence unit, warned that members of "known anti-immigration and hate crime organizations" were to arrive in Douglas during the weekend of October 27. The bulletin, which mentioned Ranch Rescue and Cochise County Concerned Citizens, noted that recruiters had been stressing to volunteers that it was legal to carry firearms openly in Arizona. The presence of twenty to thirty volunteers "may be a threat to illegal aliens and/or Border Patrol Agents," the advisory said. The bulletin listed several other organizations, including Coe's California Coalition for Immigration Reform, the Federation for American Immigration Reform, Arizonans for Immigration Reform, David Duke's group and the Ku Klux Klan, plus a couple of others.

News of the internal memo served to aggravate the ferment in Cochise County. Rancher supporters disavowed any connection to the Klan, while others said the predicted threat from volunteers was overblown, if not outright absurd. In any case, noted David Aguilar, head of the Border Patrol's Tucson division guarding 281 miles of border, including Douglas, the partisans came and went without incident. The feared trouble, he told the newspaper *Arizona Daily Star,* "simply did not occur." But the tensions around Douglas were not the only ones coursing along Arizona's border with Mexico. The state had become the main stage in the battle against illegal immigration and, with that, was to face more than its share of disruption and tragedy.

Chapter Seven

"THE BORDER CROSSED US"

Worry betrayed itself on the sweat-beaded brow of Betty Antone as she nosed the Chevrolet Suburban through a gap in the flimsy cow fence. Until recently, the string of gnarled mesquite posts and barbed wire was the most formidable barrier between the United States and Mexico along this lonely segment of southern Arizona. The fence went up during the 1930s to prevent diseased livestock from wandering into the United States. Now it was an unhappy embodiment of just how quickly border life had changed for Antone and fellow members of the Tohono O'odham Indian tribe.

The border was once but a line in the sand for the tribe and its reservation here. But the U.S. government's war on illegal immigration had instantly made lawbreakers of thousands of members accustomed to crossing from traditional lands on one side of that line to those on the other. The tribe may have been treated as a sovereign nation in many ways, but not when it came to the international boundary. Not anymore, at least. A visitor in 2000 quickly encountered bitterness toward this new, hard line among the Tohono O'odham, whose name means "desert people." They had made their isolated home for centuries among the ocotillo, sagebrush and saguaro cactus southwest of Tucson—some 150 miles west of Douglas and its ranchers. What fault was it of theirs that the tribe's home should land in the middle of this modern-day battlefield?

Antone, a fifty-one-year-old member on the U.S. side, had the job of driving a shuttle for the reservation, based in the town of Sells. Her daily assignment was to ferry ailing members of the tribe who lived on traditional lands just across the border in Mexico back to the U.S. side so that they could make use of the reservation's hospital in Sells. That task was now one of the strangest driving jobs I'd ever encountered. These days, Antone's cross-border trips put her at risk, legal and otherwise. As she navigated the back roads on the Mexican side, Antone dodged immigrant smugglers, drug runners and armed Mexican soldiers. When she made it to the opening in the cow fence—and to U.S. soil—there now was a chance she'd be stopped by the U.S. Border Patrol and her passengers arrested. She always got nervous, and this day was no exception. "I feel like a smuggler," Antone said, "but I have to do it." She had reason to feel jittery. She was, after all, breaking U.S. law, which forbids entry anywhere but at official checkpoints. And one of her passengers, an eighty-year-old man with tuberculosis, lacked the documents to cross the border legally. He'd been coughing up blood for a month and was eager to get to the tribal clinic.

Antone's unsanctioned crossing came at the end of a grueling day of driving a long loop wending three hundred miles from the reservation, along country roads past the 516-square-mile Organ Pipe Cactus National Monument and across the border into Mexico. There, her route passed through several towns and swung back north, through isolated shantytowns hidden among the cactus, as she picked up tribal members. (On the Mexican side, they still referred to themselves as Pápago, the tribal name once used on both sides.) The trip once symbolized how the tribe had remained joined as one even long after the U.S.-Mexico border was laid out following the 1853 Gadsden Purchase. Now it epitomized how a host of unexpected new troubles had befallen the tribe as the international boundary was imposed anew, nearly a century and a half after the border surveyors plotted its course.

For members of the Tohono O'odham here on Arizona's central flank, the pleas that had been heard in Douglas beseeching the government to send in more Border Patrol agents seemed ironic; the tribe now had no shortage of agents in their midst. The reservation was a three-hour drive from Douglas along Arizona's border with Mexico, but in many ways seemed on a separate planet from Cochise County and its rollicking history of cowboy shootouts, mining-town labor skirmishes and more contemporary smuggling rackets.

The sprawling Tohono O'odham reservation, covering a total of 4,800 square miles, was as isolated as it was vast. There were no boomtowns here, past or present. Through the ages, the Indians had lived a bare-bones agricultural existence, teasing tapery beans, corn and squash from the crusty ground, raising cattle and hunting javelina and antelope. Well into the twentieth century, the O'odham got around by horse. Traditional homes were built of mesquite beams and the inch-thick stalks of ocotillo, packed with mud and sand. These days, they were more likely to be built of stucco or concrete block, or to have arrived already built from the mobile-home factory. Sells, the main town, was founded in 1909 and now was a shabby collection of sun-beaten houses and treeless, bare-dirt yards. Cows ambled along the paved main drag. All around, the thorny bushes waved countless bits of windblown shopping bags from Basha's, the town's sole supermarket. There, announcements for tribal community meetings competed for attention with tabloids blaring celebrity-gossip headlines. At the center of town stood the modern tribal headquarters, a snow-bright stucco structure known as the White House.

Even by the usual grim standards of Native American life, the tribe was one of the poorest and unhealthiest in the Southwest, with an average annual family income of $8,347, a third of households unemployed and a frighteningly high diabetes rate. (A top tribal priority was to expand the twelve-bay dialysis center, for which demand was so high that it ran three shifts daily, around the clock.) The only bright spot was a pair of new casinos that had created $52 million in profits the previous year—and the prospects of a third, just under construction. No one here had anticipated a crisis over immigration. The vast reservation had never really been on the way *to* anything, really. Until recently. And in that sense, the tribe and the fed-up Douglas residents shared a similar new reality. Both were suffering the side effects of the border crackdown, though in ways as distinct as the two communities themselves.

Here, amid mesquite and bent-armed saguaro cactus an hour's drive southwest of Tucson, the widening net cast by border agents guarding the Arizona border had, quite by accident, begun ensnaring Indians. It was doing so on lands they had inhabited, without much interference or notice, for centuries. The big jump in illegal immigration and drug smuggling, diverted here from the more populous corridors, had in turn brought yet another crackdown by authorities—this time along the seventy miles of border forming the reservation's southern hem. The enforcement activity had upended life along this out-of-the-way desert swath.

The reason was a quirk of history that hadn't really bothered anybody until the current immigration crisis. The border that separates the United States and Mexico—defining the laws, customs and even the economic prospects for those living on either side—cuts straight through the middle of the traditional lands of the twenty-three-thousand-member Tohono O'odham nation. Each half is about the size of Connecticut. The border was suddenly a central, and problematic, fact of life. By the spring of 2000, the tribe was reeling from the ripple effects of a past that had failed to take them into account and an immigration crisis that raged with the ferocity of a dust storm.

The result was almost Kafkaesque. Indians, even many who were born on the U.S. side, were suddenly being treated as illegal immigrants on lands their people had traversed long before the United States and Mexico sat down to draw a boundary. There was stricter enforcement of immigration rules, such as the prohibition on crossing the border outside formal ports of entry, and citizenship was suddenly a key fact of life. But even many U.S.-born Tohono O'odham couldn't prove theirs because births at home had never been registered officially. The job of tracking births traditionally fell to designated village elders, who marked them not by calendar date, but in relation to the loose flow of community events, such as rains or droughts. That meant members had no way to assert their citizenship. Odd cases abounded, such as that of a twenty-one-year-old woman born in Mexico who was disqualified from becoming an American police officer; her mother could not prove having been born in the United States and thus gain the citizenship status that would also have been conferred automatically on her daughter. Some seven thousand members—nearly a third of the tribe's rolls— were caught in this type of predicament.

The strict border policing had created more problems for some of the 1,300 Tohono O'odham members who lived on the Mexican side. Although recognized officially as members of the U.S.-based tribe and eligible for tribal services, they could no longer venture north to visit relatives or to receive medical care at the reservation's thirty-four-bed clinic. Others had been arrested and deported. Their American counterparts faced trouble, too. Many who were born in Mexico or who lacked U.S. citizenship papers had to stop taking part in religious pilgrimages and other ceremonies in the Mexican border state of Sonora because their return to U.S. soil would be uncertain. A tribal attorney said that at least fifty Tohono O'odham members had been arrested in the past year or so by U.S. authorities while crossing from Mexico. Nonetheless, tribal officials had resolved to continue providing shuttle rides north for Mexican members who needed medical treatment on the Arizona reservation. As Antone did on this day, they often used the same informal crossings they'd always employed, despite the new risks.

Before setting out with Antone, I chatted with Cynthia Norris, a division manager at the tribe's community health office in Sells. She explained that the tribe had been running the shuttles for about four years. The medical shuttle was a service provided legally by the Tohono O'odham tribe for its members in Sonora, where the offerings of medical facilities were limited to rudimentary walk-in clinics and one poorly equipped hospital.

The tribe's drivers made daily trips south of the border, passing through O'odham villages and neighborhoods and ferrying anywhere from four to fourteen patients north across the border. Not all were headed to the Sells clinic; some of the more tradition-bound members came to see the tribal medicine man, Norris said. With diabetes rampant among the Tohono O'odham, the need for regular care was urgent, but some Mexican members had been held up for hours trying to get through U.S. immigration at the official port of entry in Lukeville, a hundred miles away. Norris said one village leader south of the border had died after going into a diabetic coma, despite having visited three doctors on the Mexican side.

Antone—short and rotund, with the broad cheeks and downturned mouth of many of the O'odham—hoisted herself into the driver's seat and guided the big Suburban onto the two-lane highway heading west out of the reservation. She looked ahead to an all-day trip, most of it on Mexican roads that in places were no more than primitive gravel tracks. Her stops were the homes of tribal members who had arranged appointments at the Sells clinic or had indicated they wanted to go. Antone was taciturn but not unfriendly. She had been driving this route for about a year and a half. She'd been a nurse, a records clerk and a switchboard operator. The fact that she could speak Spanish and the Tohono O'odham language, besides English, was a big plus in landing the shuttle position. The driving job had given her a chance to get to learn the confusing web-work of crude dirt roads connecting the tiny, out-of-the-way villages south of the border. It was pretty country and she liked her work.

Lately, though, the job had come to carry an air of danger. The desolate back roads on the Mexican side were now thick with smugglers, hauling drugs and people, and with Mexican soldiers, smooth-faced boys with rifles and baggy uniforms who had been sent in to try to catch them. During a shuttle run two weeks earlier, Antone had witnessed a shootout between Mexican *federales* and men she assumed were drug traffickers. The smugglers were showing up in these parts as U.S. agents patched holes in the border around Nogales and, slowly, in Douglas, too. Nowadays, parties of migrants were being carried by cattle truck through the open countryside to hidden pockets near the U.S. border in preparation for their nighttime crossings. Antone had gotten used to the military checkpoints, but the shooting was another matter. Her only protection was the tribal seal painted on the side of the vehicle.

After crossing at Lukeville, Antone's first stop in Mexico was in the town of Sonoyta, where the customary commerce of selling souvenirs to Arizona boaters heading south to the Gulf of California was fast being eclipsed by the trade in smuggling immigrants. As Agua Prieta's Mayor Terán had seen happen in his city, fleabag motels here in Sonoyta were filling up with young migrants arriving from the Mexican interior as smugglers trolled for U.S.-bound clients at the bus station. And as more and more migrants gathered here before attempting to cross the desert on the U.S. side, the town also was becoming a staging area for tragedy.

Antone stopped in front of a house to pick up a tribal member, Francisca Uriarte, then made two more stops in Sonoyta to remind patients that a driver would be passing through on the following day. That was the day set aside for prenatal appointments. She then swung south on the highway past a military checkpoint to Caborca, a cheerless and wind-blown city of car dealerships, shoe stores and video outlets in the heart of a region where grapes and oranges are grown. The tribe's reach extends this far—about a hundred miles south of the Lukeville cross-ing. O'odham members live scattered all over Caborca, some in tar-paper shacks, and in nearby Altar, having surrendered to the tug of the cities.

Antone wheeled past the town square to see if her passenger—the man with TB—was there. He was not, so she proceeded down a rutted dirt track to a house nearby and found him there. The man, Matías Chuhuhua, wanted to be checked at the clinic. Besides suffering a blood-streaked cough, he'd been having severe headaches and had run out of blood-pressure medicine. Considering all that, he seemed in sur-prisingly good spirits. He chatted in the O'odham language with Antone and in Spanish with me. Chuhuhua explained that he had applied for a U.S. visa under an experimental program for tribe members, but there'd been a glitch with the fingerprints and now he had to begin all over. In the meantime, still without papers, he would have to cross the border into the United States "through the back," as Antone called it.

Crossing "through the back"—far away from an official entrance—meant a bone-shaking two-and-a-half-hour ride along a maze of dirt roads, some smooth and well traveled and others as bumpy as a shack's corrugated roof. The flat landscape bristled with the spines of ocotillo bushes and prickly pear cactus. Chuhuhua said it cost $15 by taxi to be dropped off near the border crossing farther east at Sasabe. Antone's route, though, was a more roundabout course through the scrubby country-side. At a remote spot about halfway to the border, Antone was stopped by a Mexican soldier guarding a checkpoint. He asked, in Spanish, where she was going.

"Sells," Antone said.

"That's on the other side, right?" the young soldier inquired.

She answered yes.

The soldier waved her along and went back to waiting on the lone-some stretch. Next to the road was a vehicle resembling a Humvee and an old-fashioned army pup tent.

On the road ahead, a cloud of dust trailed a cattle truck packed with about twenty standing men. It, too, was headed north toward the border, and toward the reservation. As Antone drove, the roads narrowed and the ruts deepened. One by one, little O'odham villages appeared—clusters that seemed as forgotten as little ghost towns amid the shrubs. The primitive tracks crisscrossed more, throwing Antone briefly off course until she was able to find her way again.

She pounded ahead, as low branches of mesquite trees snapped and whipped at the truck's windows, until reaching the gate, known as San Miguel. She eased the Suburban through. Today, there was no Border Patrol. Antone turned onto the pavement and zoomed north toward Sells, visibly relieved. "I never know if I'm going to get here or not—every time I go out. Especially now with the shooting that went on," she said. It was the most expansive she'd been all day. Asked why she continued in a job that had grown so nerve-racking, she answered simply: "To help people out." Elaboration seemed needless. Antone dropped her passengers at the tribal center in Sells, twenty-nine miles from the gate. It was eight hours since we'd left the reservation and her strange job was done for another day.

The tribe's worries over how to continue providing medical services to its Mexican members in the midst of the new clampdown were just a part of the problem. In a broader sense, tribal members took offense at having been trapped in a bind not of their making. They worried, too, about losing their way of life in the process. Tribal members from both sides traditionally gathered each year, some on foot, for religious pilgrimages in Mexico. On the U.S. side, a cave atop Baboquivari Peak is considered home to I'itoi, the most important Tohono O'odham deity, who is believed to have made the universe in four days and to have created these "desert people" from the surrounding clay. Though many modern O'odham are now Christians, the desert remains sacred, its bounty of animals, plants and people an interrelated whole, the parts inseparable. The sacred mountain peak sticks dramatically above the range bearing its name, making it easy to find. Those in crisis often seek the cave to pray for forgiveness or guidance, perhaps to offer I'itoi a prized basket or statuette.

Family ties stretched from sun-bleached stucco homes on the U.S. reservation to the adobe shanties in Mexico, which was home to about a dozen indigenous communities but no official reservation. For years some Mexican members commuted over dirt roads through the three unofficial crossings to jobs in Sells. The Mexican O'odham have always been treated as full-fledged tribal members; some had even served in the U.S. military and held federal jobs.

One member, George Ignacio, recounted that his family had lived on both sides of the border, depending on his father's work as a blacksmith and welder. The elder Ignacio, José, was the tribe's first chairman when the nation was recognized officially by the U.S. government in 1937. He was born in Mexico, as was George Ignacio's mother. George, now seventy-seven, was born on the Mexican side, but had traveled back and forth his entire life without documents. José Ignacio brought the family north to Sells during the 1920s so that his six children would have an education. The father got welding jobs on dams all around Arizona, then periodically headed back to Mexico when the work dried up. George Ignacio grew up to be a welder, too, working in a mine near Ajo, Arizona, for twenty-seven years after marrying his high school sweetheart, also from Sonora. Ignacio, bespectacled and caramel-skinned, with sparse white whiskers on his chin, still lacked documents to be on U.S. soil. He was an illegal immigrant. "It's a thing that people don't understand," he said.

The situation grew more incomprehensible by the day. Now, as streams of illegal immigrants tried to cross, Border Patrol helicopters flew above, helping agents on the ground chase the groups that had been dropped off by the cattle trucks. You could pull off Highway 86, the main road from Tucson, just about anywhere on reservation property these days and find signs of the trend. At the base of Lookout Mountain, discarded clothes and scores of spent water jugs marked pickup spots, or "load-outs," that were favored by smugglers. Sneaker prints weaved around stands of the spiny ocotillo, which flashed with red-orange little blossoms. Several weeks before my visit in April 2000, a reservation high school had to be pressed into service as a makeshift emergency shelter after 330 migrants were caught up in a sudden snowstorm. The winter and early spring were known to carry a fearsome punch, even in the desert. The laments of overworked agents echoed those heard in Douglas a year earlier.

Border agents were given cultural sensitivity training so as not to offend law-abiding tribal members. Officials seemed remarkably sympathetic to the plight that the tribe found itself in. One commander made an interesting comparison, citing the division of East and West Germany to make the point that many Germans never accepted that their nation had been split. The supervisor acknowledged that his agents knew some Indians were using the cow-fence gates for crossings that were technically illegal. But the officers now recognized the faces and vehicles of some of the Tohono O'odham and were trying to look the other way as much as possible. Besides, there were too few agents spread over the vast zone to cover the gates all day.

Still, federal law was federal law and some Indians had been arrested, along with the thousands of Mexican migrants passing through. Furthermore, some Tohono O'odham members themselves had gotten mixed up in the smuggling. During a tour of the area, Border Patrol agent Tom J. Nix, a second-generation border agent, pointed out a home where agents twice had discovered groups of fifty-plus immigrants jammed inside a shed. On one of those occasions, agents also found a cache of dope. Another house had been found to be harboring groups on several occasions. More than a third of all the migrant arrests made in the huge Tucson region were now taking place on the reservation—2,500 during the previous month alone.

All the activity had created what the tribe's vice chairman, Henry A. Ramon, compared to a "war zone." The tribe hadn't crossed the border, Ramon had taken to pointing out. "The border crossed us," he said.

Where many once found blessed serenity in the parched landscape, there now was tension. Near the San Miguel gate where Antone crossed back into the United States, the food vendors who traditionally gathered on the Mexican side watched business go from brisk to dismal as the border grew more menacing. The tribe's education director, Rosilda Lopez-Manuel, said she no longer went to the gate to buy Mexican cheese. She was tired of being viewed as a suspect. And she now discouraged her husband from camping on remote lands because she feared drug smugglers and groups of illegal immigrants. The couple used to venture out to hunt quail and deer when the groceries ran low. It was no longer safe on either side.

"It's so distressing nowadays. It's not like it was before. And it's a result of all these illegal activities," said Lopez-Manuel, who grew up in the village of Cababi, north of Sells. "We're desert people and we don't even go out anymore." She said most people on the reservation felt hostility toward the Border Patrol, who had come to be viewed by many as an occupying force. "They act like they own the land," she said. She worried that the changes were permanent. "We'll never go back to the wonderful, free, safe, traditional lives we used to enjoy in the most peaceful manner. It's the biggest loss. That's gone forever," she said. "My childhood memories—thank God I have the memories."

Her people are not alone. A handful of tribes, such as the Yaqui elsewhere in Arizona and the Kumeyaay outside of San Diego, have members in both countries. But the Tohono O'odham are the only U.S.-recognized tribe that enrolls Mexican members and allows them to vote in the eleven Tohono O'odham districts on the U.S. side. The extent of the blending across the border became clear during a tribal meeting one Saturday morning. Vice Chairman Ramon and other leaders had come to the village of Gu Vo, a tribal district on the border west of Sells, to explain how they proposed to address the fix the tribe had found itself in.

They were proposing a provocative answer: changing U.S. nationality law to grant citizenship to enrolled tribal members in Mexico and to treat tribal identification cards as proof. The proposal aimed to repair what leaders consider a historical oversight—that the group was not considered when Mexico sold to the United States the huge chunk of the Southwest that included Tohono O'odham lands. Aggravating the matter, no arrangements for unrestricted passage were made when the tribe won official recognition in 1937. Unlike on the border with Canada, where the United States permits indigenous Canadians free passage, no sweeping arrangements exist for groups along the Mexican border.

The Tohono O'odham still consider themselves a single tribe—that was apparent at the meeting. Ramon explained before the session that what was at stake was nothing less than life and death for tribal members. He said it was unjust that his people on the Mexican side lacked the rights of those to the north; the tribe viewed its members as equals, no matter which side of the border they lived on. The answer, he said, was to provide U.S. citizenship to all Tohono O'odham members, regardless of where they were born in relation to the U.S.-Mexico border. "We want to see members of our tribe have the same rights as we do in the United States. They're members of the tribe. It's not their fault they ended up on the other side." The approach would clear up the difficulties facing the Mexican members and solve the problem of the U.S.-born members who lacked papers proving their birth. "I'm responsible for the welfare of my people," he said.

Ramon was old enough to know firsthand the strange, bureaucratic no-man's-land in which many of his elder members now existed. He, too, was born at home on the U.S. side, in 1934. His mother gave birth in the traditional manner, squatting while tugging on a length of rope dangling from the ceiling. The rope was still there, so many years later. But Ramon never obtained a birth certificate until years later, after he had served in the U.S. Army during the Korean War. Despite his military service, it wasn't easy getting the birth document, which he needed for receiving veteran's benefits. He might not have been able to get one at all if not for an uncle who was present at his birth. It would be even harder to get one today—and proving citizenship seemed more important than ever.

Ramon had been involved in O'odham government since the early 1970s, rising to the position of vice chairman in 1995. He'd grown up in the traditional way, planting beans after the summer rains and hunting deer with a rifle. The roads were dirt, cars were nonexistent. Ajo was the nearest big town—some one hundred miles to the northwest—and Ramon traveled by horseback to fetch axle grease for the wagons. Commerce with the outside world came in the form of baskets and furs to trade. Electricity and running water were unknown in many villages until the 1980s.

As we awaited the start of the meeting, Ramon's soft mocha face was a creased picture of concern. "The climate has changed. It's like a war zone, a military zone. Patrol vans are all over. Our people get caught in between. It's a real problem," Ramon said. "And it's getting worse."

Inside the low-slung modular building like that used by overcrowded schools, Ramon and nine tribal council members sat at a long table. The twenty or so rank-and-file members in attendance shifted seamlessly from the O'odham language to English, then to Spanish and back again—all without a single translation. Ramon wore a black polo shirt and the somber demeanor of a doctor explaining an impending surgery. Speaking low and soft in the language of his Indian ancestors, Ramon outlined the leaders' thinking. Congress would have to amend the U.S. law to convey citizen status at birth on anyone who was a member of the Tohono O'odham nation. This was a serious crisis for the tribe. As he spoke, the feeling in the room was quiet, dignified, significant. Sprinkled in Ramon's presentation were some words in English that apparently didn't translate into O'odham. *Register. Enrollment. Passport.*

The idea that Tohono O'odham members needed documents to move about their ancestral lands struck some, especially older members, as baffling. But everyone seemed to know of someone who'd recently had trouble crossing. At the closest official ports of entry on either side of the reservation—90 and 105 miles away—Mexican tribal members had run into trouble or been turned back because they lacked proper documents. Faustino Romero Zepeda, a thirty-four-year-old Tohono O'odham who was born in Mexico, had been deported from the port of entry at Lukeville ten months earlier after he tried to return to his U.S. home from tribal business in Mexico. The INS charged that Romero falsely declared himself a U.S. citizen. As a result, he was barred from entering the United States for five years. Nonetheless, he returned on foot through the countryside to the U.S. reservation, where he was now working as a ranch hand. He agreed to meet to describe his plight as long as I didn't identify his whereabouts. He didn't want to be deported by U.S. immigration authorities a second time. We met in the backyard of a Sells home. His black hair hung down to his chest in the style of some of the O'odham men.

Romero was born in Caborca but had split time since the 1980s living in Sells. He'd spent most of his time on the U.S. side during the previous six years and was learning English to add to Spanish and the O'odham language. He said he'd passed through the Lukeville crossing two or three times before, showing only his tribal ID to gain entrance. This time, though, Romero said he was stopped and handcuffed to a chair. He was photographed and fingerprinted and asked to sign a form. He did. He was returned to Sonoyta and borrowed money to hire a taxi. He then walked seven hours to cross back onto tribal lands through the backcountry. Romero recalled intense heat. He said he was somewhat fearful to remain on U.S. soil after having been kicked out, but said, "I don't want to be in Mexico."

The tribe had applied for a visa on his behalf as a Mexican national. But tribal officials said Romero probably deserved to be granted full U.S. citizenship. His grandmother's birth in Arizona was never registered, thereby denying U.S. citizenship to Romero's mother and, ultimately, to him. It was a familiar story here. The paucity of paperwork was central to the difficulties of the Tohono O'odham and other border tribes. It was not just U.S. birth certificates that were lacking. Thousands of Indians born in Mexico don't have Mexican papers and could not get the Mexican passport and visa to enter the United States at official checkpoints. To compound matters, many Mexican Indians were living an isolated farming existence that produced none of the documents—such as pay stubs, bank statements and rent receipts—that were required by U.S. officials to ensure that a visitor has no intention of staying. Their attempts to enter lawfully, in other words, had become an exercise in complete futility.

To their credit, some U.S. officials had begun seeking to extricate the Indians from their nightmare. They invited members of the Tohono O'odham and Kumeyaay tribes to test a program that would provide Mexican passports and U.S. border-crossing cards to Mexican members who lack supporting papers. U.S. officials had applauded the pilot program, which allowed Indians to forgo some of the usual documents and to present tribal declarations in place of others. As one key step in this process, the Kumeyaay tribe in San Diego had begun conducting a census in seven indigenous communities in Baja California. Kumeyaay leaders were hoping to enable Mexican Kumeyaay eventually to be able to work freely on the U.S. side as language teachers or to sell handmade baskets and pots at U.S. Indian casinos.

Before the program, Mexican Indians had often entered under special waivers, issued case by case, for hospital visits, funerals, family emergencies or cultural ceremonies. But that method was time-consuming and vulnerable to mix-ups because the waivers required the tribe, U.S. immigration officials and U.S. consular staffers in Mexico to fax names back and forth. Tohono O'odham leaders viewed the pilot program as helpful but only an interim step until they could get citizenship legislation passed. It promised to be an uphill fight, especially at a time when tighter borders were a national priority. A proposal to allow Mexican

Tohono O'odham to cross freely had gone nowhere in the U.S. Congress two years before, but such an arrangement was not entirely without precedent. The Kickapoo tribe in Texas won U.S. citizenship and crossing rights for its Mexican members in the 1980s. That group and a separate Kickapoo tribe were now seeking to reopen the offer of citizenship for members who lived in the United States but migrated to Mexico each winter for traditional religious observances.

Tohono O'odham members remained hopeful of changes, but resolute about who they were. One was Henry Jose. He lived in Sells, but represented a village on the Mexican side. He saw no contradiction in this. "I don't consider myself anything but Indian," he said. Now he raised cattle on both sides of the border. He described his childhood years, when tribal members in Mexico camped out during a two- or three-day journey to reach the tribe's lands to the north. "Used to be we just had roads and places to go. Now everybody calls it the international border," Jose said. "It was my place anyway, wherever I came from, whatever you call it. I call it Indian land."

By the end of 2000, the reservation was witnessing other worrisome developments. Besides disrupting the Tohono O'odham's traditions, the wave of immigrants now crossing Arizona's southern border could be gauged increasingly by a more disturbing measure: the deaths of migrants like Yolanda González Galindo, a nineteen-year-old from the southern state of Oaxaca. She perished in May during a three-day hike through the Tohono O'odham reservation with a group of ten. Her last act was to give her remaining drinking water to her daughter, who was just eighteen months old. The young mother was found under a paloverde tree; the daughter survived. It was a reminder that the tribal lands were not merely the scene of new tensions, but dangerous, too. More traffic brought the risk of similar losses. Indeed, this unforgiving section of the state promised to see more such tragedies, but another group of Arizonans was rushing to help.

Chapter Eight

A CUP OF WATER IN MY NAME

The Reverend Robin Hoover was a busy man. He was freshly arrived in Arizona, starting a new life, with a new wife, a new job. At forty-seven, Hoover had pulled up stakes in West Texas—where he had grown up, been schooled all the way to a Ph.D. and learned to preach—to take over as the new pastor of the First Christian Church in Tucson. He now had to get to know an unfamiliar congregation—and introduce himself to his new 350-member flock—in a state where he had never lived before. Even for a man of his considerable energy, the last thing Hoover had come seeking in Arizona was a crusade to add to his busy life. It didn't take long, though, for the crusade to find him.

The heartbreaking circumstances around the way Yolanda González had died to save her baby in the desert caught the public's attention in a way that few of the migrant deaths in Arizona had. Until then, the fatalities had mounted slowly, reported from time to time in news stories and brief wire-service items. They never created much more than a muffled background drumbeat amid the clamor over the ranchers in Douglas and, to a lesser degree, the plight of the Indians.

Hoover and his wife, Sue Ann, a university fundraiser, had arrived four months earlier, in January 2000. He'd been struck by news reports about the astounding number of arrests—three thousand a day—being made in the Douglas area. But by mid-year, he'd managed just one trip to the border even though it was only sixty miles south of Tucson on Interstate 19. Although Hoover had been involved in border issues back in Texas, he still knew little about what was happening in Arizona when he agreed to attend a meeting of clergy and laypeople called to address the increasingly disturbing dimensions of the border crisis.

Members of Tucson's liberal religious community had watched with growing horror as the border deaths added up, wondering how to respond. If they had needed any more encouragement, the account of a young Mexican woman making the mother's ultimate sacrifice provided the push. David M. Perkins, a Quaker in Tucson who had long paid attention to border issues, decided it was time for people of faith to step forward. He proposed that the local Quakers host a gathering of socially aware people from various denominations and faiths as the first step. Perkins got things rolling by contacting a handful of acquaintances. Each of them was to reach out to more people, who were to call others and so on. They'd see how many folks showed up.

Among those first approached by Perkins was Rick Ufford-Chase, who ran a church-sponsored group called BorderLinks that led educational tours of the border for church people and students and also was involved in humanitarian projects in Mexico. BorderLinks was housed on the grounds of Robin Hoover's First Christian Church, along a busy boulevard called Speedway—home to the University of Arizona and a lengthy string of fast-food chain outlets. It made sense to invite the newly arrived pastor to the gathering. Hoover wasn't sure what, if anything, would result from such a session, but he agreed to attend. What harm was there in going? On June 11 he joined about eighty-five others at the Quaker meetinghouse in Tucson. The group talked and brainstormed, scrawling ideas on an oversized chart pad. Hoover took notes in the moleskin pocket notebook that was one of his prized possessions. He jotted down the two central questions that confronted the gathering of religious folks: How can we respond with compassion to persons who are risking their lives to cross the border? How can we change the system?

They were big questions, capable of swallowing up the best of intentions if participants were allowed to meander aimlessly. But many of the attendees also knew that the actions of church people in Tucson during the 1980s had succeeded in sparking a daring and controversial movement that swept across religious communities throughout much of the United States. Known as the sanctuary movement, it too grew out of the moral indignation over the plight of a group of migrants who had died crossing the border in the Arizona desert. The movement came to the aid of refugees and in the process resulted in federal convictions of several clergymen and laypersons. For many of the socially progressive faithful who remained in Tucson in 2000, the effort represented an especially proud moment in the history of U.S. church activism and an inspiration for how to respond now.

The sanctuary movement was born officially in Tucson in March 1982, when a group of fifteen religious leaders including a priest, a rabbi and five Protestant ministers gathered outside the Southside Presbyterian Church in a ramshackle Tucson barrio to declare the church a haven for Central Americans seeking refuge from war and repression in their home countries. For several years, a gathering river of people had been making their way north from places like El Salvador, burned out of their villages by government troops or fearful of being persecuted by authorities as rebels or sympathizers. Latin American Catholic clergy who spoke up on behalf of the impoverished and downtrodden came under attack from right-wing regimes. Among the worst was El Salvador.

The Salvadoran social order had always rested upon a sturdy triad of military might, landed oligarchy and an acquiescent Catholic hierarchy. But there was a growing church activism, inspired by a new, so-called liberation theology that emphasized social justice themes, from political and education rights to better pay. It was seen as subversive; nuns were raped and killed, priests gunned down. In March 1980 assassins targeted the country's archbishop, Oscar Arnulfo Romero, as he celebrated mass. Romero was known as conservative, but had grown harsh in criticizing the government—and the U.S. military that backed the regime.

For many Salvadorans weighing whether to stay or leave, the archbishop's slaying was all the evidence needed that their homeland was without hope. They began leaving in droves, heading north in search of safe haven in the United States. A group of twenty-seven made their way to the border at the Organ Pipe Cactus National Monument, not far from the Tohono O'odham reservation. They were abandoned by their smuggler in oppressive July heat. Thirteen people were found dead. They were clothed in the garb of the urban middle class—some women were caked in makeup and wearing high heels—and showed that El Salvador's desperation had reached well beyond the impoverished countryside. Fourteen others were rescued over two days. It would be the deadliest incident involving border hikers on the U.S.-Mexico border for twenty-one years, until the summer of 2001, when a group of Mexicans would make a similarly disastrous journey. The shock of the 1980 incident became an uproar when the U.S. government indicated its intention to send the survivors back. Tucson churches put up bond money to allow the survivors to apply for asylum.

Among the first clergy to get involved were Jim Corbett, a Quaker rancher, and John M. Fife, a towering, stick-thin Pennsylvanian who was the pastor at Southside Presbyterian Church. Fife was also a long-time veteran of peace and justice causes, from civil rights in Tucson to the fight against apartheid in South Africa. As the refugees continued pouring north from Central America, the church activists grew appalled by the U.S. government's handling of them. Although the United States seemed to welcome those fleeing the repression of communist nations, it took a skeptical view of claims being made by Salvadoran and Guatemalan refugees, whose governments were receiving U.S. support against leftist insurgencies. The U.S. government claimed these Central Americans were showing up at the border not in search of personal safety or political liberty, but as job seekers.

The activist clergymen saw in this stance a clear violation of the Refugee Act of 1980, which had sought to even the playing field for refugees by providing access to asylum for anyone who could demonstrate a "well-founded fear of persecution" in his home country. The Salvadorans, facing death or torture if denied entry to the United States, were surely in that category, the church activists asserted. If the government would not provide haven as called for under the law, then they, as people of conscience, would. Despite legal risks, they would declare their houses of worship as sanctuaries, following a tradition going back to biblical times.

The first to be named such was Fife's little adobe church, on March 24, 1982—a date chosen for its symbolism as the second anniversary of Romero's assassination. Other churches around the country soon began declaring themselves sanctuaries. Over the next several years the sanctuary movement would swell to include more than four hundred congregations, along with eleven universities, nineteen cities and the entire state of New Mexico. It also won the endorsement of church hierarchies, including those of the American Baptist, Presbyterian and United Methodist Churches and the leaders of Conservative and Reform Judaism.

Under sanctuary, church folk created an underground railroad for the refugees. The churches made their work known to authorities by informing the INS when they brought people into the country, but leaving out the times and locations. The volunteers, ordinary citizens from all walks of American life, hired smugglers to get the refugees over the border, provided food and shelter and ferried refugees by the hundreds from one safe haven to the next along the sanctuary trail. Church ladies relied on coded messages to sneak their charges past Border Patrol checkpoints. Pastors hosted refugees in their parishes and homes. The actions put the activists into conflict with U.S. law, which called for terms of up to five years in prison for helping undocumented immigrants enter the country.

In 1985, Fife and fifteen other sanctuary workers were indicted on federal immigrant-smuggling charges that resulted in part from the work of a paid INS informant who infiltrated the church group and made secret tape recordings. INS officials said the movement had no basis for protection under U.S. law. INS Commissioner Alan C. Nelson labeled it "a political protest involving lawlessness."

In 1986, following a highly publicized six-month trial, Fife and seven others were convicted on criminal charges relating to harboring and transporting illegal aliens. Fife, two Roman Catholic priests and a Catholic nun were given suspended sentences and placed on probation. Four lay workers also got probation. (Corbett was acquitted.) But the widely publicized federal proceedings in Tucson did little to quell the movement. By 1986, the movement had shepherded some 1,500 to 2,000 refugees to homes in the United States. Around the country, congregations and other institutions added themselves to the list of self-declared refugee sanctuaries. "I plan for as long as possible to continue to be the pastor of a congregation that has committed itself to providing sanctuary for refugees until their lives are no longer in danger," Fife said defiantly after his conviction.

Fourteen years later, he and other people of faith in Tucson and elsewhere in Arizona found themselves wrestling with the tricky moral and ethical questions over how far they were willing to go to lend their help to a new group of border crossers—one they viewed as being in the sort of mortal danger that again urgently demanded action. But this latest group came as job seekers, not as political refugees. This time the deadly perils lay not in the threat of repression back home, but in the act of crossing itself.

By the middle of 2000, the Arizona border was alive with activity. In Douglas, the local authorities were blaming the U.S. government for their troubles and trying to squelch fallout from the "Neighborhood Ranch Patrol" flyer. In Sells, the Tohono O'odham were pressing forward with their campaign to gain U.S. citizenship rights for tribal members from both sides of the border. Over in California, Claudia Smith was publishing running counts of deaths along the California border. But the activists there had gained little ground yet with their year-old human rights complaint to the Organization of American States charging that Operation Gatekeeper violated international rights standards. She and the other activists continued to hold vigils along the fence in San Diego and Tijuana, but it was here in Arizona that the crisis was becoming most acute. It was here also that the single largest tragedy would soon occur.

At the Quaker meetinghouse, Robin Hoover jotted notes as the group neared consensus on how to react to the deadly risks facing the Mexican migrants who entered Arizona's desert wasteland. Some of the ideas were concrete, others grandiose. The list included creation of a faith-based movement, one that would stretch across the border into Mexico so as to be truly binational in character. Among the tactics of the movement would be to "organize organizations," a long-held technique in social-justice activism. On the list of aims was to change INS policy. But at the top, the church folk had assigned themselves a more straightforward errand, ingenious in its simplicity: put water in the desert.

The result was a group named Humane Borders. Its symbol would be the Big Dipper, a logo with double meaning. The dipper would evoke the pouring of water; its North Star was also used by the Underground Railroad movement to guide runaway slaves north. Hoover was named to a steering committee of three members, but soon was selected to be the campaign's president and its most visible spokesman. As the death count rose in Arizona, it fell to the newcomer Hoover—a pipe-smoking, straight-shooting Texan with the baritone of a late-night disc jockey—to channel the rising moral outrage into humanitarian action.

Hoover warmed quickly to the challenge. Though he was new to the area, he did not lack for self-confidence and had encountered controversy before. In 1980 he got his first pastor's post in Freeport, Texas—a job that enabled him at last to put into practice his long-held ambitions and commitment to righting social wrongs. In his sermons, Hoover borrowed from the issues of the day. In one about Abraham's land promise, he cited the Falklands war, bombing in Beirut, reparations for U.S. slaves and apartheid, noting that God was the ultimate arbiter. Twenty-four hours later the church was torched. The arsonist used Hoover's preaching stoles to ignite the blaze. If he had doubted it before, Hoover learned then that his words had impact. He moved through a series of pastor's posts around Texas in Fort Worth, Floydada and Lubbock before making the shift to Tucson. Alongside him was his wife of fourteen months, Sue Ann Goodman Hoover, whom he had met while working on a border ministry project.

Throughout his work in the realm of the spiritual, Hoover remained deeply concerned about the practical and the political. His doctoral dissertation examined the interplay between social theology and the work of nonprofit religious groups in immigration policy. He helped out on a project for refugees in South Texas, arranging shipments of truckloads of rice and beans to migrant shelters along the Rio Grande. He had sought to have his own congregation join the sanctuary movement, but had to be satisfied with an auxiliary role providing clothing and supplies for the South Texas churches that did sign up. In the mid-1990s, when the INS began to roll out its border offensive in Texas, Hoover joined other faithful in vigils on the banks of the Rio Grande. He also launched a ministry program to work with political refugees and asylum seekers.

For all his socially committed works, though, Hoover remained a far cry from the caricature of the touchy-feely, politically correct liberal activist. He favored peace, yes, but he was a proud gun owner and did not mind telling you of how close he had come to having to use one against more than one human being. He hated being tagged a liberal, preferring instead to consider himself a "postmodern philosopher." He wearied of the constraints of conventional rationality and its limiting labels. Political correctness held no appeal—Hoover saw it as the sign of an unexamined life.

Nor was he much of a committee man. He'd always preferred working alone and had little interest in being pious. He was playful and delighted in not being easily boxed. He cussed. He liked playing the slots. Hoover said the cause of empowerment must be preceded by figuring out "who's screwing who." To his way of thinking, INS policy was screwing the migrants. When Hoover said "the shit's gonna hit the fan," his Texas drawl carried no hint of apology.

Placing drinking water along well-traveled migrant corridors in the desert was an act with utilitarian and symbolic value. On a religious level, it displayed the Judeo-Christian belief in compassion and tolerance, the same kind shown in the biblical parable of the good Samaritan and elsewhere in the exhortations of Jesus: "For whosoever shall give you a cup of water to drink in my name, because ye belong to Christ, verily I say unto you, he shall not lose his reward." Politically, the water campaign would draw attention to what the religious activists saw as glaring contradictions in a government attempt to toughen the border in some spots while doing little to curb the economic appeal of migrating. And, practically speaking, if people were dying of thirst, wasn't the immediate answer a lifesaving drink of water?

Not long after signing on to the still-evolving effort, Hoover was listening to a public-radio broadcast when he heard a story about a California man named John Hunter, who, in the summer of 2000, launched his own one-man mercy campaign by installing water stations in the desert stretches of Imperial County. When the piece ended, Hoover started making calls. It didn't take long for him to track down Hunter, a quirky physicist and entrepreneur whose concern over the fate of illegal border crossers struck many as supremely ironic.

Hunter's brother is Duncan Hunter, the Republican congressman from the San Diego suburb of El Cajon who had made a name for himself as a hard-liner on illegal immigration. Congressman Hunter had called for the yearly increase of a thousand agents mandated in the 1996 immigration reform law and for years advocated for the steel fences that separate San Diego from Tijuana. Hunter kept the heat on the Border Patrol to move forward with the directive to complete the triple layer of fencing along the fourteen miles leading to the Pacific Ocean. Even at a time when nearly all elected officials were scrambling to be seen as tough on border matters, Duncan Hunter stood out for his outspokenness.

John Hunter was no weak-kneed liberal, either. A scientist who now worked as an inventor, he tended to vote Republican and counted himself a George W. Bush conservative. But as he watched the news about migrants dying in southern California's deserts, Hunter decided to act. This had nothing to do with whether the country's immigration policy should be tightened or loosened, he reasoned. This was a more fundamental matter. If lives are being lost in the desert, then you must go to the desert to save them.

Hunter asked the Imperial County coroner's office for maps of the areas where the people were falling dead. Most of that land was owned by the government, from the Bureau of Land Management to the military, so he got his brother's help in navigating the thicket of bureaucracies for permission to place the water stations out in the desert. Even with that help, John Hunter found it extremely complicated to put a simple plastic jug of water in the wilderness. In some cases, he went ahead without waiting for permission.

He chose spots along routes that had been identified as thruways for the hiking migrants. Each station consisted of three or four one-gallon jugs; each cluster was marked by a thirty-foot pole topped with a blue banner. A handful of volunteers helped set out the stations and returned on weekends to replenish them. By late summer 2000, Hunter and his helpers had installed nearly a hundred stations along three separate stretches—admittedly mere pinpoints of relief amid a vast, five-thousand-square-mile desert.

Hunter wasn't alone in trying to save migrants' lives in Imperial County. In the same area where he was focusing his efforts that summer, teams of Border Patrol agents had been assigned to keep special watch over the desert to prevent heat-related fatalities. Since the previous October, the beginning of the federal government's fiscal year, nineteen migrants had died of heat-related causes. The teams were one way the federal government was trying to respond to the death toll and to dampen public consternation about it through a multi-pronged effort called the Border Safety Initiative, launched in 1998.

As part of the campaign, the INS released public-service announcements aimed at persuading would-be migrants against making the risky cross-border journey. A thirty-second video spot featured Jackie Gallegos, whose husband had been part of the group of eight who had perished near Salton Sea in Imperial County in August 1998. The INS hoped that its two-year-old safety initiative would have more credibility with the help of someone directly hurt by a border-related death. The twenty-five-year-old widow, who lived in Los Angeles, cradled her eight-year-old son as she spoke to the camera in Spanish. "My husband was one of the people who died in the desert that day. We had a promising future—and so many dreams. Now all I have are memories. The border can be dangerous. The smugglers won't tell you that, but I will. Think twice. Don't risk your life. Think of the lives you'll leave behind."

Those who ignored those warnings would have to rely on good fortune, or the Border Patrol's desert teams. The agents, equipped with all-terrain vehicles, a dune buggy and medical gear, crisscrossed the desert in search of signs of wayward migrants. The border crossers faced a trek of up to thirty miles amid merciless heat, plus an untold number of unexploded bombs hidden in the scrub on a military practice range northwest of El Centro.

Border Patrol officials had credited the team with rescuing more than thirty migrants in distress while arresting about 1,870 others so far that year, and I decided to accompany the agents on an August day. Not long before, the desert agents had found twenty-four people stranded without food or water after a smuggling van broke down miles from the nearest road. As we drove along the edge of a bombing range, we passed Hunter's blue flags, with jugs beneath. The border agents expressed skepticism about the effort, saying migrants had told them upon arrest that they were steering clear of the blue-flagged stations because they feared a trap.

Still, it seemed worthwhile that somebody was thinking about water, since the migrants themselves were not. It was also obvious that officials' fears were accurate—migrants were plunging headlong into life-threatening conditions with no idea about the kinds of travails that confronted them. Soon after setting off into the desert, the agents this day came upon five men from the Mexican state of Michoacán resting in a dusty creek bed. They'd brought compact duffels stocked with canned sardines and tortillas—but little water—for a hike that would have taken them at least twenty-five miles across searing countryside to the nearest highway. They said they were heading ultimately for Fresno, in central California's farm belt. When asked how they planned to get there, one of the men gestured vaguely toward distant mountains to the north. Getting arrested, it seemed, was the best thing that could have happened to them that day.

Back in Arizona, Robin Hoover invited John Hunter to come tell his group about the water effort. Hunter visited in September, staying with the Hoovers in Tucson and speaking at the First Christian Church and at Fife's Southside Presbyterian Church. Hoover then took the Californian to a Catholic parish in Agua Prieta, Sonora, to describe his work there. In planning its own work, the Humane Borders group borrowed some of Hunter's methods, such as choosing sites carefully and deciding upon flags to mark water locations.

Hoover began meeting with Border Patrol officials in Tucson, gathering information on where migrants had died. The new chief of the Tucson station, David V. Aguilar, provided maps showing the locations. With those, Hoover and his group made plans to place stations along the state's wide-open southern border region. The volunteers would begin by year's end by placing a test station on private property south of Tucson where border crossers were known to travel, and then expand their efforts, hopefully by getting permission from the federal agencies that oversaw the largest and most dangerous segments to the west. They hoped to install stations on the Tohono O'odham reservation, inside Organ Pipe Cactus National Monument and on lands that were protected as wildlife refuges farther to the west. In the end, Hoover spoke of establishing a vast network of water stations, perhaps as many as eight hundred across the state.

Even before setting out its first jug of water, Humane Borders was generating attention—and some controversy. To Hoover's way of thinking, every time a newspaper mentioned his group's name, it was good news. Some were already comparing the new campaign to the sanctuary movement of the 1980s. Fife had signed on with Humane Borders, and other veterans were enlisting, too. It was a key moment. The Tucson area, by 2000 the second-deadliest zone along the Southwest border, saw seventy-four migrants die in the fiscal year that ended September 30, more than half of them due to the heat. The Humane Borders effort showed that "Arizona [had] finally developed a conscience about what's happening along its southern border," one Phoenix newspaper columnist declared.

Not everyone was charmed. Some Arizonans saw the act of placing water in the desert as naïve, if not wrongheaded. In letters to the editor, residents along the border complained that migrants would be more encouraged to try crossing illegally and would now have even more plastic containers to discard on private land. ("Is Hoover of Humane Borders going to pick up all these bottles after they toss them?" one Sierra Vista woman wrote.) Down in Douglas, Roger Barnett took a darker view of the efforts of these so-called humanitarians. Providing water to people who were knowingly entering the United States illegally was, he thought, at best "a feel-good service." At worst, it was anti-American.

For their part, Border Patrol officials were somewhat uneasy with the program. Though he applauded the humanitarian instincts of the volunteers, David Aguilar worried that publicity over caches of water in the desert might aggravate the dangers by giving migrants a false sense of security about a journey that was fundamentally foolhardy. He considered each of his 1,600 agents a mobile water station and believed there was little chance that a group of church volunteers could possibly establish enough stations in the vast desert lands to make a difference. "It could possibly increase the dangers out there to the people they're trying to help," Aguilar warned. "The perception is what I'm afraid of. The real message we want to send is, 'Do not risk your life by crossing in these areas.' "

But Hoover proved tenacious. Inside Humane Borders, he resisted the kind of doctrinal hand-wringing that tends to mire well-meaning religious causes in unending internal debate. Humane Borders would avoid that pitfall by not spelling out a specific theology. The drinking-water campaign was a means, not an end, Hoover believed. The group wrote a mission statement that steered clear of a limiting theology. Humane Borders would create a "just and humane border environment. Members will respond with humanitarian assistance to those who are risking their lives and safety crossing the United States border with Mexico. We will encourage the creation of public policies toward a humane, nonmilitarized border with legalized work opportunities for migrants in the U.S. and legitimate economic opportunities in migrants' countries of origins," the statement said. "We welcome all persons of good faith."

Outside the organization, too, the pastor was plain and clear. He was a natural with a microphone stuck in his face. Crossing the border illegally was a fairly minor offense, he argued. "You shouldn't have to pay the death penalty for it." And in answer to those, like Barnett, who saw the water project as tantamount to complicity in illegal immigration, Hoover argued that migrants likely were going to come anyway. "If you have someone on the highway who has been in an accident and is bleeding to death, you stop and render aid," he said. "It's a purely humanitarian effort." He talked about "taking death out of the immigration equation."

A thirty-year-old bus rattled down Interstate 19 south of Tucson, through a parched rolling plain hemmed by a rim of mountains. It was early December. On board the Nogales-bound bus were twenty representatives of church organizations from around the United States. They'd descended on Tucson for a weekend-long "border summit," a gathering of hundreds of rights activists and others concerned about the deteriorating climate along the international boundary. Some of the key religious workers had signed up to join Hoover on a BorderLinks tour of the twin border cities that both carry the name Nogales.

The border visit by some of the nation's most prominent church groups dealing with immigration—including the Lutheran Immigration Service, Church World Service, U.S. Catholic Conference and United Methodist Church—was fresh evidence that events on the border were beginning to strike a troubling chord among many American religious leaders. The representatives this day had hoped to get an up-close look at the border many knew about only through news accounts.

Their trip carried a much loftier assignment: to begin, as their sanctuary brethren had two decades earlier, to formulate for the nation's faith communities a broad and coherent stance on a border-enforcement policy whose deadly results were becoming increasingly evident. Though many of the groups had worked with refugees and asylum seekers for years, few had paid much attention to the Mexican border and therefore were poorly equipped to weigh in on the matter of Mexican immigration. The Tucson gathering was a chance to brainstorm and learn.

As the bus rolled south, the church workers introduced themselves to the others over a tinny speaker system. Outside, canyons bit sharply into the landscape as the group approached Nogales. Hilltops became visible across the border in Mexico. The bus grew quiet when the boundary itself appeared, in the form of a steel fence and a towering row of high-powered stadium lights, like the ones illuminating the border in San Diego. The bus crossed into Nogales, Sonora, a quintessential bustling border town of assembly plants and cantinas, where the makers of *Traffic* shot film scenes depicting Tijuana.

The group's main stop was a migrants' shelter in Nogales, Sonora, that had seen a growing workload since the U.S. border crackdown began drawing border crossers to Arizona. The shelter, housed in a white brick building at the top of a scraggly hillside neighborhood above the city's main drag, had been active as a way station for Central American refugees during the sanctuary days. Now its clients were mainly Mexicans.

The manager, Fernando Loreiro, met the church group in front and, through a translator, described the shelter's work. The shelter had been in operation for eighteen years, but it was only in the last two that its volunteers had needed to warn migrants about the fatal consequences of continuing their journey. A sign inside reminded would-be crossers of the perils. The building was an austere bunkhouse; its beds were covered with blankets donated by Hoover's church. The shelter accommodated twenty-five to thirty-five people daily, depending on how many got arrested and returned by the Border Patrol. No one was turned away from the shelter, Loreiro said. He described his goal as promoting a sense of Christian mercy: "to feel the way we do and feel moved to help people in need." His guests nodded, hearing in his words a call to action.

On the ride back to Tucson, Hoover laid out the various levels of activity that the Humane Borders group was pursuing. It hoped to change immigration law to allow more migrants to travel north legally to fill the jobs that everybody seemed eager for them to do. And he hoped the group would serve as an umbrella for like-minded groups along the entire border, where activism traditionally was fragmented according to the particular needs of each location. So far, eleven churches in Arizona and Sonora had joined Humane Borders; Hoover expected a dozen more to enlist anytime.

The following week, the group was to install its first test station near Rio Rico, one of the settlements of tract homes that had begun popping up along the sparse corridor between Tucson and the border. Later, the group planned to set out stations from Douglas in the east to Yuma in the west.

The group was already handing out bumper stickers with the Big Dipper logo. The stickers symbolized protest of the U.S. border policy, but also were meant to signal to migrants which residents were willing to give aid. There was no sign yet that anyone south of the border was familiar with the logo's meaning. But to the activists, the water effort marked the stirrings of a different version of the sanctuary movement. The churches added "moral suasion and legitimacy" to the border protests, Hoover said. "It's a different voice," he said. "We heard it in sanctuary and we're hearing it again."

Still, the looming shadow of the sanctuary movement raised ticklish questions for the church workers as they pondered what to do on the border now. How far should they go? Should they break the law? Was the current border crisis analogous to the refugee conditions of the 1980s that, for many, had justified defying U.S. immigration law? The questions the church people were asking themselves revealed telling splits in their thinking over how ambitiously people of faith ought to act out their humanitarian impulses.

Hoover was sure of one thing: Humane Borders was not about to break any laws. "Individually, that's a personal thing. Institutionally, we're going to put out water," he said, clenching his unlighted pipe. Back in Tucson, the group gathered for a vigil in honor of deceased migrants at El Tiradito, a sacred wishing well listed on the National Register of Historic Places. The church workers formed a circle and prayed, ending their ceremony with a song about the desert.

But the harder work of crafting a church strategy on the border remained. A brainstorming session was arranged that evening. It seemed historically appropriate that it would take place at Southside Presbyterian Church, the cradle of the sanctuary movement. Some thought it was time for a new version of the grassroots movement. Father Carney, the Catholic priest from Douglas, drove up for the session. Though he had signed on to Humane Borders, he and other activists had their doubts. Carney, like Fife of Southside Presbyterian, was queasy about working so closely with the Border Patrol. Fife's dislike for the INS was legendary. Moreover, Carney and others in Douglas were skeptical that the ranchers, who controlled vast tracts of land where migrants were traveling, would allow the do-gooders to put more plastic jugs out there.

After watching the situation in Douglas decay for more than two years, Carney had decided that a more radical solution was required. Perhaps that involved openly offering sanctuary to Mexican migrants, just as parishes had done for Salvadorans and Guatemalans in the 1980s. He had been a sanctuary volunteer in San Antonio while in seminary, though the movement was winding down by then. That kind of action now would have a dramatic effect, he thought, by sending the government a message that people were suffering along the border. Carney had already taken to sheltering and feeding the growing numbers of travelers who showed up at his church doors, and a few times had given rides to Yuma or Phoenix. Still, that was nothing like a concerted sanctuary drive.

Not everyone agreed the border situation could be compared to the previous immigration crisis. While church workers saw rough similarities between the two groups of border crossers, especially in the common risks to life and limb, they also acknowledged that impoverished Mexican migrants choosing to travel to the United States in search of decent jobs did not necessarily represent the same moral imperative as refugees fleeing civil war or brutality at the hands of a dictator's army. This current situation, lacking the clear and immediate threat posed by war, was messier. "People have more diverse opinions about who we should let in in terms of immigration policy," said one Franciscan brother who had been involved in sanctuary.

The U.S. Catholic Church, whose hierarchy had sat out sanctuary, was only now becoming familiar with the scope of problems at the border. A month earlier, the National Conference of Catholic Bishops had issued a call for broad changes in federal immigration policies, including easing the border crackdown. The bishops acknowledged the responsibility of the U.S. government to secure its borders and said they did not condone illegal immigration. "We nevertheless affirm the dignity of undocumented persons who live in our midst and must make every effort to ensure their human rights are respected and protected," the bishops said.

Meanwhile, observers on both sides of the border were still coming to grips with a watershed event in Mexican history: the election in July of reformist rancher Vicente Fox, who toppled the country's long-ruling PRI to capture the presidency. The PRI had ruled for seventy-one years straight, a reign whose longevity had less to do with enduring popular support than with the clever use of party largesse, electoral trickery, episodic repression and classic Mexican resignation. Discontent and hopelessness spurred many Mexican peasants to join the march to the United States. Now Fox promised a new start. Before taking office in December, just before the U.S. church people gathered in Tucson, Fox mused aloud about his hope of creating open borders within a generation's time. It was a revolutionary concept.

The leadership change in Mexico, which some equated with the felling of the Berlin wall, would undoubtedly send ripples to the border. But what kind? For church activists trying to devise an understandable stance on border issues, it was one more huge variable that made consensus no easier to achieve. "There's a genuine quarrel going on—or discussion—over to what extent the residents of the borderlands have a responsibility in providing help or aid," Fife said before the strategy session at his church.

The gathering resolved little beyond showing the disparate philosophies that were emerging. There were calls for list-making and network-forming, the dreary drudge work of activism. Hoover stressed the need to change public opinion on immigration. Fife urged turning more to Mexico in hopes of forming a binational movement. There were suggestions, too, that the time had come for 1960s-style acts of civil disobedience aimed at the fence that symbolized the stricter border.

"How long are we going to pray at the wall on Day of the Dead?" asked one church activist.

"Until it's down," another called.

"How do we get it down?" queried the first. Then he mused aloud: "Maybe next time we take a blowtorch."

Not everyone was waiting for church direction on how to proceed. The same humanitarian impulses behind Hoover's water stations project had taken a different form down near the border. There, self-styled Samaritans, drawing their own lessons from the Scriptures and history, had begun offering aid directly to the immigrants. If Aguilar, the Border Patrol chief in Tucson, wasn't thrilled about the Humane Borders water plan, he would have been even less pleased to know about the steps that some residents were taking to help immigrants continue their trip north past Arizona. While the church groups were assiduously avoiding violating U.S. law—so far, anyway—some Arizonans were now sheltering migrants temporarily and even shuttling them north past the checkpoints that the Border Patrol had set up along highways to the interior. Church leaders and other activists around Tucson during the border summit had been trading whispered comments about the actions of these residents. Why would they risk running afoul of the law to assist total strangers?

I made discreet requests for leads and got a call in my hotel room one evening from a woman who said she'd meet me for coffee in Bisbee, a little over an hour's drive from Tucson. Bisbee, on the road to Douglas, had been described as the center of this informal underground railroad. A restaurant owner there had served sandwiches to the migrants who were showing up, and a newly formed group called Citizens for Border Solutions was said to be looking into what types of assistance its members could provide legally. The caller said she was familiar with a small network of U.S. citizens who were helping to spirit immigrants north to Phoenix, but would talk only if her name was not published.

Bisbee, perched in a natural rock bowl off Highway 80, is a surprisingly pretty bust town. By all rights, the place should have dried up and blown away years before, after the shutdown of the Copper Queen mine in 1975. Everyone predicted that it would, especially after hundreds of its residents packed up and moved on, abandoning the tottery hillside shacks, the steep, heart-straining stairs throughout downtown and Bisbee's winding commercial avenue, called Tombstone Canyon. Instead, hippies came, drawn by word-of-mouth accounts of cheap digs—or free, if you were willing to squat—and of a place where it was easy to live off the radar screen of ex-spouses, the law, whomever. The tin-roofed houses took on fanciful pastel tones. Artists settled, crafted bracelets and earrings, painted portraits and desert scenes, bent steel into lizard shapes. The grand turn-of-the-century buildings were renovated. Galleries and restaurants opened in spaces that had once housed jail cells and the company store. Eventually, Bisbee was a thriving arts colony, a tidy left-tilting burg whose sandaled denizens questioned authority as dutifully as they splashed themselves with patchouli. If you were a Mexican migrant on the run from the Border Patrol, it made for a warm oasis of sympathy amid an otherwise hostile countryside.

In the months before my arrival, the undocumented immigrants had been turning up regularly in the big drainage ditch in front of the Renaissance Café near downtown. They'd come to the café to buy a bus ticket north or get a ham sandwich or a donut. The manager, Kim McGee, pointed out the ditch, a concrete culvert under the main street, and described her numerous encounters with the migrants, many of whom were shivering and hungry after long hikes. Word had gotten out at the border that the café was "safe," McGee said. If one member of a group came inside to buy a soda, she often invited the others, too. "I'd get 'em in there, make sure the coast was clear. They were nervous wrecks. They were hiking all night," she said. The restaurant doubled as a bus station and migrants knew they could buy tickets there.

McGee said the flow through town had slowed in recent months, as the Border Patrol worked to plug the gaping hole at Douglas. She said she was willing to give the migrants advice. Two weeks earlier, a pair of men popped up from the ditch and bought two tickets to Phoenix. She drew a map showing where the Border Patrol's highway checkpoints were located and an alternate route around the road check. Lately, she'd been telling them there was little chance of making it without getting caught. Their immigration status did not concern her; their need for help did.

A sign in the front window proclaimed a no-questions-asked policy toward visitors. "We will not, under any circumstances, now or in the future, give information to the INS," it said. "We will do everything in our power to make sure that everyone gets the services they need, regardless of their immigration status."

Down the street, I met my caller, whom I will call Beatrice, at another coffee house. Beatrice, the co-owner of a small hotel, said she had been providing free lodging and food to migrants for months. She said she had taken in thirty-four people who became lost or ill on the trip north. Some stayed for as little as two days, others as long as three weeks. She had even helped sneak them past Border Patrol agents on the highway. One might have expected a wild-eyed zealot probing the limits of law enforcement; Beatrice was anything but. The person seated at the small café table was a grandmother in her late fifties, a lifelong Republican, raised as a Baptist and with the earnest certitude of a Sunday school teacher. She spoke softly but with intense conviction. She was unapologetic about aiding in an illegal entry, but there was no fanaticism, not even puckish mischief. As the coffee machines whirred in the background, Beatrice explained her actions simply, in terms of morality and religion. They, she said, are what had motivated her since the first two bedraggled women had shown up at her door fourteen months earlier.

The pair of Mexican women had been discovered hiding in a ditch one weekday morning in October 1999 by an eleven-year-old neighborhood girl, who led them to Beatrice's front door and asked if she could help. To Beatrice, the women, draped in layers of clothing, looked desperate and exhausted. She thought they were about to fall into shock. Beatrice had only rudimentary Spanish, but brought them inside and listened to their story as she fed and cared for them. They had come from Veracruz, on Mexico's Gulf Coast. One of the women, about thirty-one years old, had lived in the United States for eight years. She'd worked at a McDonald's in Chicago and spoke some English. The woman was desperate to return to her three U.S.-born children, aged two to eight, in Chicago. She had gone home to Mexico to visit her ailing mother, never expecting the return to be so difficult. She remembered it being easy when she came across the border previously. She brought along her brother's mother-in-law, a forty-eight-year-old woman with seven children who all had moved to the United States. The two women had crossed the border on foot at Douglas but then were left in the desert. They made it the twenty-two miles to Bisbee, crawling at times in the darkness out of fear of tripping and falling.

The women stayed with Beatrice for eight days, helping out around the house by cooking and cleaning. The trick was going to be getting them to the airport in Phoenix and then onto a plane to Chicago without detection. There was a Border Patrol checkpoint on the highway near Tombstone, and once at the airport, the women would need to be ticketed without identification. Beatrice worked out a plan. Her husband, a businessman with a private pilot's license, agreed to fly the two migrant women in his airplane to Casa Grande, south of Phoenix. That would take care of the checkpoint problem. Beatrice would drive there, along with two American women who had bought plane tickets to Chicago in their own names. They'd pick up the Mexicans, proceed to the airport and switch tickets with the migrants.

The plan worked perfectly. At the airport, the American decoys checked in and, during lunch, handed their boarding passes to the Mexican women. In those days, nearly two years before the terrorist attacks on the World Trade Center and the Pentagon, ticketed air passengers seldom had to present identification once they held a boarding pass. The two migrants were on their way.

After that incident, the local kids kept finding beleaguered migrants in the hills around Bisbee. Beatrice's doorbell would ring again. Every two to three weeks, there'd be another group in need. Neighbors and store owners would call, too. She almost never said no. There was a man and woman from El Salvador who were discovered on a Bisbee street "in terrible shape." They'd traveled by rail across Mexico, lain in layers inside a cattle car. They watched four fellow travelers die on that leg. Once north of the border, the young man, who was eighteen, kept falling. Eventually the smuggler grew tired of waiting and left the pair behind. After they got to Beatrice's, they took to the sickbed and didn't emerge for days. Another time, a Honduran man turned up on the leafy street in front of her house, sobbing. Most of her guests, though, were Mexicans. They stayed as long as they needed to rest and regain their strength. Most required some nursing. When that occurred, Beatrice summoned friends who were doctors or nurses. She fed her weakened guests plates of spaghetti, bologna sandwiches and hamburgers until the day she realized that, after subsisting on crackers and water for weeks, the migrants were getting sick from the unfamiliar diet. She switched to clear broths, fortified with chicken and vegetables, and saltine crackers.

As the year went on, the whisper network jelled, though it remained informal and very much out of the public eye. The helpers went as far as they dared. Some were comfortable providing water or a place to sleep for the night. The more adventurous—and this included Beatrice— gave the migrants rides away from the heavily patrolled border area.

They developed a variety of tactics aimed at keeping their charges from being identified as illegal immigrants if stopped by agents on the highway. Female migrants might be given a haircut, then dressed in fashionable clothing and jewelry to look more "American." Sometimes, migrants huddled under a blanket in the back seat while an Anglo woman would join Beatrice, who also is Anglo, in the front. "Give me a blonde and a dog and I can get through anything," she would say. Once past the checkpoint, the migrants would be dropped off in Benson to catch a bus to Phoenix or Los Angeles. It worked surprisingly well.

Beatrice's husband didn't much care for her activities. He thought her heart was too big and would soon land her in trouble. She didn't care. A fourth-generation Bisbee-ite, Beatrice saw her help for migrants in much the way the rancher Barnett viewed his roundups of them: as the well-intentioned actions of a private citizen during a chaotic moment in history. The motivations differed, but the imperatives were just as compelling; both saw their rural way of life suddenly under attack. Beatrice had grown up watching Mexicans cross the border to work, then return. Back then, nobody cared. Trying to curb that ebb and flow now, by building fences and sending battalions of border agents, struck her as the equivalent of interfering with the passage of migratory birds. It was, Beatrice thought every time she saw another white-and-green Border Patrol truck, as if nature itself were being interfered with.

Beyond that was what she saw as Christian obligation. "This is tough stuff. You have human beings. Regardless of anything else, these are human beings," she said. She cited biblical teachings, such as the story of the good Samaritan, that urged kind treatment for strangers. She even drew parallels to the Holocaust. "This is a real moral and spiritual issue. It's like man's made this law that says these human beings are off limits. God doesn't say that," she said. "I could not stand by and watch this happen. If I don't follow what I know is right and turn my head and look away, who's to say? When I watch them rounding up people like criminals, one thing that sticks inside of me says, 'This is dangerous.' These people are not criminals."

But didn't her actions amount to immigrant smuggling? After all, the law clearly forbids helping people enter the country illegally. She answered quickly in the negative. "We're not trafficking," she said. "We're just helping. This is serving life."

She then invited me to the hotel she owned—there was someone she wanted me to meet. It was a short drive from downtown Bisbee. There, in a second-floor room, the bed held a thirty-one-year-old widow from Acapulco. The woman, named María Luisa Ramos, was swaddled beneath blankets, staring at a Spanish-language program on the television. She was lucky to be alive. She was still suffering the effects of pneumonia after falling ill during a four-day hike across the border. It was Beatrice's husband who had found her, five days earlier. The woman had made her way to the roadside and flagged him down. She had hiked for four days and nights, without food or water and clad only in a T-shirt and light fleece jacket to fend off the cold. The temperature had fallen into the low thirties the night before she broke off to seek help.

After a day at Beatrice's house she was breathing with increasing difficulty. Beatrice called a doctor friend, who dropped by and found Ramos's pulse and blood pressure elevated. They later took her to another friend's house and put her on oxygen there. She seemed to be improving. Beatrice had been feeding her hot broth and letting her doze. Ramos slept almost around the clock, but she spent an hour recounting the depressing chain of events that had landed her, very sick, in this bed hundreds of miles from home.

In a soft voice, Ramos said she had been headed to North Carolina. She joined a group of thirty-two people, all from the southern state of Guerrero, that included two women and three children. She got caught by the Border Patrol on her first attempt. She tried again, this time with a group of forty-five. The hiking went on and on, endlessly, it seemed to her. Desert, then hills. More hills. The cold was nothing like what she had expected, and her clothing was no match. Ramos weakened from lack of food and water. She fell back. Finally, she decided to break from the group and go to the highway for help. That's when Beatrice's husband saw her and stopped, despite his usual reservations. She just looked so helpless there in the early-evening darkness.

It had been a bad year. Ramos's husband was killed by an errant bullet in Acapulco eight months earlier. Despite its glitter-and-white-sand reputation, much of Acapulco and its surroundings are grindingly poor; those who venture away from the beach strip of discos and high-rise hotels can encounter a world of wobbly, dirt-floor huts, without running water, on the outskirts of town. The contrast is eye-popping, even by Latin American standards. Ramos lived in the Acapulco of the have-nots, with four children. But she was not without resources. She said she had a godfather living in the United States—in North Carolina. He owned a restaurant and she could work there. So Ramos took to the road.

It was a familiar story line. Most migrants don't just decide to make their way north out of the blue. Many are uprooted from their rural homes in Mexico by one setback or another—a death in the family, an anemic harvest. Like Ramos, most have the name of a family member or acquaintance to help carve a new existence in the United States, even if it is a seasonal one. Social scientists have a term for this kind of connection. Social capital, they call it. It is expressed in the U.S. telephone numbers carefully written on a scrap of paper in the migrant's pocket. It's seen in the crowded apartments of immigrant enclaves where there always seems to be room for one more person. It helps explain what simple economic statistics do not: it is not merely the promise of jobs that inspires Mexicans to head to the United States, but social ties and tradition as well. It is one more reason simplistic approaches to illegal immigration from Mexico are likely to fall short.

Ramos finished telling her story and expressed deep gratitude toward her hostess, this American woman with the tourist Spanish and bottomless soup kettle. I asked what she planned to do. She smiled a little, flashing a silver filling, and said she would go back home to Guerrero. Beatrice was arranging a bus ticket back to the border. Ultimately, however, Ramos did not go back. She stayed at Beatrice's for three more weeks. Her condition turned worse. She had seizures, her eyes rolled back in her head, mouth foaming. Beatrice finally took her to Copper Queen Community Hospital in Bisbee, where doctors made a grim discovery. Ramos was six months pregnant; the fetus was dead. She was helicoptered to Tucson Medical Center and a friend of Beatrice's checked on her there. Ramos gave birth to a boy three days later, and they had a funeral.

Ramos's seizures persisted after her release. Beatrice, in Bisbee, started working the telephone, looking for help. She had already contacted the Mexican consulate, but she also had a North Carolina phone number that Ramos had used during her stay in Bisbee. Ramos's "godfather" in North Carolina, it turned out, was a brother. There were other siblings, too: a brother and two sisters in Tennessee. The relatives had lived in the States for nearly fifteen years. One of the sisters spoke perfect English on the telephone. They arranged to have their ailing sister fly to Tennessee. Beatrice bought a ticket in her own name, then met Ramos at the Tucson airport for the boarding-pass switch. It was January 2001—twelve days after the young woman was airlifted to Tucson. Beatrice watched a nearly depleted figure get on the plane. Ramos had appeared to be on the mend a few weeks earlier. Now she leaned on a cane, dragging a heavy foot behind her. She could barely make words and her eyes were blank as stones. At the very least, however, she would stay in the United States.

Six months after Beatrice had nursed Ramos, a group of more than two dozen Mexicans, including five men from her home state of Guerrero, would throw themselves on the mercy of the Arizona countryside in the ghostly desert near Yuma. Their enemy would be heat. As harrowing as Ramos's hike had been, she would have to count herself among the blessed if she compared her experience with the hell her countrymen were about to endure.

By early 2001, Hoover's water project was hitting its stride. The Humane Borders group, pleased with its test run north of Nogales in December, won permission from the National Park Service to install its first water stations in the desert. On March 7 the group set up water stations in two spots along a power line in the Organ Pipe Cactus National Monument. Of late, the monument had been identified as a route frequently used by border crossers entering from Sonoyta. The Humane Borders water stations were slightly different from those installed by John Hunter in Imperial County. Rather than setting out gallon jugs, the Arizona group opted to put out sixty-five-gallon tanks made of blue plastic. The canisters, which were converted soft-drink syrup containers, were now marked "AGUA." Above each station flapped blue flags modeled after Hunter's.

The Organ Pipe stations marked an encouraging breakthrough. The group was now supplying water in a stretch where migrants were known to have traveled and died. The fact that it was on publicly owned land demonstrated that it was possible to get the federal bureaucracy to commit to such an endeavor on terrain under its protection. Such cooperation would be crucial if the project was to succeed, since most of the desert locations where Hoover's team wanted to provide the water lay in protected lands. No one liked the prospect of putting tanks and flags all over the desert wilderness—potentially disrupting an ecosystem that was home to endangered species such as bighorn sheep and the Sonoran pronghorn antelope—but Hoover's plan was to place them along roads and power lines to reduce the potential environmental harm.

On March 27 the group wrote to the refuge manager of the Cabeza Prieta National Wildlife Refuge, making formal application for permission to deploy water sites on that sprawling desert preserve west of Organ Pipe. Measuring 1,344 square miles, the Cabeza Prieta refuge is vast and heavily regulated. It, too, hugs the border, but unlike Organ Pipe, is almost completely inaccessible to outsiders, except for a few primitive dirt roads. Hardly any souls stir there on a given day except for a few hardy wildlife buffs, the animals they hope to spot and the migrants who don't know better. To the north lies the Barry M. Goldwater Air Force Range.

The Humane Borders group, in a letter written by Mick Beyers, proposed putting the five Cabeza Prieta stations along a way called Christmas Pass Road, on a segment running through the Tule Desert. A second deployment would involve stationing two tanks along Charlie Bell Road as it notches west through Daniels Arroyo. As at Organ Pipe, the tanks would be designated by blue banners on poles. Humane Borders would maintain the sites, replenishing the tanks on a weekly basis and monitoring usage to ensure that one tank at each site was adequate. The group also agreed to have volunteers take part in an orientation session led by refuge staffers. Beyers enclosed a copy of the group's liability insurance for the Organ Pipe project and promised the same coverage for the proposed work in Cabeza Prieta. "We must work together to become increasingly responsive, resourceful and resilient in the face of the dynamic circumstances impacting our wilderness and our communities," Beyers said in closing.

As the group waited for an answer, it won permission for a separate plan to set up two stations in the Buenos Aires National Wildlife Refuge, a finger of protected land stretching north of the border at Sasabe, well to the east, plus a few privately owned sites. Things were beginning to click.

Soon after, in a letter dated April 18, came the reply from the Fish and Wildlife Service, which runs the Cabeza Prieta refuge. The answer was no. "After much deliberation and consultation, I must inform you that your proposal is denied," wrote refuge manager Donald Tiller. He said that under the government's rules, the water project "has been determined to be non-compatible with the Mission of the National Wildlife Refuge System and the goals, objectives and purposes of the Cabeza Prieta National Wildlife Refuge and Wilderness Area."

The reason was environmental. "Due to the extreme situation with the endangered Sonoran Pronghorn currently, we cannot allow this use in 'critical habitat' for this imperiled species." Tiller added that there also were "many other reasons why the use is being denied."

Hoover was disappointed at the decision. He thought it was silly to put the pronghorn first when the threat to people trying to cross in that zone was so starkly evident. A month later, the deaths of fourteen Mexicans of heat exhaustion in that same area would turn the preacher's frustration to rage.

Chapter Nine

THE DEADLY SEASON

To enter the southwestern corner of Arizona even weeks before the on-set of summer is to sink into a vast inferno, as beautiful as it is pitiless. Once May arrives, no one here is too surprised if the heat in this expanse—an area bigger than Connecticut and Rhode Island added together—climbs above 115 degrees. There is only scant shade beneath the scattering of paloverde trees, which punctuate a landscape of sa-guaros, greasewood bushes, bone-dry arroyos and low mountain ranges that seem to repeat endlessly.

This is the lower Sonoran desert, a broad belt of aridity that spans the international border. It carpets the region east of the Gulf of Califor-nia on the Mexican side and then sweeps north to include a portion of Arizona, some three hundred miles south of the Grand Canyon, as well as a slice of California. Ground temperatures can reach 150 degrees and the wildlife that exists here has had to adapt to the intense heat through extraordinary means. One type of burrowing ground squirrel survives by hunkering down in a trancelike state that has been compared to death. To move on sandy surfaces, lizards grew special flaps on their feet; a type of kit fox has hairs on the undersides of its paws for the same pur-pose. Many creatures are never seen in daylight. The landscape is, without doubt, beautiful, although it's a beauty of the most severe kind.

Lieutenant Nathaniel Michler of William Emory's surveying team saw little to like in August 1855 when his sun-ravaged crew traversed the desert between Sonoyta, near the present-day Tohono O'odham reservation, and Fort Yuma, on California's border. "It was the most dreary and tiresome I have ever experienced. Imagination cannot picture a more dreary, sterile country, and we named it the 'Mal pais,' " he writes. "The burnt lime-like appearance of the soil is ever before you; the very stones look like the scoriae of a furnace; there is no grass, and but a sickly vegetation, more unpleasant to the sight than to the barren earth itself; scarce an animal to be seen—not even the wolf or the hare to attract the attention, and, save the lizard and the horned frog, naught to give animation and life to this region. The eye may watch in vain for the flight of a bird; to add to all is the knowledge that there is not one drop of water to be depended upon from the Sonoyta to the Colorado or Gila [River]. All traces of the road are sometimes erased by the high winds sweeping the unstable soil before them, but death has strewn a continuous line of bleached bones and withered carcasses of horses and cattle, as monuments to mark the way."

Nearly a century and a half later, the region hosted both the Cabeza Prieta National Wildlife Refuge and the Goldwater bombing range. It is a place so remote that a person could trudge fifty miles in a straight line without hitting a paved road. In the heat, it is not possible for hikers to carry enough water to sustain themselves for those distances, and the immigrant smugglers who plied their trade along the crude dirt tracks here normally picked more direct, shorter routes. But they sometimes veered off course to avoid Border Patrol agents cruising in four-wheel-drive trucks near the international border, which is unfenced and marked only by white concrete pillars, not all of them standing. Sometimes, the guides simply got lost. It was easy to see how; once you make your way deep into the desert here, it appears pale and infinite.

Border Patrol agents assigned to the station in Wellton, about thirty miles east of Yuma, watched over one of the most difficult stretches of the entire two-thousand-mile international boundary. It was not just the loneliness and the heat; the stakes were higher, too. Immigrants who slipped through along the gravel tracks represented more than just a successful unlawful entry; they could easily end up in the kind of emergency that required rescue. Here in the Wellton area, the jobs of captor and rescuer blurred into one. Unlike the agents in Imperial Beach near

San Diego, the agents in Wellton, such as veteran Glen Payne, had honed a special set of skills: they could gaze at the desert and see countless things an outsider would miss. Payne, who had perfected his eye during more than two decades working in the desert, teased clues from the desert floor. A scuff mark here or an upturned stone there would betray the route taken by migrants once they'd sneaked across the border. Here in one of the nation's most unforgiving tracts, his skill in the ancient art of tracking—or, in the argot of the Border Patrol, "sign-cutting"—could mean the difference between life and death.

No other law enforcement agency in America depends as much on tracking humans as the Border Patrol, which provides cadets with only an hour-long introduction to the technique during their nineteen weeks of academy training. Most of the training comes later, on the job. Nowhere was sign-cutting more central to the daily work of agents than in the three-thousand-square-mile desert expanse patrolled by Payne and the forty-two agents he supervised. In an era of high-tech border defenses that turned night into day and converted the whorls of a migrant's fingerprints into digitized data, this was a skill harking back to the agency's cowboy roots. Although the Border Patrol had planted seismic sensors in key spots of this sixty-two-mile segment near Yuma, the area was just too big, and agents too few, to rely on much else than simply eyeballing the ground.

Sign-cutting combines a hunter's canniness and a prospector's patience. Each day, agents in four-wheel-drive trucks and sport utility vehicles prowl the vast web of primitive, sandy roads that carve the desert into huge, uneven patches. Despite the area's desolation, it was surprising to learn how frequently this bleak corridor had been traveled over the centuries, by ancestors of the Tohono O'odham, Spanish colonizers and later by Mexican fortune seekers on their way to California's gold rush. Some of the roads patrolled by border agents in Wellton and Yuma today were remnants of those ancient trails, including a dirt track that the Spaniards named the Camino del Diablo, or the Devil's Highway. The road slices northwest from Mexican Sonora and then tracks roughly along the modern-day border before veering toward Yuma.

Indians coursed the desert routes for centuries before the Europeans came. Coronado's ill-fated quest for the Seven Cities of Cíbola brought

Spaniards north from Mexico in 1540. The Spaniards drove westward into the Sonoran desert, whose terrifying vastness is matched by its geological variety. There are dormant volcanoes, known as the Pinacates, and their black, glassy remains. Underlying lava, revealed over the centuries by erosion, has given some of the mountains striking black crowns—thus the name Cabeza Prieta, which in Spanish means "black head." To the west are broad, sandy dunes. Basalt lends hills a bluish quality and there is also granite and mica to be found. Andrew B. Gray, who would explore the area south of the border while searching for a decent railroad route during the 1850s, describes finding "ridges of rocks containing much feldspar and mica" and "myriads of black boulders, from the size of a paving stone to that of a ton weight, and occasionally very large masses. These rocks seem as if they had been ejected during the eruption of some powerful volcano, and showered like hailstones upon the surrounding country."

The same sights no doubt greeted the earlier Spanish missionaries, who made use of the Indian trails and guides. Fray Melchior Díaz was thought to have roughly followed the Camino del Diablo during an expedition in 1540. A century and a half later, Father Eusebio Francisco Kino, who had explored the Baja California peninsula, founded a string of mission towns as he pressed north through Sonora, Mexico, and reopened the *camino* as he crossed lands that are now divided by the U.S.-Mexico border.

Along what is probably the most parched stretch between the Atlantic and Pacific Oceans, travelers found relief in a chain of ancient water holes, or tanks, called *tinajas,* that pocked the mountains along the Camino del Diablo, collecting water in small ponds that descended the granite hills like steps. The Tinajas Altas Mountains next to the border grew to become a kind of rest stop for desert travelers, but as crossings accelerated into the thousands during the gold rush of 1848–49, they became impromptu graveyards for those who fell short or who could not climb to the highest tanks where water remained. Estimates of the death toll along the Camino del Diablo during that decade reached into the hundreds. An account related by one gold rush–era traveler, quoted in William K. Hartmann's *Desert Heart: Chronicles of the Sonoran Desert,* describes the Tinajas as "a vast graveyard of unknown dead and the road from there to the Colorado was marked the whole way by the dried carcasses of mules, horses, and cattle and the scattered bones of human beings, slowly turning into dust."

In contemporary times, the hidden tanks still contain water, but as U.S. border agents pointed out, you could die of thirst fifty feet away if you didn't know where they were.

For Glen Payne's team, the desert was a giant slate onto which were scribbled telltale clues—for those attentive enough to spot them. The agents here maintained about a hundred miles of gravel tracks, called drag roads, that were smoothed each day, sometimes several times, by a truck towing a chain of tires laid side by side. "Our big eraser," Payne called the devices, and they created a grid of roads, blank as newly groomed ski slopes, that made it easier to detect footprints.

In proper light, a trail of footprints would show as tiny shadows, dappling the soft gravel like droplets on paper. Long scuffs could suggest the hiker was falling ill. A knee print might signal collapse. Vomit meant worsening distress. A meandering trail or cast-off clothing often suggested the delirium that typically precedes death in severe heat. "You might find a shirt and a hundred yards down the road, shoes and pants," one agent said. "A lot of times when you see that, you know it's getting short—you don't have much time." Once they detected tracks, the agents methodically followed them, on foot or by driving ahead in their four-wheel drives to see if the trail showed up farther north. The hunt was often joined from the air by helicopter pilots skimming above the ocotillo and paloverde trees in search of more tracks. (Agents marked their own treads to make it easier for fellow agents to distinguish the trackers from the pursued. Payne, for example, had carved an X into the heel of his spit-polished boot.)

To do their job, agents were required to read the footprints in sufficient detail to gauge the size of the migrant group, so that all were accounted for at the end of the search. The trackers working a "trail" talked to each other by radio in an arcane lexicon of shoe-tread patterns that described what the agents saw etched in the dust: wavy line, chevron, starburst, honeycomb, heel within a heel. Bare feet were harder to follow. Lacking sharply defined lines, they tended to leave only a shiny spot where the desert sand was pressed slightly into the firmer subsoil.

The clues could be remarkably detailed. Tracks often gave a hint, for example, about the time of day they were made. Those skirting neatly around bushes probably were left in daylight, when the hiker could see. Those slashing through the brush were likely created at night. Even the presence of bug trails or animal tracks, which are typically left at night, helped agents estimate when the human prints were made. Footprints endured well here, but the tracking work was made difficult by the subtly varied desert surface—light, nutty gravel giving way to darker, packed earth and to tumbles of the black volcanic rock.

Smugglers and migrants knew about the trackers and tried to foil them. The border crossers crafted tread covers from foam mats or from squares of carpet, tricks that agents conceded worked pretty well. Migrants sometimes walked in single file to disguise their tracks, or swiped away prints with a tree branch. Despite the cover-up tactics, it was next to impossible to traverse this area without leaving some kind of trace. It was those traces, which trackers referred to collectively as "sign," that agents had to spot amid greasewood bushes and ironwood trees, darting lizards and the ubiquitous tracks of rabbits and coyotes. Sign could be anything—a cigarette butt, a piece of paper, discarded clothing, a broken branch, human vomit.

Sometimes, agents would find just a sliver of track. Retired agent Joe McCraw, who remained something of a legend here in Wellton for his superb tracking abilities, related how he had been haunted for years by his failed search as an inexperienced border agent in Imperial County during the late 1960s for a nine-year-old boy. During that search McCraw passed over two scrapes in the dirt, then moved on to search further. He realized only later that what he had seen were the child's indistinct tracks. The boy, a U.S. citizen, was ultimately found on a mountainside, dead from a fall. "I didn't have sense enough at the time to know what I was looking at," McCraw recalled many years later. "Nine times out of ten, you're not going to see a whole track." Araceli Garcia made the same point when she searched out tracks in Imperial Beach.

These challenges in reading such clues demanded persistence and Zenlike calm, commodities often in short supply among some green recruits, whose formal academy training in sign-cutting was quick. For his part, Glen Payne had patience long before joining the Border Patrol. He had grown up in the New Mexico countryside and spent much of his youth tramping among the junipers and pines around Arenas Valley, hunting deer and fowl and fishing the rivers for trout. His tracking skills came in handy when in 1979 he joined the Border Patrol station, which at the time was located up the road from Wellton in the town of Tacna. In the ensuing years, Payne had acquired a reputation as an exceedingly good tracker. Puffing a Winston, he often shook his head at the ways of some of the greenest agents, who tended to drive too fast to spot sign or to detect brush-outs.

But the tedious work could also turn suddenly heart-pounding. "Anytime you've got a trail and temperatures are 100-plus, you've got to move quick. Or if you find discarded clothing, you know darn well something's not right," Payne said, guiding his Border Patrol truck along the dirt roads, checking for tracks. "We come out here in an enforcement mode, but it can turn into a rescue or humanitarian mode in no time." Such was the case only a week earlier, during an early heat wave that turned the desert skillet-hot. For three tense days in May 2001, the skill and endurance of Payne's agents were tested in ways few of them could have anticipated, as their bleak but panoramic workplace became the setting for the worst fatal disaster among a single group of desert crossers ever recorded along the U.S.-Mexico frontier.

It would be difficult to find a place more distinct from the dust-caked environs where Payne's agents worked than the emerald lushness of Veracruz state, a saber-shaped slice of Mexico's Gulf Coast. It was 1,650 miles away and a world distant from the stately saguaros and burnt gravel of the Arizona desert. There, in villages like El Tesoro, Cuatro Caminos and San Pedro Altepepán, the fertile earth and tropical moisture had yielded an agricultural life for generations of rural *veracruzanos*. It was coffee country—a green-canopied highland that also was home to banana plantations, citrus and fields of sugarcane. Industry had made inroads, in the form of a Coca-Cola plant and clothing *maquiladoras*, but the rural economy of north-central Veracruz over the years had thrived or suffered according to the caprices of nature and the vagaries of far-off market forces.

The year 2001 was no different, coming at the end of a highly unstable decade for the region's coffee farmers. Even as coffee houses seemed to sprout overnight in aspiring U.S. urban enclaves, a glut of coffee production worldwide, including big exports from Brazil and Vietnam, had sent prices plunging for growers. Some traditional exporters, such as Mexico and other Latin American producers, found a dampened appetite for their brands. In 2000 the coffee industry in Veracruz lost $84 million, according to one report. The losses meant that growers could keep fewer workers and pay them only $25 a week. Furthermore, the region's coffee and banana crops had already been ransacked by insects.

Lacking the sort of safety cushions that shield U.S. workers, such as unemployment insurance or disaster relief, the men of Veracruz's countryside did what Mexicans have done for decades when beset by economic shock and acts of God: they left for *el norte.* So many workers poured out of the region—more than 400,000 during a five-year period— that by 2000 Veracruz was second only to Mexico City in the rate at which the residents were leaving faster than newcomers arrived. The exodus was significant enough that the state's population had grown just 2.5 percent since 1995—well below the national rate of 7 percent. Indeed, the number of residents actually shrank in about half of the towns in Veracruz. Even those who were able to find work at home often didn't earn enough to sustain ambitions of getting something more out of life.

For Mario Castillo in Cuatro Caminos, a town of six hundred, aspirations were as simple as a new kitchenette and indoor plumbing for his two-room house.* The twenty-five-year-old Castillo had hired himself out to coffee and citrus plantations—jobs always susceptible to price dips. Like other farm workers, he was earning 35 pesos, about $4, a day. Even then he was lucky, compared to others in his village, where the number of residents designated by the census takers as "economically inactive" outnumbered those who were "economically active." Meanwhile, only about half the grown-ups in town knew how to read.

---

* Some of the material about Castillo's journey and the migrant trail northward described in subsequent pages was gathered in 2001 by the *Los Angeles Times*'s Mexico City bureau chief, Jim Smith, who interviewed Castillo's relatives in Veracruz and traveled to the border.

By May 2001, it was clear to Castillo that with his uneven earnings, he could not improve his modest house. He would need to make another trip north. He had crossed illegally before and found work washing farm machinery in Galena, Illinois. It wasn't long before U.S. immigration officers nabbed him and sent him home, but even that short stint earned him enough to pay for a cinder-block house, with a corrugated tin roof, for his wife and two children, a boy and a girl. In preparation for his second journey, Castillo borrowed $1,200 toward the $1,900 smuggler's fee and got ready. He planned to go for a year or two. Although many U.S. and Mexican officials were then expressing worry that too many migrants embarked unaware of the risks, Castillo thought he knew them well.

Other young men from the same rural area would go, too; seven of them would not come back alive. Among them were Raymundo Barreda, fifty-four, and his fifteen-year-old son, who shared the same name. The boy hoped to buy a truck with his earnings. The elder Barreda carried with him a U.S. green card, giving him the right to enter the country legally, and other documents indicating he had been to the States previously. He had three different Social Security cards and a Blue Cross & Blue Shield card from Mississippi. He also bore a letter from the human-resources manager of an Ohio-based packing house affirming that Barreda was promised a job on the production line there once he had gained work authorization. Joining the group was Edgar Adrián Martínez Colorado, a twenty-three-year-old from Cuatepe, Veracruz, who worked at the Coke plant and played on the company soccer team. He had never been to the United States before, but had lined up work in Phoenix, with hopes of saving enough to build a house for his bride-to-be. Enrique Landero García, a thirty-year-old, planned to send money back in order to improve his family's small house. There was Reyno Bartolo Hernández, thirty-seven, who also borrowed to pay the fee, and several other men.

A smuggler, a local fellow known to the men as Sierra Moisés, had arranged everything. The travelers would be picked up from their town by truck, then escorted to the border and guided across to Phoenix, where they were to get rides to jobs. A labor contractor in Lake Placid, Florida, was promising orange-picking work for the Mexicans. Workers could count on earning $7.50 per crate; a good picker could fill ten or eleven in a day—enough to make $75 or more. It was a long trip, but the men's hopes were high.

Crossing to *el otro lado,* the other side of the border, had become almost a rite of passage in many rural Mexican communities like Cuatro Caminos. It wasn't always about money, or the treasures that the migrants showed off when they returned, like satellite dishes and cars. The migration trail was best seen less as a south-to-north conveyor than as a looping circle between Mexican hometowns and work sites in the United States. The movement ebbed and flowed according to growing seasons and holidays, producing a back-and-forth flow that over the years had been as predictable as the tides. But many left, got jobs in the States, found girlfriends or had kids and stayed north of the border. There were small towns all over rural Mexico that were all but empty of men in their peak working years because so many had gone north. It wasn't just remote villages that had offered their able-bodied. Migration scholars were noticing that a growing number originated in small cities, where privatization and the rise of foreign-owned factories—the heralds of economic transformation in Mexico—had upset the way that people once lived. In the countryside, small-time farmers were uprooted from their communal land holdings; in the towns, factory jobs were filling with growing ranks of women. The dislodged men were hitting the migrant highway. Some came back only sporadically, especially now that it had become so difficult to cross the border.

In any case, by early 2001, the Border Patrol had noticed a curious phenomenon: a drop of 25 percent in arrests along the Southwest border. Everyone had a theory. Some U.S. officials suggested that fewer migrants were making the trek because they were optimistic that Mexico's reform-minded new president, Vicente Fox, was going to improve living conditions, and because of the toughened border enforcement. Skeptics said the drop in arrests more likely reflected that many of the migrants who had made it into the United States were staying put north of the border to avoid the challenge of having to cross again. There was a theory, too, that fresh talk of a new binational agreement on migration had inspired some laborers to stay in the United States in hopes of another amnesty. Signs were pointing toward some kind of immigration reform that would allow more Mexicans to enter legally and legalize many who were already here. Fox had made clear his ardor for a new migration arrangement. President George W. Bush, who took office in January, just a month after Fox, seemed eager for a close, trusting relationship with this fellow rancher and with an emerging new Mexico. Bush, who had been governor of Texas, spoke some Spanish and appreciated the swelling political clout of U.S. Latinos. He seemed well positioned to ply a new course, and even chose Mexico as the destination for his first foreign trip as president. The session in Guanajuato produced a joint presidential statement placing migration—long a touchy issue that tended to be pushed to the rear of binational talks—squarely on the front burner.

While the politicians postured, the migrants stayed on the move. The Veracruz group left before dawn on May 15 and rode to the border. On May 19 some relatives received calls saying the group had arrived in Sonoyta, the burgeoning smuggling hub across from the Tohono O'odham reservation. The gateway to Sonora state—and for many Arizonans, to the boating playground that is the Gulf of California—Sonoyta had also long enjoyed a less savory reputation. As far back as the 1850s, the place stood out to visitors for its seedy character. In his chronicle of the boundary survey, Lieutenant Nathaniel Michler describes Sonoyta as "a resort for smugglers, and a den for a number of low, abandoned Americans, who have been compelled to fly from justice. Some few Mexican rancheros had their cattle in the valley nearby. It is a miserable poverty-stricken place, and contrasts strangely with the comparative comfort of an Indian village of Papagos, within sight."

By 2001, Sonoyta had returned to its roots with a vengeance. This time, the smugglers were trafficking in people. The industry was in full swing. There were as many as 1,500 migrants awaiting passage on any given day—a clientele visible at the storefront bus station, at the town's small park and in the boardinghouses that had blossomed like desert weeds. Around twenty had opened in the past two years alone. Their customers were packed six to a room. The migrants killed time as they waited for the pay phone to ring with word on when they would cross.

Many of the calls came from the U.S. side. This border enterprise was a binational venture, with entrepreneurial opportunism aplenty in both countries.

Many locals watched the developments in Sonoyta—including a rise in drug trafficking—with dismay, fearing that their small-town life was giving way with each arriving busload to a new air of criminality and corruption. The tempting power of quick money was strong for the young men of Sonoyta, who stood to make $1,000 by acting as couriers, or mules, for the big-time drug smugglers. One local priest bold enough to speak out against smugglers said he had been the target of shouted threats outside his home and once had his car run off the road.

Once they were picked up by the *coyotes*, migrants fell instantly under their command. They were told when to move, when to stay put, what to eat and what to carry. The migrants were usually instructed to pack light—a jug of water, canned tuna and beans, crackers, a loaf of bread or packet of tortillas. Some carried a change of clothing, but many toted only what they wore. The better-prepared invested in new sneakers for the hike, while others set out in sandals or cheap shower flip-flops.

Because of limited communication, the Veracruz relatives would know little of how their loved ones fared during their brief stay in Sonoyta. For many, there would be no more contact until the bodies came home. The Veracruz group was joined by five Mexican men who had traveled from Baja California, where they were working in the tomato fields. The smaller group included three brothers named González—Mario, Isidoro and Efraín—from the southern state of Guerrero and two friends who also were hoping to make money working the crops on the U.S. side. Not yet thirty and with only a sixth-grade education, Mario González was the most worldly of his group of *campesinos*. He was the only one who'd been across the border before and he had useful contacts at a Florida-based firm called Vásquez Harvesting, which had hired him twice. He had called before the group headed north and been told there were jobs available picking oranges.

The González group took the bus to Sonoyta and checked into the San Antonio Hotel. Upon instructions from their smuggler, known to them as "El Negro," they moved to a boardinghouse run by a woman named Nelly. El Negro, who was later identified in court documents as Evodio Manilla Cabrera, told them to pack light for the trip across the desert: no more than two gallons of water. Their first attempt, crossing by van, didn't last long. On their first night the group was nabbed by the Border Patrol soon after crossing the barbed-wire fence dividing the two countries and sent back to Mexico. They returned to the boardinghouse and called the owner of the Florida company to send money because they had run out. They were soon wired about 850 pesos, or a little less than $100. A few days later—before the fateful trip—they received another $50. The loans would be added to the tab for being smuggled across, $1,400 each, to be repaid through their labors when they got to Florida.

By May 19, the González party merged with the Veracruz group and took the bus out along the border road west toward El Papalote, a rural community, or *ejido*, marked by a food shop and a couple of shacks along Mexican federal Highway 2, which runs northwest from Sonoyta toward San Luis Río Colorado. Then the migrants were packed into a van for the trip into the United States. Once inside, they would continue on foot. As instructed, they each carried two gallons of water and a little food. Their goal was the city of Ajo, Arizona, a hike that they were told would take a day and a half. Including the three smugglers who led them, the group numbered close to thirty people, all men, when they crossed the border.

What happened to the migrants before their discovery by border agents four days later would have to be pieced together from agents' recollections and deductions, and from the incomplete versions of survivors who were unfamiliar with their surroundings. The account provided here is based on several sources: the testimony of several survivors and formal allegations by U.S. authorities that became public through U.S. court documents and legal proceedings; the comments of U.S. officials; and interviews with Border Patrol agents who found the migrant party in the wilderness and then spent the better part of three days hunting for survivors.

While U.S. authorities initially reported that the group crossed at Los Vidrios, they later said the point was farther east at El Papalote, some fifteen miles from Sonoyta. Border Patrol agents who traced the trail of footprints back toward Mexico said the tracks had led to a spot on the U.S. side called Quitobaquito Springs, just northeast of El Papalote, in the southwestern corner of Organ Pipe Cactus National Monument.

The van drove for two hours through the desolate countryside on U.S. soil before the smugglers had their first problem: they spotted the lights of what they thought was a Border Patrol vehicle. To evade the agent, the driver of the smuggling van turned back south and retreated to a spot called Pozo Nuevo, still on the U.S. side, where the migrants and their three guides were dropped off and instructed to start walking. The group was told to head north and to aim for lights that would appear in the distance. The lights would mark Ajo, about twenty-five miles away on Highway 85, a north-south artery between the border and Interstate 8.

It is unclear precisely when the group veered off course, or why. It's possible that the guides mistook a distant transmission tower on the interstate to the northwest for the lights they were originally seeking to the northeast. In any case, the hikers, instead of approaching Ajo, headed into the desert's vastness. It appears that the group trudged north along the west side of a mountain chain called the Growlers and into the Cabeza Prieta National Wildlife Refuge. Their trail came within two miles of a low saddle in the mountain range that held Charlie Bell's Well—one of the places where the Reverend Hoover's group had been denied permission a month earlier to install its water stations and blue flags. The hikers then made a critical mistake: rather than continuing toward the saddle, where they might have found a pool of water and spotted the lights of Ajo, the group turned west, away from safety. The hikers would eventually round the southern tip of the Granite Mountains, a full day's walk away, and then head north along the western flank of the range. It was along that stretch that most would be found.

The trip had gone poorly from the start. After the hikers were dropped in the desert following the brush with the Border Patrol truck, it soon became obvious that the guides were poorly prepared for the journey. They bickered over the right route. By the second day, one of the smugglers lost his nerve and decided to head back to Mexico, taking at least one of the migrants with him. The group soon found itself short on water. As they struggled on along the base of the Granites, the migrants explored the nooks and folds of the narrow range, perhaps in search of water deposits or passage through the wall of rock. At some point, probably the third day, another of the smugglers, José López Ramos, and the remaining guide collected $90 from the immigrants. The guides said they were going to get water and went away. For the migrants, waiting in the desert heat began to take its toll. By that night, at least one of the twenty-four travelers was dead.

The survivors, losing hope that the guides were ever coming back, gave up waiting. On their own, they stumbled on in small groups, crisscrossing sandy washes and shedding shoes and clothes, piece by piece, in a misguided attempt at relief from the unrelenting desert sun. They tried to find shade. The clothing was all they had to get rid of; by now, none carried so much as a duffel or a bottle of water. Crazed for fluids, they found liquid where they could. Before the first were discovered by Border Patrol agents, the desperate men had resorted to sucking at the moist cores of cactus. Mario González watched his traveling companions drink their own urine.

Well before noon on May 23, four days after the group had departed Sonoyta, the sun had already turned the desert floor into a furnace. Border Patrol agent David Phagan turned his Chevy Tahoe south on Papago Road, a dirt road leading from the highway south through the Mohawk Valley. Phagan's shift began at 7 a.m. His assignment that morning was in the east desert, an enormous tract that marks the easternmost limit of the Wellton station's patrol zone and covers some of the nation's least touched territory, including the Cabeza Prieta refuge. He was one of two agents covering that section today and among just six patrolling the three-thousand-square-mile Wellton zone. Phagan had swapped his life as a probation officer in Douglas, where he'd grown up, for that of a border agent three years earlier. Working in Wellton had placed him in some of the loneliest spots along the border, but he liked being on his own out there. The onset of late spring and summer only added more significance to his job. Wellton agents knew that on any given day, a migrant's life might depend on their ability to spot tracks in the sand. Most agents didn't go for long here before encountering the fatal results of these desert treks. Phagan, however, was an exception. He had remarked to a fellow Wellton agent just a week earlier that he had yet to encounter a dead border crosser.

Phagan wheeled east onto an even more primitive track, a seven-and-a-half-mile stretch known to the border agents as the Vidrios drag road, to cut for sign. In the morning, sign-cutting was best done going east, into the rising sun. That was when the odds were most favorable that the angled light would create shadows where it struck the indentations of footprints in the sand, making them easier to spot. Late in the day, it was best to cut in a westerly direction. In the middle of the day, with the sun straight overhead, it was hard to see much of anything. By ten that morning, the temperature was already over 100. The Vidrios drag jutted into the desert just short of the Granite Mountains and outside the limits of the refuge, whose protections kept even patrol agents out, except on the few established dirt roads. This was the heart of the desert—a solid hour's drive from the highway even on decent dirt roads.

Phagan was within a mile of the eastern limit of the drag road, near the end of his cut, when he caught sight of a man, in jeans and a T-shirt, running toward him about a hundred yards off the road. It was Mario González. Then three others approached—Mario's brother Isidoro and their two travel companions. All were desperate for water. Phagan pulled out a five-gallon plastic water jug, resembling an old jerry can, like the one all Wellton agents carried in their trucks. The men gulped the water from their hands and from two old soda cans that Phagan found on the truck floor and turned into cups. He told the men to slow down—they'd get sick swallowing so much water at once. They told him the water was hot, but drank hungrily. The agent sprinkled water on their heads to cool them.

Phagan had never seen people so severely dehydrated. The men's bodies were nearly empty of fluids. Unlike other desert crossers he'd encountered, these men had no body odor. It was over 100 degrees out, and they weren't even sweating. Phagan asked in Spanish if there were others. Mario González said yes, his brother Efraín was left behind somewhere out there. "How far?" Phagan asked. About two hours' walking, the migrant replied. They had last seen the brother the day before.

He had wandered off alone. Phagan knew that he would have to summon help for a search. He continued cooling the men with water and then repeated his question: "Were there any others?" This time the agent was stunned by the answer. "There is a group of twenty farther back," the migrant said. "But they're all dead."

Phagan could scarcely believe what he'd heard. He radioed the report to his day-shift supervisor, Kevin Kimm, back at the Wellton station and asked for help, including Border Patrol pilots. Kimm told Phagan to follow the quartet's footprints backward in hopes of finding the brother, then quickly ordered the five other Wellton agents on duty to make their way to Phagan's spot. Glen Payne, the station chief, was in Yuma on his way to a dentist appointment when he heard the radio traffic. He called the Border Patrol's air base in Yuma and asked for emergency support. The sheriff's office was alerted and some of the top trackers in the Border Patrol's Yuma station were mobilized. No one knew yet if the migrants' report was accurate. If so, it could easily be the worst disaster involving migrants on the border in recorded history. Perhaps there was a chance to find survivors, but if the men who flagged down Phagan were any indication, there would be little time. By morning's end, the desert was alive with frenzied movement.

Aaron Heitke was the first of the other Wellton agents to make it to the end of the Vidrios drag road. With the help of the four migrants, he and Phagan maneuvered their vehicles slowly along the difficult terrain in search of the wayward brother. For now, the agents would ignore the ban on taking their vehicles off-road into the protected confines of the wildlife refuge. The progress was painfully slow. The ground's thick crust gave way under the weight of a truck to a silt so fine that agents called it "moon dust." One truck could proceed well enough, but it was difficult to maneuver a second vehicle through the deep sand.

To make matters worse, this stretch of the desert harbors countless ironwoods, gnarled and prehistoric-looking trees as hard as steel and capable of piercing a truck's shell. Broken-off stumps were hell on tires and the bane of desert agents. They would plague the Wellton rescue from start to finish. Phagan had driven barely half a mile off the drag road when he got a flat tire—the first of four he would suffer that day. All told, Wellton agents had twenty-six punctured tires in three days of searching. As more agents showed up, and the flat tires mounted, agents began leaving their disabled vehicles behind and hopping into a fellow agent's truck until it, too, fell victim to the ironwoods. Spares became so short that agents began taking usable tires from the disabled trucks. As the search wore on, the Wellton station sent tires along with fresh agents; the local service station shuttled needed parts to the search area. Trucks, too, soon were in short supply. Wellton supervisors became so desperate that they dispatched the station's "ice-cream truck," a boxy vehicle used to transport arrestees that won its nickname because it looks better suited to delivering dairy goods.

Phagan's search soon was foundering and Heitke's truck had quit. Three of the migrants were taken away, while Mario González, mostly recovered, rode in the passenger seat of Phagan's truck to help guide him to the spot where his brother had disappeared. They had found a wash where the men had attempted to light a signal fire, but no sign of the lost hiker. The chances of getting to any survivors from there on the ground were looking more and more remote.

Helicopter pilot Stuart Goodrich was summoned at about 11 a.m. A fellow Border Patrol pilot said Goodrich was to get into his helicopter, a little two-seater known as an OH-6 Cayuse, and fly out to the Wellton zone to help on a search and rescue. There were no further details. Goodrich topped off the fuel tank in the chopper—on loan from the Border Patrol's office in El Centro because Yuma's four helicopters were in the repair shop—and lifted off. He couldn't raise the Wellton agents on the ground as the mountains blocked the radio signal. But as he skimmed east above the desert from Yuma, Goodrich got the early report from the Wellton station of a possible disaster involving a large group of border crossers.

In four years as a pilot in Yuma, the thirty-year-old Goodrich had come to know the ribs and furrows of this parched landscape the way a homeowner learns the lumps and divots in a backyard. When he first arrived, it had all looked the same. The dun-colored hills, their repetition, the apparent blankness of the land—it all seemed to create an endless pale sea. The desert topography played tricks on the eyes, but by now, it had revealed itself to Goodrich. There were ridges of tan, pale gray and coffee brown, but also of black—short ranges arrayed in rows of rough humps and wrinkled like elephant skin.

On a typical day, two Border Patrol helicopter pilots split the border zone between Yuma and the Organ Pipe monument, which falls into the zone patrolled by a separate unit of the agency, based in Tucson. A three-hour overflight would usually take Goodrich down to the border-line and then east across the Tinajas Altas range, north through the Cabeza Prieta Mountains, then east again over the wildlife refuge to check the remote washes and protected canyons off limits to agents on the ground. His path would pass over the Sierra Pinta Mountains and parallel to the borderline along the Camino del Diablo. On a slow day, he might jog north a bit and head into the western edge of Organ Pipe, since the overwhelmed Tucson agents seldom made it that far.

The pilots were critical to border enforcement. They could cover stretches that were out of the range of truck-bound agents, or give early warning of footprints headed into hostile territory. The pilots could zip above drag roads at sixty knots or slow to the speed of a person walking, or just hover above. Peering down through his bubble-shaped wind-shield or hanging his head out the open door, Goodrich could track foot-prints from twenty to thirty feet overhead as capably as if he were tramping in the same dust, without kicking up the sand. But it also was brutally hot work. The burning desert air blew hard through the open cabin, creating an effect that Goodrich likened to "sitting in a clothes dryer." Pouring sweat inside his flight suit, he could guzzle a gallon and a half of water during a single flight.

Because the Yuma helicopters had been sidelined for repairs, none of the pilots had flown over the border area for two days prior to the res-cue. Whether the pilots would ever have seen the migrants is debatable, since the migrants' path curled west into the pilots' patrol zone at a point farther away from the border than the Border Patrol flights usually passed. The group's looping trail may well have taken them out of the range where anyone could have helped in time.

Around noon, Goodrich located Phagan and brought the helicop-ter to the desert surface to compare notes with his fellow agent. They agreed that the best course was to search for the missing brother, who was alive when last seen and believed to be close by. They thought it might be easier to find him from overhead. Phagan plugged along on the ground, maneuvering between greasewood bushes and the terrible iron-woods, while Goodrich slowly hunted for tracks from thirty feet in the air. No luck. They simply could not pick up the solo man's sign.

Goodrich decided to head south along the range to try to confirm the migrant's report of a large group, all dead. It wouldn't have been the first time that a sun-addled hiker had offered a story that proved not to be true. Goodrich had come across migrants so delirious from the heat that they reported having been accompanied by ten others, triggering a search when, in fact, they had traveled alone. The pilot flew to the south end of the Granite Mountains and began cutting for sign, working his way back north. Around the range's midsection, Goodrich found what he was looking for: the tracks of a sizable group of walkers, tracing the mountain's flank. Oh man, Goodrich thought to himself, this guy's probably telling the truth.

He began to search the dry gulleys for the shapes of people. It didn't take long. Strung along a wash leading from one of the canyons were about a half-dozen human forms. Goodrich was about six miles south of where he had left Phagan. Even before he touched down in a clearing, Goodrich knew it was bad. The men were sprawled here and there under the sparse bushes. Most were naked, or nearly so. The pilot radioed his discovery to the ground agents and informed the Border Patrol's dispatch center in Yuma that they would need the services of the Marine Corps's search-and-rescue helicopter, a much larger Huey. The marines based in Yuma served as the area's medical-evacuation air service since there was no private air ambulance to respond to emergencies.

It would take Phagan and the other agents in trucks some time to pick their way to Goodrich's location. For now, the pilot was on his own to sort out a scene that grew more grisly with each bush he searched. Still, what the migrant had told Phagan wasn't entirely true: not everyone was dead. Of the eight people Goodrich first encountered, four were alive. He helped them to their feet and ushered them together under the same shaded bush. They were barely able to walk, and couldn't speak. The best way for Goodrich to tell the living from the dead was by the low, constant moaning coming from those who still hung on. Goodrich grabbed the five-gallon water jug from his chopper and helped feed water to the four survivors. One was in better shape than the rest, so Goodrich left him with the jug and instructions to pour water into the mouths of the others. The pilot needed to get back in the air to look for more survivors, and to guide the ground agents to the spot. From the air, Goodrich located more people. He repeated his prior actions: he landed, identified survivors and shepherded them back to the original group of four who were still alive. Then he'd lift off again, each time spying another cluster of two or three people, and then land to help them. Within the same hundred-yard radius, he discovered twenty people, nine of them dead. A little farther to the south, Goodrich later found two more bodies, for a total of eleven dead.

It took Phagan and two fellow agents an hour to link up with Goodrich, who was now working feverishly. By 12:45, the marine search-and-rescue helicopter was en route. Kimm, the Wellton shift supervisor, was headed to the scene, joined by Rob Roll, the Border Patrol agent in charge of the Yuma station. The temperature was approaching its peak that day of 117 degrees. Because of the prohibition on off-road travel in the wildlife refuge, Phagan had never been this far south before. He could barely believe his eyes. The first man he saw there was dead. The migrant had stripped down to his boxer shorts and socks. The man was facedown, his head dangling into a hole he apparently had dug while trying to find cool. He had tried to bury his body in the loose sand but had succeeded only in covering his buttocks and thighs.

Another man, still alive, stood in his underwear, his arms draped over the branch of an ironwood, hanging on for dear life. When he looked at the agent, it was unnerving; the vacant eyes gazed straight past without seeing his rescuer. The agents got the same unsettling stare from most of the other eleven survivors. Phagan moistened the men's discarded shirts and used the wet cloth to cool them. Their skin had been burned to a furious, stop-sign red by the sun. The extreme loss of body moisture had peeled back their lips, giving them a sickly grin, and left darkened pits where their eyes should have been. All Phagan could think of was documentary films about survivors of the Holocaust. These men had the same sunken look, "like skin draped over a skeleton." The dead lay scattered where they had last sought refuge. All were shoeless and bare-chested; some had kept their pants on. They wore black or tan jeans, leather belts. The ground next to one man was sprinkled with the shreds of torn U.S. $20 bills. Phagan wondered why the man would have ripped up his money before death. Was it so the smugglers wouldn't get it? Was he conceding the impotence of cash in his last moments? Among the dead were Mario Castillo and the Barredas. Castillo's death certificate would list his cause of death as hyperthermia. In the space provided for the place of death, the document would say simply "base of Granite Mountains."

The marine helicopter arrived and survivors were helped aboard for the ninety-mile ride to Yuma Regional Medical Center. One of those men would not survive the trip. The rest made up a grim parade as they were wheeled into the hospital. Their faces and hands were peppered with spines as a result of their attempts to draw water from cactus. Others were still delusional. Most had suffered kidney distress, the result of extreme dehydration. The lack of fluids left the survivors wan and shriveled-looking; one emergency-room doctor said they resembled "mummies from ancient Egypt." It was likely, the doctors said, that the men had been but a few hours from death at the time Goodrich spotted them. Amazingly, all of those who made it to the Yuma hospital would survive.

Back in the desert, the search continued all afternoon for any others. The migrants had been uncertain of the size of the group. Twenty-six, maybe. Perhaps thirty. The border agents knew that the wandering brother still hadn't been found and they went on scouring the ground for traces of others, too. Sheriff's personnel had arrived to begin the official death investigation and an air force helicopter, a Blackhawk, was dispatched from Davis-Monthan Air Force Base in Tucson to retrieve the bodies of the deceased and ferry them to coroners' workers out at the road. By now, a team of border agents assigned to BORSTAR, the search-and-rescue team, had arrived from Tucson.

Phagan kept working past the end of his assigned shift. He was exhausted and thirsty. He'd used up both hundred-ounce bladders of the flexible water carrier that was strapped to his back. Only hours later, when he called it quits for the day at around 9 p.m., did he realize that he had labored all day in the inferno conditions without ever removing the bulletproof vest from beneath his green uniform shirt.

By mid-afternoon, the Wellton station's night crew was coming on duty. Jerry Wofford, one of two evening supervisors, knew nothing of the roiling drama until he was driving to work from Yuma. When he pulled through the immigration checkpoint on Interstate 8, about ten miles outside of Yuma, a fellow agent told him there were six or seven people already confirmed dead. Once at the station, it was decided that Wofford would head into the field. There were no patrol trucks left, so he headed out in an unmarked vehicle. He grabbed ten or fifteen gallons of water in jugs and several spare tires. By the time Wofford made it to the area an hour later, agents were following two sets of tracks: that of the missing brother and a second trail, with the footprints of two people, heading north through a gap at the north end of the Granites.

Wofford, a thirty-eight-year-old veteran agent who had cut his teeth patrolling Imperial Beach during the chaotic late 1980s and early 1990s, was now in charge of the search effort, which was certainly headed into nighttime. He pulled aside his best tracker, Jerry Scott, and a second agent from Yuma, and told them to head north after the trail of the pair. Wofford and three other agents joined in the search for Phagan's solo hiker, Efraín González, by tracing the path of the brother's small group a few miles to find the point where it went from five men to the four who found Phagan. The men's trail was puzzling. Agents following the tread patterns saw places where some of the men appeared to take their shoes off, then put them back on. At another point, some of the shoe patterns changed mysteriously. Were they switching shoes? the agents wondered. (It would later turn out that they were; two of the men had carried a second set of shoes and changed them along the way, for reasons that are unclear.)

At last, they found the brother's trail. Wofford followed it, in darkness now, as it wobbled east, then north, then south and north again. There was little moonlight to help; on nights like this it was easy for agents to lose their bearings. Wofford and the other searchers carried handheld spotlights as they traced the zigzagging footprints, on foot and in trucks, across a dry wash running east to west, perpendicular to the mountain chain. It was shortly after 11 p.m.

Then the trail disappeared into a thicket of trees and waist-high elephant grass that already had been trampled by animals. Making track-

ing harder, the surface had changed to hard clay, which betrays hardly
any traces of footprints. The agents were about to skirt around the patch
and try to pick up the trail on its opposite side when one of the agents
made the discovery about fifty yards inside the thicket. Efraín González
was dead. He lay on his back, naked, about five miles south of the Vidrios drag road where Phagan had come to the aid of his brother Mario
and the three others. Efraín González's path had come within just a half-
mile of the same road and then veered away, for reasons that would be
impossible to ascertain.

The search for the last pair of footprints—the ones headed north
toward Interstate 8, thirty-five miles away—wore on past 3 a.m., when
the midnight shift took over. Finally, at about 5 a.m., the searchers
found one of the two men dead along the San Cristobal Wash, which
runs south from the highway. An hour later, the second hiker was found
a little farther north. He was alive. It was López Ramos, the smuggler.
He was in bad shape, and one of the BORSTAR agents administered
CPR. He and the deceased man, who was believed to be the second
guide, had traveled a remarkable distance since leaving the migrants
behind near the Granite Mountains. López was within four miles of the
interstate, near the farming town of Dateland. He was transported to
the hospital in Yuma, where he recuperated. He was the twelfth and
last survivor; all told, fourteen were dead, including López's travel
companion; Edgar Adrián Martínez, the soccer-playing Coke worker;
and Reyno Bartolo, who had borrowed money to make the trip. The
searching continued throughout the day and overnight into a third day,
May 25. Agents found no more people, nor any footprints to suggest anyone remained missing.

In Tucson, the Border Patrol's commander, David Aguilar, called
Robin Hoover with the news in the middle of the afternoon. It was a sign
of how close the relationship between the two men had become in the
months since Hoover first kicked off the water-station campaign.
Aguilar told Hoover that a number of bodies had been found in the
Cabeza Prieta refuge and that a rescue effort was under way. He invited
the pastor to come to the agency's Tucson headquarters to monitor the
search operation. Hoover accepted the invitation. He then phoned an
associate in Yuma, Fernando Quiroz, who had helped with the water ef-

fort. Quiroz was furious. He said the government, which had denied permission to place water in that part of the desert, was to blame for the disaster. Hoover agreed, though it would be months before broad outrage over the tragedy would take the form of legal action. Hoover, ever media-savvy, first had a message to get out. That same afternoon, as the agents searched for life deep in the desert, the preacher drove to the studios of KGUN 9, the ABC affiliate in Tucson, and sat for a live interview on the 5 p.m. newscast. "This is a horrible tragedy," he declared. "It is precisely what we've been trying to avert."

The incident would make front-page news in the United States and Mexico as reporters poured in from all over. The scale of the incident was lost on no one. Border-crossing hikers had never died in such numbers, at least in anyone's memory. Officials from both countries rushed to Yuma to express their horror. The next day, even as searchers were still combing the desert, the INS's Johnny Williams, Wellton chief Glen Payne, Yuma assistant chief Maurice Moore, and Yuma's sheriff, Ralph Ogden, joined representatives of Mexico's Foreign Ministry at a press conference in an air-conditioned Yuma hotel. The officials displayed a map showing the Camino del Diablo and the locations where the survivors and the dead had been found. Moore said the group could not have picked a worse time to get lost: an unusually early heat wave had pushed temperatures up by ten degrees during the previous week. "Unfortunately, these people got caught right when the weather shifted," he said. A ten-degree margin was enough to "make a big difference," he explained. Agents calculated that the surface temperature on the desert floor that day might have reached 133 degrees.

Williams was well familiar with the ravages of Yuma's heat from his stint there as a Border Patrol supervisor. Grim-faced, he described the long odds facing an ill-prepared hiker in these surroundings. Even a direct route between the border and the interstate could mean a trek of seventy miles, with "virtually zero" water available in the wild, he said. A person would have to carry at least five gallons to survive such a journey—more than the two gallons the migrants were instructed to take—and that was nearly impossible to do. "If you want to find out what isolation is, you should go to this part of the desert," Williams said. He referred to the smugglers as "leeches" and described a slow agony that typically accompanies death in the heat—a steady withering that leaves its victim delusional and disoriented as the body's organs shut down, one by one, from lack of water and overheating.

Under normal circumstances, the body's machinery works together to maintain a steady temperature of 98.6 degrees. A part of the brain known as the hypothalamus bears primary responsibility for that job, directing the body's cooling mechanisms much as a living-room thermostat tells the air conditioner to kick on when it's hot. The body tries to cool itself in several ways. Sweat glands produce perspiration to the skin's surface; evaporation draws heat from the skin, cooling it. The brain also orders the heart to pump harder and steers blood from the body's core to its surface. This is done by restricting the flow of blood to the internal organs and opening the vessels to the skin to vent heat from the core. To accomplish all of these jobs, the body requires enough fluid to produce cooling sweat, to maintain the proper volume of blood plasma and, with the help of salts to escort the water past cell walls, to keep organs and muscles working right. A hiker in normal hot weather needs at least a gallon a day. The heat pounding down on the Yuma migrants was extreme. The air outside was doing nothing to help cool the migrants.

Dehydration is like not having enough water in your car's radiator; the body keeps struggling, but there is no way for it to dampen the rising core temperature. As a person succumbs to heat exhaustion, muscles cramp and nausea can set in. The pulse and breathing quicken. The person may feel weak, suffer a headache or go faint as a result of the body's decision to steer blood from the organs—brain included—to the skin.

Without treatment, and the body's temperature reaching 105 degrees, the condition worsens to heat stroke. The skin can turn hot to the touch. The heart and lungs labor even harder. The pulse can reach 160 to 180 beats per minute, the same level achieved during a vigorous workout at the gym. Eventually, the body's attempt to divert blood away from the core falters, and the temperature rises more. Because the central nervous system is vulnerable to excess heat, the hiker in such a state becomes confused, squandering his last strength circling aimlessly, or even loses consciousness. It is not uncommon for seizures to occur. The body is overwhelmed down to the tiniest cells; tissue perishes. The organs begin to fail as the critical chain of life-sustaining chemical reactions collapses. The eyes dry up and the kidneys shut down. The person takes on a shrunken appearance due to moisture loss. The body's final throes can be frantic. Desert trackers who have encountered dead hikers noticed that the sand around the body had been kicked up by the flailing, as if it had been tilled.

"It's one of the most terrible deaths that can happen to a human being," said Williams. "It's a grisly, terrible, terrible death."

The tragedy rippled to the nations' capitals. Juan Hernández, a former University of Texas professor who was named to a newly created post as Mexico's point man for migrant affairs, flew to Yuma, where he visited survivors at their hospital beds the next day. U.S. Attorney General John Ashcroft, monitoring the search from Washington, D.C., labeled the incident nothing short of a disaster. The same day, in an unusual move, U.S. Secretary of State Colin Powell and his Mexican counterpart, Foreign Minister Jorge Castañeda, issued a joint declaration on the deaths.

The joint statement said, in part: "The governments of the United States and Mexico condemn the actions of smugglers who put the lives of would-be migrants at risk. We are committed to ensuring a safe and orderly border, and both governments reaffirm their commitment to spare no effort in combating the trafficking of migrants along the border. These tragic deaths highlight the pressing need for our governments to continue their work to reach new agreements on migration and border safety." The communiqué noted that delegations from both countries were scheduled to meet in Texas two weeks later to discuss how to prevent such tragedies and to promote "safe and orderly migration."

A subtle rhetorical shift was under way. Where two-fisted control had once been the watchword along the border, safety was now on everyone's lips—not just those of Claudia Smith and the other activists. The two governments had already appeared headed toward some kind of program to permit more Mexicans into the United States to work. That momentum seemed to gather after Bush's promising summit meeting with Fox in Guanajuato a few months earlier, when the two presidents agreed to launch high-level negotiations "aimed at achieving short- and long-term agreements that will allow us to constructively address migration and labor issues between our two countries." Now they had another reason to do so. As some advocates of a more liberal policy had predicted, it seemed that change had been propelled by disaster.

But the deaths also raised the volume of the immigration debate. Claudia Smith latched on to the incident as the latest proof of what she saw as the nation's flawed enforcement strategy along the border. On the other side, U.S. Congressman Bob Stump, an Arizona Republican who had long advocated a get-tough approach toward illegal immigrants, told the *Arizona Republic:* "I don't know what the answer is. I'm more interested in trying to stop them than doing more to help them. I don't mean to sound inhumane, but it's only going to lead to more crossings if you take the danger away. The people should know the risks, unless they're abandoned out there by those *coyotes* or whatever you call them, who take their money and don't give a damn about them."

For all the official expressions of dismay and promises of action to come, there remained little sign that the fatal episode had changed life much where the risks were highest—in the arid death zone where Payne's trackers continued prowling daily for ill-advised hikers. A week after the incident, I returned to the desert for several days to get a ground-level view of this peculiar game of hide-and-seek in its most dangerous setting. It was a sobering reminder that it would take far more than good intentions and impassioned rhetoric to stop the dying here. And in the short term, there was only luck and the efforts of dusty-booted border agents.

Rick Sanchez, a Yuma-based border agent, was working the Camino del Diablo and other roads southeast of Yuma. It wasn't yet noon, but the mercury approached 100 degrees. Other agents working the same region had come upon the tracks of a group of about ten people. Seismic detectors, buried in the desert floor near Yuma, had been set off by human movement, further confirming the migrants' path. The trekkers had crossed southeast of Yuma, at a different point than that employed by the ill-fated group a week earlier. But judging from the direction taken by this latest group of migrants, it was apparent to the agents that they were headed deeper into the desert.

The agents steered around cactuses and twisted ironwood trees. From low overhead, a helicopter pilot radioed repeated directions as he followed the meandering tracks north through a break in the mountains, called Smuggler's Pass. Another agent, Buster Hummel, picked up the trail on foot. A fine, sugary dust, kicked up by the patrol trucks, filled the folds of his dark green uniform. The agents lost the trail in spots, only to relocate it farther along. They hopped out of their trucks, scanned the ground, got back in and drove more, heads jutting out their windows in the heat. They'd get out again when the trail grew faint. In Sanchez's truck, the air conditioner put up a weak fight against the desert breath that blew in his window.

It took three hours, but the hunt paid off. Small clusters of people—seven in all—emerged from beneath the paloverdes where they had sought shelter from the noontime heat, now up to 106 degrees. Sanchez asked in Spanish how many more there were. No one answered. He then announced sternly to the group that fourteen people had died here a week earlier: "We don't want any more deaths out here, OK?" he pleaded. Apparently persuaded, someone in the group let on that there were thirteen people all told. Soon, the remaining six people were located amid the scrub. All were in good condition.

The migrants told me they had set out from the San Luis Río Colorado end of Mexican Highway 2 about sixteen hours earlier. They walked about twenty miles to get this far, and were not yet halfway to their goal: Interstate 8. Worse, the hikers were pitifully equipped for such a desert trek. In sneakers and jeans, each began with a gallon of water. Not yet into the first afternoon, most of the jugs were close to empty. One more day in the desert heat and this group, too, could have found itself in jeopardy. Three men and two women, all from the same town in the state of Nayarit on Mexico's Pacific Coast, appeared stunned to learn that they faced a walk of at least twenty-five more miles. For many, it was their first crossing—and their introduction to the desert. "We had no idea how far it was," said Maximiliano Valdivia Vásquez, a thirty-two-year-old construction worker. The migrants, bound for the orchards of

Washington State, insisted they were not traveling with a *coyote*. But that was a common denial; they had every reason not to snitch, as the same guide might be leading them again the next day, once the group was returned across the border.

Slumped in the back of a Border Patrol truck, one of the migrants, thirty-year-old Santiago Jara Ramírez, said he had successfully crossed the Arizona desert during one of five previous journeys north of the border. He fit a pattern: studies had shown that once a migrant had crossed north even once, his or her chances of making another journey again escalated. Neither he nor any of the other migrants had heard of the fourteen deaths a week earlier, but they listened, rapt, as I described the events. It was Jara who spoke up. He had grown beans back in Nayarit, but business was bad. To illustrate, he pulled out his wallet and extracted a carefully folded invoice. It recorded a sale he had made in March, nearly three months earlier. The price of beans had dropped to 5 pesos a kilogram—less than 30 cents a pound, Jara said. That was no living. His solution to the crisis in the desert was simple: open the border to temporary workers so that nobody had to risk such a dangerous crossing. Four others who sat in the back of the Border Patrol truck alongside Jara nodded in agreement.

The perils were not unknown to many who made the trip, though. Migrants on the U.S. side talked often with friends and relatives back home and were able to convey word about the potential dangers. But like Mario Castillo, many migrants set out anyway, placing their faith in the competence of the smugglers, in divine protection, or both. They figured they would not end up among the dead. One such person was eighteen-year-old Yadira Graciano. Standing outside the truck where Jara and the others waited to be transported to Yuma for booking, Graciano, her pretty smile edged in silver fillings, said she knew full well that the trip was dangerous. Her parents had even tried to talk her out of coming. "They warned me. They said not to go. But I wanted to look for something better," she said, squinting into the bright sun. "And to help them." This day's brush with danger might frighten others into giving up. But this young woman was unbowed. As soon as she was returned across the border to Mexico, she said resolutely, she would cross again.

On the afternoon that Graciano's group was rounded up, a graver drama faced a separate band of Mexican migrants in a different stretch of the desert. They were about a hundred miles to the east, directly north of Sonoyta, the smuggling town. Six migrants, three of them cousins and all from the same town in the southern coastal state of Oaxaca, had set out on foot from the border two days earlier. They were part of a group of sixteen that was guided by a pair of Sonoyta smugglers. It had taken some doing for the Oaxacans to make it north, their first trip to the border. They borrowed money from relatives to pay for the two-day bus ride to Sonoyta, then lined up a *coyote* to get them to Los Angeles. The smuggler's fee, at $600 each, was to be paid when they arrived, as was customary.

But far short of California's farm country, five of the men watched one of their party—Armando Rosales Pacheco, a fit if slightly chubby twenty-five-year-old *campesino*—die before their eyes south of Ajo, Arizona. They would recount their story the next day at a Border Patrol detention center in Tucson. Their clothes were still dust-smeared and their expressions were somewhere near shell-shocked. They agreed to chat, outside of the presence of any border agents, in order to share their account. They spoke softly and without tears. What they conveyed instead was exhaustion and lingering disbelief at how suddenly their hopes had been swallowed in the desert.

According to their account, the men had hiked all night from Sonoyta. The next day, Rosales complained of feeling ill and weak in the legs. One of the travelers, David Soriano, rubbed his ailing friend's legs to recharge them, but Rosales kept falling behind. The two smugglers grew impatient, but nonetheless were decent enough to replenish the migrants' bottles with cloudy water they had found nearby, probably from a cattle pond. Still, Rosales faltered. Eventually, the smugglers and the ten other migrants couldn't—or wouldn't—wait. They pushed on, leaving Rosales and his five companions not far from Highway 85, the highway to Ajo. Alone the next day, the men swabbed Rosales's face and neck to cool him. He vomited the brackish water. Two cousins, Rosebel Miguel Rosales and Oscar Morales Rosales, propped him between them as the little group hobbled north. They still held out hope of making it to Ajo, where they hoped to pool their money to buy a junk car and then drive on to California.

They made it another hundred yards. When Armando Rosales went faint, his cousins laid him down and watched helplessly. He trembled.

His lips turned purple. And just like that, Rosales was dead on a scratchy bed of gravel. He was more than 1,500 miles from home, a verdant Oaxaca countryside of cooling ocean breezes and broad-leafed papaya and fields of corn. "It happened fast. He shook and his eyes went back in his head and he was gone. He didn't say a thing," recalled Morales, one of the cousins. Two of the men trudged on in search of help. They succeeded in flagging down a Border Patrol agent out on the highway. Their trip was over. The next day, as the five survivors sat in an air-conditioned room in the Border Patrol's station in Tucson, they seemed concerned about making it back to Oaxaca in time for their travel mate's funeral. Their awe over the meanness of the desert took few words to express. "This is the last time I try—too dangerous," Morales said. "It is my first time—and my last time, too."

Meanwhile, the Yuma disaster continued to resound. A month later, in June, Mexico and the United States unveiled their latest joint safety program, one that officials described this time as a key first step toward a broader accord to create orderly and safe migration. The safety pact, announced simultaneously in Mexico City and Washington, called for a U.S. review of the controversial tight-border policy that had steered Mexicans into dangerous and remote crossings. At the same time, Mexico agreed to consider ways to prevent migrants from traversing the most deadly deserts, canals and rivers. A joint U.S.-Mexico statement repeated the governments' shared commitment "to create a process of orderly migration that guarantees humane treatment of migrants, provides protection of their legal rights, ensures acceptable work conditions for migrants and also recognizes the right of nations to control the flow of people across their borders."

In announcing the effort in Mexico City, Mexican Deputy Foreign Minister Enrique Berruga said the fourteen deaths near Yuma had served to hasten action on this safety accord. He was quick to stress that the policy emphasized humanitarian efforts, such as joint search-and-rescue operations, over police action. "We are not talking of raids, of arrests," Berruga told reporters. "We are using very different language to address a problem that ultimately is common to us both. We are seeking to change the chemistry on the border." The plan called for stepped-up publicity campaigns, better aerial surveillance of the desert regions on the U.S. side and more agents assigned to a Mexican migrant-protection force on the border known as Grupo Beta. The program also called for a joint crackdown on migrant traffickers such as those accused of abandoning the Mexicans in Arizona.

In San Diego, U.S. officials announced separate border-safety plans to equip agents with nonlethal weapons as a way to decrease the odds of fatal shootings. Agents there would test a new weapon, called a pepperball gun, that launches capsules of powdered pepper up to a hundred feet. The idea was to reduce the number of shootings involving agents who fired to defend themselves against rock throwers along the fence. Of fifty-two shootings by San Diego border agents since the outset of Operation Gatekeeper in 1994, nearly half had occurred amid rock attacks. The five fatal shootings, including three in 1999, had stirred official consternation in Mexico and inspired numerous calls for reform from U.S. rights activists, such as Roberto Martinez.

Johnny Williams was there also to announce steps to keep migrants from the swift waters of the All American Canal in Imperial County, where seventeen people had drowned during the previous eight months. As part of the new safety push, Williams promised that the U.S. government would beef up night patrols and put up lights on ten miles of the irrigation canal where it hugged the boundary near Calexico.

Critics of Gatekeeper scoffed at the safety plan. They compared it caustically to throwing a man into perilous waters, then heaving him a lifeline and asking to be congratulated. When Attorney General John Ashcroft visited San Diego a month later, in July, Claudia Smith and a handful of activists were there to greet him. A day earlier, Ashcroft had traveled to the edge of a grassy field near the border fence to address the newest class of the Border Patrol's BORSTAR team. There, four agents put on an impressive display of their techniques, rappelling from a hovering Huey helicopter to show how they could be lowered into inaccessible canyons to save migrants in distress. Ashcroft awarded citations to agents who had taken part in several rescues in San Diego, including one in the rugged Otay Mountains weeks earlier that had required use of that same rappelling technique. Similar teams were being planned for all nine Border Patrol sectors along the Southwest border.

Under a sun-bleached sky, Ashcroft ticked off some of the signs that the border had changed—at least in San Diego. Arrests were down by 70 percent since 1995 and stood at their lowest level in twenty-six years. The crime rate along the border had fallen, too. The attorney general mentioned the summit meeting between Bush and Fox in February and the creation of a high-level working group on migration, a committee to which Ashcroft had also been named. "One of our chief concerns is how to improve safety along this shared border," he said. But he insisted that smugglers remained a threat: "Neither government can address the problem alone."

Now, a day later, Ashcroft was greeted by protesters outside the hotel where he was due to announce a new plan to improve cooperation between prosecutors of the two nations. The protesters held giant mock death certificates and placards alluding to the certificates he had awarded the day before. "Mr. Ashcroft: What About These Types of Certificates?" one of the posters asked. Others bore lists of the number of dead in each border state since 1995. Arizona was up to 227, California 683. Claudia Smith darted from one television interviewer to the next, hoping to punch holes in the Bush administration's border-safety drive. "The terrible irony that underlies this," she said, "is first putting migrants in mortal danger and then asking for credit when you rescue them." The Yuma disaster had given fresh ammunition to both sides in the debate over enforcement. To the government, it reflected just how desperate the smugglers had grown under the intensity of the crackdown on more populated sections of the border. To the activists, it exemplified the unconscionable results of squeezing the immigration bubble into hostile environs.

Although Yuma had made headlines, no place on the border proved deadlier in 2001 than Imperial County, California. The place sat remote from the site of debates over tactics and responsibility or whether the answer was a retooled guest-worker program or a tighter lid. Beneath the summer's pressing heat, such political discussions were a luxury there was little time to indulge because of the immediate physical dangers. And in two short months—on September 11, 2001—attacks on the World Trade Center and the Pentagon building were to drastically alter the terms on which any discussion about the border took place.

. . .

In October 2001, López Ramos, the surviving guide in the Yuma tragedy, would plead guilty in federal court in Phoenix to twenty-five smuggling counts stemming from his role in the fatal trek. He later would be sentenced to sixteen years in prison as federal prosecutors vowed to "go up the chain of command" in search of others involved in the smuggling case. A month after López's guilty plea, U.S. authorities arrested Francisco Vásquez Torres, a forty-six-year-old labor contractor in Lake Placid, Florida—the firm that Mario González had called from Mexico in search of work. Evidence against Vásquez included the migrants' statements about his promises of work, records of money transfers to Sonoyta and telephone logs showing calls from the offices of his company, Vásquez Harvesting, to the Arizona number of a man agents considered an important smuggler in the Sonoyta area. In April 2003, Vásquez would be sentenced to six and a half years in prison for luring the group north. Evodio Manilla Cabrera, the man known as El Negro and thought to be López's boss in the smuggling hierarchy, was indicted, but he remained a fugitive in 2003.

The Yuma survivors were allowed to remain in the United States to act as material witnesses in the prosecutions. Mario González, for example, was given a work permit by the U.S. government and found employment in a slaughterhouse. At López's sentencing hearing in U.S. District Court in February 2002, the guide expressed his remorse at the tragic results, according to a news account. "I am very sorry for the fate of the victims and the families," he said in Spanish through an interpreter. "My intention was not to lead them to their deaths. My intention was to lead them across so they could find better lives."

One of the survivors, José Colorado Huerta, also got a chance to speak. He recounted watching his nephew Edgar Adrián Martínez, the soccer player, succumb to the heat. "I will never forget the sadness in my nephew's eyes when he looked at me shedding tears and I wasn't able to do anything, only tell him not to die," Colorado said, also through an interpreter.

He described having questioned López about two people who had been left behind. "I asked him, were they not going to help them because otherwise they would die," Colorado recalled. "He answered, 'What do you want us to do?'"

Chapter Ten

BURYING JOHN DOE

Ricky Macken got the call shortly before 1 p.m.—his quiet day was officially over. In the cool of his air-conditioned office, he had known the lull wouldn't last long. It had been like this all summer. Nearly every day since the weather had turned hot back in May, Macken and the two deputy coroners he supervised had run at full tilt. It was worse than the previous summers, worse even than the bad time in 1998, before Macken took over, when the bodies started piling up.

Besides the usual call-outs—the midnight car wrecks, the shut-ins dead in their easy chairs, the odd passion killing—the trio of coroners now struggled to cope with the summer's steadily mounting count of undocumented border crossers who did not make it. Although the Yuma episode had demonstrated spectacularly the high risks of backcountry border crossings, it was here in Imperial County that the death toll was the highest now in 2001. Yuma had made for front-page headlines and much official consternation, while in California's southeastern corner, Macken and his team toiled mostly without public notice. "It's a continuous syndrome," Macken said.

One-third to one-half of all the coroner's cases now involved migrants. All summer long, the team had scrambled into the county's most far-off nooks, by four-wheel-drive truck or sweating on foot, to fetch the bodies of deceased immigrants who had succumbed—one here, two more there—to Imperial County's varied hazards.

The coroner's team included an office assistant and had the help of a pair of sheriff's deputies who took death-scene photographs. The squad, part of the sheriff's department, occupied a corner suite in the sheriff headquarters complex, which also housed the county jail. In the shared lobby outside the locked door of the coroner's office gathered a listless collection of people—mostly women, dressed for the heat in shorts and flip-flops—who had driven past El Centro's hay fields, cattle lots and pop-up subdivisions to wait around on the molded plastic chairs until they could visit their jailed loved ones.

Hardly anyone came by to see Macken and his men. They were very busy as it was, due to a disturbing paradox that was baffling everyone from the local Border Patrol to officials at the Mexican consulate a few miles away in Calexico: although arrests of undocumented immigrants in Imperial County were dropping—suggesting fewer crossings—the number of fatalities continued to rise. The new measures announced for Imperial County in the wake of Yuma were clearly overdue.

Powerless to stop the trend, Macken's team tried to make better sense of it. When they had time, the coroner's workers had begun trying to plot each new fatality on their computer, using map software purchased at Costco. The cases showed up as rust-colored dots the size of BBs. On a section of the map showing the most heavily traveled desert route, the markers formed a wobbly string resembling a trail of dried blood droplets.

Macken, forty-seven, had joined the coroner's unit fourteen months earlier. He was an affable former cop, nearly bald, with a crisp, prematurely white mustache and the open, ruddy face of a TV country doctor. His voice seemed surprisingly high-pitched for a man of his portly build. He and his deputies, Gary Hayes and Richard Williams, traded corny, G-rated jokes and hoarded Slim Jims, which they gobbled by the fistful. Despite the levity, the death investigator's creed posted on the main bulletin board was an immediate reminder of the macabre world Macken and his team inhabited.

It wasn't just the number of deaths. The scenes that Macken, Hayes and Williams encountered in the wilderness would break their hearts if they thought much about them. Just a few days earlier, a woman had been found dead in a distant wash. Her five children survived. For the coroners, there was little to do but head once more into the heat, make the "recovery," plot it on the map and set about trying to determine the identity of the decedent. They wouldn't have long to wait for the next call.

Today's victim was a "floater." Mechanics tending a power-generation station along the All American Canal east of El Centro had come upon a dead man in an eddy at the base of the station, known as a "drop," that regulates the flow of water like a dam. It was unclear how long he had been there or who he was. As I climbed into the coroner's van for the ride out to the site, some thirty-five miles east of El Centro at a spot called Gordons Well, Macken warned gently that the ride back might be unpleasant. There was no telling how long the man had been dead in the water, or how advanced would be his state of decomposition—or "decomp," as Macken called it. An upholstered plywood shield separating the cargo area from the driver's compartment would help quell the stench, but floaters were often the worst.

Macken peeled open a convenience-store sandwich and sped east on Interstate 8. The lush farmland around El Centro gave way quickly to scratchy desert. The heat outside was punishing. Inside the white coroner's van, the air conditioner was cranked high. It carried a dry, antiseptic smell like that in a veterinarian's office. On the sun visor above Macken's forehead was a sticker that said "I See Dead People."

Macken had grown up in the valley and moved back after a stint in the Coast Guard. He was a cop in Brawley and Westmorland before joining the sheriff's department in 1989. Over the years, he'd worked as a gang specialist and a jail investigator, busting up inmate smuggling schemes and the other low-end enterprises to which convicts continue to devote themselves once behind bars. He was a child-abuse specialist and, after making sergeant, served briefly as commander of a sheriff's substation up the road in Salton City.

When an opening in the coroner's unit came up, though, Macken jumped. Most cops were only too happy to turn the nauseating work of death scenes over to the coroner investigators, but Macken was intrigued by the notion of delving into the medical causes of each death. At first he wondered if he could stomach the worst cases, but quickly found he could. It no longer bothered him to watch chest and stomach tubes extracted from a body during autopsy, for example, or to have to recover body fragments strewn during an especially severe auto crash.

The migrant calls, however, had begun to nag at Macken. He'd always been more or less indifferent to the illegal immigration issue, though his vote in favor of Proposition 187 came from a middle-class taxpayer sensibility. It seemed wrong to shell out more money for immigrants who had no right to be in the country while cash-hungry schools were rationing pencils and paper for American children, he thought. But Macken also saw U.S. policy as lopsided when it came to immigration. As a young man in Imperial County, he'd seen the Border Patrol swoop into a field to round up immigrant workers. Although he favored a tight border, he thought it was unfair to arrest the workers but not to lay a finger on the fat cats who were hiring them. The government's Operation Gatekeeper had only added another problem. San Diego was now peaceful, but the strategy had simply shifted the crisis out here into Macken's area, too often with deadly consequences. It was illegal to cross the border without papers, Macken the cop certainly recognized. But dying seemed too severe a punishment. His frustration grew with each new Mexican body.

Macken was dressed informally today, in black jeans, a sky blue short-sleeved shirt, white sneakers and a black baseball cap. A holstered pistol rode on his right hip. Between bites of his sandwich, Macken explained some basic truths of his trade. Migrants here died mainly in two ways—by exposure to the heat and by drowning. It seemed supremely ironic—and as eloquent testimony to California's refusal to be limited by Mother Nature—that a person could perish in the outdoors by such completely opposite means. Where else but California could you drown in the middle of a desert?

The All American Canal is a shimmering man-made river in a land as dry as emery paper. If food grows where water flows, as the highway sign proclaimed, it is because of the canal and a network of branches and related irrigation works overseen by the Imperial Irrigation District. The scale of the project is stunning. The canal, whose sides are lined in concrete, measures two hundred feet wide at its broadest point and in spots twenty feet deep. It carries enough water to nourish nine cities and a half million acres of farmland. From its source at the Colorado River, the canal travels west for eighty-two miles, much of it so closely hugging the international boundary that almost everyone, including the

Border Patrol agents who police the area, treat the waterway as if it were the official dividing line.

Because of its proximity to the border, the canal also serves as a barrier in the path of migrants. Smugglers had begun using cheap blow-up rafts to usher groups across the water. Border Patrol agents had noticed that the shelves for rafts at the Wal-Mart store in Calexico were often empty because of the brisk aquatic trade. Like abandoned getaway cars, the rafts, deflated, littered the banks of the canal, or became snagged in the half dozen or so drops, where grates filter debris from the canal. Too often, the unstable little rafts, overloaded with adult passengers, capsized. Other times, the migrants simply fell out. Sometimes people had tried to float on inner tubes or with the help of a makeshift craft fashioned from empty milk jugs.

The canal's surface appears placid as a pond, but underneath the waters move fast over a silt and clay bottom, whose V shape creates thumping up-and-down swirls. Experienced divers know the powerful currents below can beat you like eggs in a bowl. Richard Williams, one of Macken's deputies, was familiar with the canal's awesome force. He had been a sheriff's diver and once went into the canal in search of a van crashed by an elderly driver. Almost as soon as he hit the water, Williams said, he was wrenched and "got sucked into a vortex that spun me like a top." In a matter of seconds, Williams tumbled fifty yards downstream, his swim mask and diver's regulator jostled loose before his diving partner yanked him out. "This stuff stomps you to pieces," Williams said.

Imperial County also presents immigrants with a second aquatic peril, as odd as the All American Canal. It is the New River, a sewage-filled channel that flows north across the border through a breach in the fence near downtown Calexico. Carrying up to 25 million gallons a day across the border, the waterway sweeps pesticides from the farms of the Mexicali Valley and chemical refuse from Mexicali's factories. In look and smell, it bears closer resemblance to a cesspool than to any river. As a Mexican official once starkly put it, "We're not talking about a real river." The New River has been named one of the most polluted waterways in the United States.

But if one could ignore the putrid-smelling toxins carried downstream from Mexicali, the New River was a smuggler's ally. For years, drug traffickers floated their wares to the U.S. side; now the immigrant smugglers were making use of it. Immigrants would wade across in the chest-deep water, cloaking their presence as they went by hiding amid tufts of floating foam. Smugglers wouldn't tell migrants how dangerous the poisoned waters were, and the river's toxicity was actually an asset: Border Patrol agents watching from shore refused to set foot in the pea green water out of fear of contamination. People had reported getting severe rashes after being splashed with merely a few drops.

While the two countries were working on a long-term cleanup plan, the more immediate danger for migrants was drowning, which they were doing now with regularity. On top of its other demands, Macken's squad was now plucking more souls from the river's wretched depths.

There was no answer to the New River problem, but John Hunter, the man behind the water jugs in the desert here, had been proposing a response to the dangers posed by the All American Canal. Hunter had suggested that the Imperial Irrigation District (IID) install a series of cable lifelines across the waterway. (The district would later approve such a system, then change its mind.) The segment of the canal to the east, before it reaches Calexico, had presented the most trouble— exactly where Macken was headed today. Although the desert cases tended to involve one victim at a time, the canal drownings could claim several at once. This afternoon's call-out, involving one reported victim, was an exception to that.

By the time Macken pulled off the highway at Gordons Well, a team of four sheriff's deputies and canal workers had already gotten an eyeful. The body, facedown, lolled amid a pillow of foam and floating reeds at the base of the station. The drop is essentially a dam through which water passes and falls to a lower elevation in order to create hydropower. This man did not die here; he was carried downstream and stopped by the apparatus, Macken said. Soon a sheriff's dive team pulled up.

Macken began filling out his paperwork for the incident. Keith Roussel, one of the irrigation-district mechanics, watched from atop the dam as three deputies tried to recover the body using a twenty-foot pole fitted with a rope loop. By now, Roussel's work had put him in regular touch with such scenes, but he still hadn't gotten used to them. He said he'd seen twenty to thirty drownings in these waters in two years, almost all of them immigrants. "It makes you sick, really," he said, looking away. The deputies continued to fumble with their hoop device. They would lasso the body, only to lose it as they tried to tug it out. Then they would start again by restringing the hoop. The heat was blistering.

Finally, they opted to hoist the body by using a mechanical lift built as part of the power station. It resembled a giant rake and normally was used to clear branches and debris from the canal waters. The deputies used their hoop to guide the floating body onto the rake and an IID worker activated the device. Slowly the body rose to the top of the dam.

Macken pulled on rubber gloves and began his examination. The man's face, grotesquely inflated by decomposition, had gone the color of lead, with patches of purplish green, like the bruise on a thigh. He wore two wool shirts, pleated black pants, dingy tube socks and church shoes. A gold belt buckle bore the initial "L." A quick once-over told Macken the man was almost certainly a migrant. He had probably been in the water a day at most, the coroner figured, since the hands had yet to "glove," the postmortem process by which the skin begins to slip off.

Now came the hard part: figuring out who the man was and where he came from. Determining the identity is as important a function of the coroners as establishing a cause of death. Whether the deceased was a longtime resident who perished alone in his mobile home or a solitary hiker in the middle of the desert, the coroners were obliged to carry out a complete death investigation, starting with figuring out the identity. For the coroner workers, this was in many ways the most demanding and time-consuming aspect of their job now that migrant deaths were so common. Unlike the victims of fatal car crashes, for example, many of the border crossers who died in the wilderness carried no identification. The *coyotes* often told them to get rid of any identification cards to enable them to offer an alias to Border Patrol agents if arrested. It was a tactic of dubious worth now that fingerprints were taken electronically and entered into the INS database, but it remained a common ploy.

Macken and his two deputies tried mightily to make their identifications, often with the help of officials at the Mexican consulate in Calexico. In about nine of ten cases, their efforts succeeded. "Our job," Macken and his men were given to say, "is to speak for the dead." Their main

hope was to make the identification based on the clues the migrants carried. Some toted ID cards, despite the smugglers' urgings. Migrants also
had been known to sew birth documents, along with carefully folded
Mexican peso notes, into the waistband of their pants. Macken had one
desert case where the hiker, apparently certain he was near the end,
took off his boots and tucked his ID card into the laces before lying down
to die. Sometimes a slip of paper was enough to make an identification;
other times it was a description of the clothing. (The investigators were
able to identify one man after photographing his red-checkered Jockey
underpants and showing the picture to his wife, who identified the distinctive pattern. Another time the breakthrough came because of a belt
buckle that was embroidered with a distinctive horse-and-saddle design.) "Little things like the brand of the tennis shoe and the belt buckle
are just really important when we don't have facial features we can use
for identification purposes," Macken had said during the ride out.

With these little things in mind, Macken went through the drowned
man's soggy pockets. A slip of paper bearing telephone numbers in Tijuana and Los Angeles was wadded inside a plastic bag—a sign the
man knew he was going near the water. The numbers, including one for
someone named Rosa Elia in Los Angeles, could prove helpful leads.
His pants pocket yielded a gray wallet with just two items: a Mexican
factory ID card for a young woman—his wife or girlfriend, Macken
figured—and a faded thumbnail photo of an older woman. His mother,
maybe? There was nothing else. For now, he was just John Doe.

The body, zipped inside a yellow vinyl bag, was loaded into the Ford
van for the ride to Frye Chapel and Mortuary, a funeral home in Brawley
that was one of two facilities under contract with the county to receive
the coroner cases for cold storage and autopsy. In a few days, Macken
would oversee the autopsy. It was the practice of the Imperial County
coroners to conduct an autopsy on each deceased migrant, even though
the cause of death might have seemed patently obvious. Every unattended death merited an autopsy, including those on U.S. soil illegally,
Macken said. Once he discovered during an autopsy that a male border
crosser who seemed to have died of heat exhaustion had, in fact, suffered a crushed windpipe. His murder was never solved. Such cases
were rare, but one never knew.

At the funeral home, the body of the canal victim was transferred from Macken's van into a storage tank on wheels that snapped tightly shut to prevent the stench of decomposition from wafting through the rest of the funeral home. The funeral home's octogenarian owner, Francis Frye, had to buy these tanks to cope with the growing number of migrant bodies ending up here. In addition, Frye had to bear the cost of keeping the victims stored inside his cooler for weeks until they were identified or sent for burial in the pauper's graveyard in nearby Holtville. Today's victim became the third John Doe held in the walk-in refrigeration unit in the rear of the funeral home. The storage unit was cooled to 40 degrees. In a room nearby, morticians worked on a migrant woman who had died several days earlier. In years past, there were fewer heat-exposure cases. Now there were so many migrant cases that Frye was starting to complain that he might give up the county contract.

"We wouldn't do this again because of all this exposure—all these cases. Years ago, you didn't have such exposure. If San Diego would ease up a bit, they wouldn't come this way. They're going to come, though. No matter what advertisements you put out, no matter how horrible the conditions you say—the heat—it won't make a difference," Frye would say later. "The last three years have been miserable."

The heightened caseload had also led county officials to consider building their own morgue. There was no sign of a letup in the number of migrant cases, which now were routinely numbering more than a third of the coroner's two-hundred-plus cases each year. The private contract arrangement was costly, even though Frye grumbled that it was now hardly worth the trouble. It was costing the county about $225 to store each body, plus another $500 to $700 for the autopsies by an out-of-town pathologist. Adding in the time spent by the coroners and the sheriff's photographers, Macken conservatively estimated the cost of each migrant death at about $2,000.

That expense was one of the reasons that Imperial County's supervisors had declared a state of emergency in 1998, arguing that the costs associated with the new tide of illegal immigrants—from hospitalizing those injured during the trek to burying those who perished—was breaking the bank of the impoverished county. Macken's team had to buy a four-wheel-drive pickup truck in order to be able to drive into the remote off-road areas where the bodies were turning up with growing frequency.

A similar financial toll was being felt by a number of border counties, which were now shelling out $108 million a year in police, court and emergency-medical-care costs associated with illegal immigrants. Slightly more than half of the total costs across the entire border were borne by California's two southernmost counties, San Diego and Imperial. Nationwide, the border counties, including some of the poorest sections of the United States, had formed an association in an attempt to draw attention to their plight. Officials at the Tucson Medical Center in Arizona said costs related to illegal immigrants amounted to $10 million a year; in Bisbee, uncompensated services forced the Copper Queen Community Hospital to close its maternity program and long-term care unit.

All along the border, local officials had been arguing for three years that the costs of providing emergency medical care, incarcerating immigrants, and autopsies and burials should be shouldered by the federal government since it was federal immigration policy that had flooded their communities with undocumented border crossers. So far, little had come of their lobbying.

Back in his office, Macken went to work. From the dead man's pocket he had the phone numbers and from the wallet an employee ID card for someone named Rebeca Hernández Azamar at Lear Corporation in Mexico. Macken tried an 800 number listed on the card but got a recording saying there was no listing. He turned then to the Los Angeles number for Rosa Elia and punched it in. The person on the other end didn't speak English. Macken tried a few words in Spanish—though once married to a Mexican-American woman, he had only a rudimentary grasp of Spanish—before a girl was brought to the phone who answered in English. Macken continued.

"We found a gentleman who had drowned. I'm with the sheriff's office in Imperial County," he said, then stopped. "How old are you? . . . You're nine? Well, what I'm trying to find out is, we found a person who drowned, who died. . . . What I'm trying to find out is if you know someone who might have been coming through El Centro, Calexico, who didn't show up yet." Another pause. "A man drowned," Macken said. "In the water." Macken asked the girl to get her mother, then summoned his bilingual office assistant, Elsa Guzman, to act as interpreter on the telephone. Macken started over, explained the situation—that a man had been found dead without identification, that he had this phone number on a slip of paper. The woman on the other end asked for a description and Macken provided one: he was in his twenties, six feet tall, 150 pounds, black pants, leather shoes and carrying Rebeca Hernández's ID card.

The woman said her name was Rosa Elia, but she seemed nervous. She said she knew no one matching the description of the deceased. Elsa explained in Spanish that the coroners were not immigration officers: "The only thing we're here to investigate is the cause of death and so the relatives can recover the body," she said. With that, the woman's tone changed abruptly. Yes, she said, someone from her family was planning to cross the border, a cousin from Durango named José García. Maybe the young victim was her cousin. She began to cry. She would be his only relative in the United States. Rosa Elia said she would call her family in Mexico and find out when and where he was to cross, what clothes he wore. Who else would have her phone number? she wondered aloud, fearing the worst.

Macken ended the call by suggesting that the woman speak with Francisco Torres, an officer at the Mexican consulate in Calexico who worked closely with the coroners on these cases. Torres was perhaps the hardest-working Mexican bureaucrat on the border. Assigned to a section in the consulate known as protection services, he was part detective, part grief counselor. He worked out of the consular offices in a strip mall near the border entrance to Mexicali.

Lately, much of his job was devoted to fielding inquiries from callers in Mexico who feared that something terrible had happened to a loved one along the journey north. He would jot down identifying information—name and date of birth, of course, but also clothing, scars, tattoos. He checked his missing-person reports against the lists of those arrested by the Border Patrol and local police agencies, and against the coroner cases. Mexican consulates around the United States shared missing-person reports via electronic mail. It helped, but Torres still had a backlog of unsolved cases going back several years. So far this year, twenty-nine of eighty-seven deceased Mexicans here and in Yuma remained unidentified.

He had been a godsend to Macken and the coroner investigators, none of whom spoke much Spanish. When they needed to track down information in Mexico—fingerprints, dental records, next of kin—or to relay a photograph or a description of the recovered clothing for identification purposes, they worked through Torres. If this latest drowned man was to be identified, it would be Torres who would make arrangements for transferring the body. And it would be Torres who likely would greet the grieving relatives who came to take custody. The previous week he had five bodies from four Mexican states. Torres had consoled relatives and cautioned some against opening the coffin to confirm that their family member was inside. The condition of many of the bodies was often too ghastly for any loved one to behold. But many could not stop themselves. "It's a bitter drink," Torres would say, "but they need to know." His voice was heavy with a resignation born of three years of this grim work.

The folks at the consulate were as confounded as everyone else about the mounting fatalities in the face of fewer crossings. The missing-person reports had been coming in daily. Some days there were two, other days ten. The Mexican officials shook their heads. There was little else they could do. Stopping migrants short of the U.S. border was out of the question. They had to hope that somehow their warnings would take hold. By now, northbound Mexican express buses were playing videos on board that warned migrants of the dangers of crossing. Public-service spots were playing on TV and radio. Meanwhile, the government's warning posters grew more gruesome: one carried the photograph of a drowning victim, in advanced stages of decomposition, being pulled from the water. The canal's surface is deceptive, it warned in Spanish. "Don't try it! Your life is more important!"

The smugglers plying their trade along the Imperial County border, however, told migrants it was the easiest place to cross. Not surprisingly, they didn't tell them, one Mexican diplomat noted acidly, that it also was the easiest place to die.

. . .

Rosa Elia had called back. Her cousin from Durango never left home. But another relative from Sinaloa might have been on his way north. She would check some more. In the meantime, Macken gave Torres the information from the factory ID. Maybe he could track down the woman on the card. First, there was the autopsy. You never knew what might turn up there. A distinguishing mark, maybe. A document hidden inside the clothing. On a bright Sunday morning, Macken headed back to Frye's for the procedure, which would be performed by John Eisele, a forensic pathologist who formerly worked in San Diego and had been handling autopsies here since 1996.

A refrigerated body doesn't stop decomposing, though it does so more slowly. It had been nearly three days since the drowned man was placed in storage; the stench would be severe. The decision was made to perform the autopsy outdoors, behind the funeral home. Even in the open air, two big fans were positioned near the body, which was lifted from the special tank in which it had been stored. As Eisele went to work, Mike Ruiz, a sheriff's deputy working with Macken as the photographer on the case, handed out breath mints. They helped dampen the odor, he said with a weak smile, if only a little. Macken examined the body for tattoos, checked the waistband for any stowed documents. Eisele dictated into a miniature recorder as he turned the man inside out. Some of the heart blood was saved, as was a section of rib, for a possible DNA sample. Other bits of organ went into plastic containers. The skull was sawed off, the brain removed. Flies darted in the sunshine. The jaw was detached. Two teeth were missing. There were no fillings. The man's bulging eyes stayed open the whole time. He measured five feet six inches tall.

For Macken, it was usually the fingertips that had proved most useful in helping him identify a body. As long as the tissue remained largely intact, the fingerprints were still good. In desert cases where the skin had dried to a state of brittle leather, it could be soaked in a mixture of lye and water to rehydrate it to salvage usable prints. This man's were fine. The fingertips slid off in neat sheaths. Investigators could use them to make prints by slipping the tiny flesh sleeves over their own gloved fingers. Nonetheless, fingerprints were often of limited use in Mexico because there was no centralized databank. The availability of dental records was likewise spotty.

But Macken would need none of those tools this time. Torres had succeeded in tracking down the woman in the ID card. She lived in Ciudad Juárez, across the border from El Paso. She was too poor to travel to California to identify the body. Instead, she faxed to the consulate a copy of the man's driver's license. Macken, in turn, relayed, via e-mail, autopsy photographs of the "L" belt buckle, shoes and shirts. The driver's license offered poor fingerprints, too low in quality to serve as a decent comparison against the fingertips Macken had removed. But the woman was certain about the clothing. It belonged to her husband, a twenty-five-year-old auto worker. His name was Quirino Lara Primo.

How he ended up with the telephone number of the woman in Los Angeles remained murky. He was not one of her relatives. Officials at the consulate pieced together a fractured account. They said it appeared likely that the victim had gotten the telephone numbers from a man in Tijuana named Agustín, with whom he apparently intended to cross the border. But Agustín, who was thought to be a smuggler, was arrested first. And so the man apparently went on, crossing far to the east of Tijuana and carrying little besides the wadded plastic bag with a telephone number inside. It is possible that, if he had made it, the migrant's best hope on the U.S. side was a total stranger. It wasn't unusual; thirdhand contacts and friends of friends were often the closest thing the border crossers had to go on.

From its sun-bleached surface, the huge desert covering western Imperial County appears flat and featureless, but it is coursed by deep sand washes and sharp ribs of stony gravel. Dotted with ocotillo and creosote, the floor surrenders sharply to the boulder-studded mountains that march toward San Diego, another seventy-five miles to the west. In late August, the temperatures routinely exceed 110 degrees. The heat takes a toll on all it touches, human and otherwise. Even the roads are paved with a special compound to keep from melting into the consistency of Play-Doh. Sunset offers little relief. In Imperial County, triple-digit heat at midnight is not uncommon.

On this afternoon in late August 2001, Border Patrol agents near the tiny crossroads of Ocotillo had come across an undocumented man along Interstate 8. He was alive, but lapsing into unconsciousness. He was able to communicate that he had not been alone. The agents back-tracked to find his traveling companions, a man and a woman, on a sizzling expanse half a mile off the highway. They were both dead. This section, about ten miles from the border, had been patrolled more intensively due to the more frequent crossings. But it was rugged country, full of crannies. Agents can miss people until they're practically on top of them. Most of Imperial County's migrant victims were dying in the desert, and this was the worst section.

It was deputy coroner Gary Hayes's turn to make the trip. Hayes liked to joke around and he was in especially high spirits today, his thirty-eighth birthday. Dressed in a tropical-print sport shirt, khakis and work boots, he roared off in the coroners' newest tool, a four-wheel-drive, three-quarter-ton Chevrolet pickup. The investigators had acquired the truck the previous summer in order to reach bodies now turning up in places that were all but inaccessible. Before, they had to rely on border agents to give them a ride into the sites, by Border Patrol truck or helicopter, or have the agents extract the bodies. It was an arrangement nobody liked much.

Beefy and six feet three, Hayes must have cut an imposing figure in his past jobs as a cop, bailiff and jailor. His gregariousness and goofy jokes were disarming, however, and he was more scoutmaster than hard guy. Hayes had gotten to know the desert through years of hunting dove and deer. But it was during his year-and-a-half-long stint as a death investigator that he had hiked into some of the county's most remote pockets, huffing over mountains and through canyons he never knew existed. He'd once even had to rappel while removing a body from a particularly out-of-the-way spot.

Hayes had a realist's view about the people he and his two partners had seen in such numbers lately. The previous year there had been seventy-six dead migrants; there were nearly that many this year and it was not yet September. And those were only the ones that were known. Hayes was fond of saying that if the skeletons of all the dead who remained undiscovered were to stand up at once, the desert would suddenly look as crowded as Manhattan. That was exaggeration, of course, but few realized better than Hayes, Macken and Williams how incomplete their recovery work probably was.

Hayes, whose father was a detective, was fond of the forensic aspect

of police work. He had enjoyed reading a book by John Douglas, the famous FBI profiler, and tuned in to the Discovery Channel's program on
forensic cases. He liked to say that he spent 95 percent of his working
hours outside of most people's comfort zone. As for immigration, he had
voted against Proposition 187 in 1994, mainly because he feared it
could usher in an age of national identity cards and an incipient police
state. He'd always considered America a nation of immigrants. His
own grandfather had been born in New York Harbor while the great-
grandparents were en route from Germany and Holland; his grandmother had immigrated from Canada.

But more than a year on the coroner's detail had surprised Hayes.
He found himself admiring these migrants. He had not realized the
lengths people would go to in order to make the trip north, the sacrifices
involved in leaving behind families and homes in exchange for a long-
odds march through this hellish countryside. He thought the United
States would be a better place if the citizens who took their rights for
granted would demonstrate as much moxie. Hayes, who had earned a
degree in public administration from San Diego State University, saw
the migratory trend as a simple matter of economics. A nation has to
control its borders, he believed, but you couldn't ignore the powerful
pull that even its lowest jobs exerted across the border.

A father himself, Hayes also detected fundamental human obligation at work. "You've got to ask yourself: 'If I was in the same boat,
would I be doing what they're doing?'" Hayes asked. "Odds are,
I probably would—if I could support my family. There but for the grace
of God."

Hayes pulled off the interstate onto the shoulder, where a border
agent briefed him on the incident. There were more agents deeper in.
They were still looking for other possible victims. Hayes set out in a
four-wheel drive, navigating the sharp edge of a steep bank overlooking
the highway, and then headed into the desert itself. He had a partner on
the call, Sheriff's Deputy Ida Din, who had become one of the department's first female deputies when she passed the test in 1987 at the age
of forty-two. She'd been a clerk in a furniture store when she decided on
a career change; she made her way to deputy by first working as a file
clerk and corrections officer in the county lockup.

Din, now fifty-six, was along today to take photographs. She exulted in her job. Scientific investigations mean collecting the tiny traces of physical evidence—fibers, hairs, fingerprints and tire tracks—on which cases often rise or fall. Migrant cases offer less suspense, but they are hard. Din herself was Mexican-American, the daughter of a farming family in the town of Imperial. The sight of fallen migrants had hardened her views toward the smugglers who had guided them into her morbid realm. They should be charged with murder, she thought.

The coroner's team now was spending so much time out in the desert that they were familiar faces to the Border Patrol agents, who were usually the ones to find the bodies and make the call. Din jerked back and forth in her seat, clutching her camera bag, as Hayes hammered over the demanding terrain of soft sand, black volcanic rock and crumbling rises. The dusty washes are carved like veins throughout the area, presenting a confusing maze of possible trails for Hayes. At one point, he jerked to a stop to scout for a better route. "Recon!" he shouted, hopping out to survey. He clambered back in and zoomed off, fishtailing through a stretch of deep sand until the tires found purchase again on the bumpy ground. The truck chattered as Hayes steered through a fifteen-foot-deep wash. His Gatorade spilled. Pens and other items flew loose around the cab and the truck mounted a final rise. Carly Simon was singing softly on the radio as the first body came into view.

The woman appeared to be about thirty. She lay on a low rocky slope, face up, with one dust-covered arm extended outward. Someone, probably one of the border agents, had covered her head with a blue T-shirt. Din removed the shroud to begin taking photographs. The woman's left eye remained open. A trail of dried mucus smeared her upper lip. Her left sneaker—bearing an Air Elway brand name—was half off, unlaced. Most of her fingernail polish, colored the orange of traffic cones, had long since worn away. Three Border Patrol agents milled about as Hayes fetched one of the yellow zip-up body bags. The agents carried "camelback" canteens, worn on the back like knapsacks, and were still sweating profusely from the exertion of backtracking the footprints. Less than a mile away on Interstate 8, sunlight flashed off the sides of tractor-trailers. The traffic sound, carried on the hot desert breeze, reached the site as a faint hum.

The woman was clad in black—a black corset, black pants. It was a common sight. One of the Border Patrol agents, a young woman, said all the migrants seem to wear black. The immigrants are instructed by their guides to dress in dark clothing to avoid standing out at night. Hayes said the clothing should be the subject of a new campaign of public-service announcements urging migrants to wear white for safety. Dark clothing might cloak its wearer at night, but in daylight it absorbs the desert heat, cooking a person inside her own sweatsuit. "You might show up more," Hayes said, "but we can spot you from a helicopter." Another agent, a man named Chavez, looked to the distance and sighed. "They should stay home," he said quietly.

The victim fit another puzzling trend that had unsettled the coroners, Mexican officials, and border agents: the desert dead had begun to include women in greater numbers than anyone here remembered. Torres had mentioned that already this year, sixteen women had died in Imperial County. This woman would make seventeen. The death rate for women now was about four times what it had been in the past—a sign that more and more women were being steered through the backcountry. Women were also showing up more often among the dead in the Arizona desert. Previously, male migrants were the ones guided through the demanding terrain while women more often were sneaked across the border in other ways. Sometimes they were crammed into the trunks of cars and driven through official ports of entry, such as SanYsidro. Many resorted to buying false documents to get across, while their husbands and fathers trekked through the wilderness.

No one knew what to make of so many women now traveling routes once used almost exclusively by the men. INS officials suggested that it was yet one more sign that the smugglers were being squeezed as never before—and therefore resorting to desperate gambits to get their clients over the border. Others suggested that the flow of women might be a sign that Mexican families were seeking to consolidate north of the border in preparation for a hoped-for amnesty. There was speculation, too, that the trend reflected a growing number of city dwellers, including women, among the ranks of migrants, who traditionally tended to come from the countryside.

The discovery a week earlier of the woman who had been traveling with her five children, ages ten to seventeen, had underlined the horrifying new reality. The group had been led on a day-long hike through the Jacumba Mountains and into the Yuha Desert before the woman, María Isabel Pacheco Madera, who was thirty-eight, began to falter. The two smugglers decided to leave her behind, ushering the children along until they, too, fell into distress. Border Patrol agents, alerted by the sheriff's office, flew by helicopter to a section of the Anza-Borrego Desert State Park, where they found the group in an isolated wash. The two smugglers, both Mexican nationals, were arrested. The children recovered, but were left without a mother. In a separate case, a woman was left dead by her two children, who covered her with a blanket, using stones to anchor the corners.

Back in the desert, Din had finished taking her photographs. She, Hayes and three agents carried the bag containing the woman's corpse to the truck and slid it into the camper compartment in the back. She carried no identification. For now, she would have to be registered as a Jane Doe.

It was easier to identify the second victim, a man lying 150 yards from where the woman had collapsed. He was heavyset with a neatly trimmed black mustache. He lay sprawled at the base of a wash. His eyes were closed and his skin was already going dark. He, too, wore black—a short-sleeved shirt that had come untucked from his gray chino slacks.

Hayes began going through the man's pockets. With scissors, he snipped open the pants pockets. In the right pocket, inside a plastic bag, Hayes found a Mexican voting card, which contained a photograph, name, address and thumbprint. "Cha-ching!" he called out. The man had come from Mexico City. The card said his name was Gonzalo Mora Carrillo, age thirty-two. The picture matched the expressionless face of the man at Hayes's feet. The migrant had chosen to wear a pair of brand-new soccer cleats for the trip. He had also brought along two copies of a birth certificate, folded into quarters, and telephone numbers in Tijuana and Los Angeles. In the shirt pocket, for some reason, was a rock the size of a walnut.

A few yards away, near the man's footprints, the gravel bore an odd set of squiggles. One of the agents bent down to look more closely. Four shallow furrows broke the gravel surface, making little wavy lines, like a child's fingerpainting. There was little question what they were. The indentations had been left by human fingers, digging at the ground.

The mystery of the woman's identity lasted less than a day. Hayes and Din made their way to El Centro Regional Medical Center to meet the man who was rescued from Interstate 8. He had been kept overnight and treated for heat exhaustion. The man, Santiago Ochoa, was still in his hospital gown when the pair located his room. Din made the introduction, in Spanish, and served as interpreter. Ochoa wore a thick five-o'clock shadow and a dazed expression. As Din described what the coroners had found the previous afternoon, Ochoa forced his eyes shut and then began to cry. The woman, Socorro Arroyo, was his wife. He had not known she was dead until now.

His account, which unfolded as he sobbed and quaked, was now sadly familiar. The couple had set out from Mexicali at night, part of a group of seven people, but in the morning the woman was overcome by the heat. They were able to bring only a gallon of water, which went quickly. They crossed one rural road, then separated to evade a Border Patrol agent. He, his wife and Mora—the dead man with the rock in his pocket—continued north. His wife grew dizzy. He helped her walk for as long as she could, then trudged ahead alone to the interstate for help. She was still alive then.

Ochoa said he had previously worked in Sacramento, California. His life was fully binational. He had two children, a seven-year-old in Michoacán and a four-year-old living with his brother in the United States. Now he would have to decide which way to go. Ochoa rocked on the edge of the hospital bed, his empty stare aimed at the window. The morning sun was still climbing. It was hot already.

Miles from any paved road, fraying blue flags fluttered over the desert atop thirty-foot shiny poles. Each marked a water station. These were the stations that had been put out by John Hunter's volunteers, some of whom drove three and a half hours from Los Angeles to help. The movement begun the previous year had grown beyond its original core of Hunter and a few hardy souls from San Diego and Imperial County. An activist Catholic priest from Los Angeles and parishioners were now on board, along with a wide smattering of other volunteers, from suburban real-estate brokers to Boy Scouts and state legislators. Since the publicized disaster in Yuma, putting water in the desert suddenly didn't sound crazy anymore. Indeed, the project seemed to be just a celebrity-volunteer shy of becoming a major happening.

At the base of each pole sat a white cardboard box, labeled "WATER" and "AGUA." Rocks were piled on top to keep the flaps closed. Inside were bottles of water—three one-gallon jugs and a couple of quart containers—a packet of powdered replenishing electrolytes and a plastic cup. Hayes and the other coroner investigators applauded the charitable impulses of the volunteers who drove far and endured the withering temperatures on the off chance that someday one of these water kits would save a border crosser's life.

But the coroners also knew that even plenty of water couldn't protect against the worst heat. They'd made removals where a half-full jug of water sat at arm's length from the corpses. Dehydration certainly worsened the threat, but the killer, quite simply, was the heat. Macken had put it this way: "If you're in 115-degree temperatures and you're climbing mountains and your body temperature reaches 107 or 108, you're going to die."

Hayes guided the coroner's pickup past the line of flapping banners, which lined a dirt road along the military bombing range forty miles west of El Centro. He was on his way to the latest case, a day after his visit to the El Centro hospital. It was the week's fourth victim. Unlike the other cases, this man would defy the efforts of Hayes and Torres at identification. He would finish his journey in the plain box in the pauper's graveyard in Holtville. He had apparently found none of Hunter's water stations.

The coroner's team had been out to this area many times this summer. They'd recovered half a dozen bodies along an area known roughly as Carrizo Wash. It is one of several long depressions that finger north from the border through a landscape of salt cedars and creosote bushes surrounding the Anza-Borrego Desert State Park. Hayes wondered if this man had been part of the prior group but had been missed when the others were discovered. A Border Patrol agent met Hayes on the road into the range to escort him to where the body lay. "You're going to have quite a job," the agent warned Hayes, who was dressed today in a short-sleeved denim shirt and tan cargo pants. Coyotes—the four-legged kind—had gotten there first.

Upon examination, Hayes figured the corpse was a month old. Little had survived the coyotes' scavenging. It was mainly a skeleton—an incomplete one at that—bound with sinews as dry and leathery as jerky. There would be little hope of identifying the man by his face. Strewn about nearby were scraps of clothing, a baseball cap with the logo of a Mexico City soccer team and a dozen rib bones, which Hayes collected one by one and placed in a plastic bag. He never found the man's right boot.

There were a few clues to the migrant's trip. He apparently had passed through Mexicali, based on the bus ticket found in the pocket of a checkered shirt that lay a hundred feet from the body. He had 126 pesos, worth less than $13, a packet of antacid labeled in Spanish and a pair of used cotton swabs. Hayes pointed at a stain on the ground beneath a creosote bush. The gravel had been pressed down slightly, as if it had been ironed. It was probably where the man had died. If so, he spent his last moments curled like a fetus.

That was all that would be known. The remains, weighing no more than thirty-five pounds, would be scooped into a body bag to take a place on the shelf of Frye's refrigeration room. The tag would read John Doe, 01-177. For three months, the body remained there. No name would emerge. The coroners could find no useful clues, even after having a forensic anthropologist look over the remains, as they sometimes did in skeletal cases. At the consulate, Torres scoured his files but found nothing with which to make a match. The remains were then assigned to the custody of the county public administrator's office, the agency responsible for disposing of bodies when identification proved impossible. Two months had passed since he was found.

Claudia Smith was by now pressing the Mexican government to do more to help find the names of the fallen migrants. Her idea, inspired by reading accounts of attempts to identify the remains recovered from the September 11 terrorist attacks, was for Mexico to establish a centralized database of DNA samples. The idea struck Hayes as noble but impractical. To match a sample taken from a corpse found in the desert, you would need to extract samples from close relatives, or have them banked somewhere. Would you store samples from thousands of people? The process promised to be unwieldy and expensive.

For John Doe, case number 01-177, there remained still the sparest of funerals. On burial day, the remains were placed in a cheap coffin with the case number written in black marker. The box was loaded by the Frye mortuary workers, along with the casket of a female migrant who likewise had not been identified, into the back of an aging Suburban for the ride to the Holtville graveyard.

Funeral director Greg Marr took the wheel and drove the pair across the flat topography of a farming world that was morphing into what the rest of southern California looks like. A beet-sugar plant. A field of grazing sheep. A John Deere dealership. The cookie-cutter subdivisions, with names like Sunset Ranch Estates. A sign cheerily promoted El Centro as the place "where the sun spends the winter."

The Terrace Park Cemetery sat across from a cabbage field. The main section of the cemetery was quaint and grassy, neatly manicured, obviously fussed over. Marr drove past, through a dirt field, and on to the potter's field, a muddy rectangle next to a trash-strewn gulley. It would normally have been a dismal site, but Claudia Smith and other migrant-rights activists had decorated the graves for Day of the Dead, the traditional Mexican celebration of the deceased. Sugar skulls, marigolds and bright carnations injected a festive splash to the squalid tableau. Alongside were two-foot-tall white crosses that the activists had brought previously. The crosses, like those placed along the Tijuana airport two years earlier, were lettered *No Identificado* and *No Olvidado*. Unidentified. Not forgotten.

The thirty-one-year-old Marr had deep roots in Imperial County. His grandfather had been an Assembly of God preacher here. The young funeral director took these rituals seriously. He helped the three cemetery workers lower the caskets into two holes that had been dug side by side. Short segments of plastic pipe, sealed at each end and containing the case numbers, were thrown in, too, as an aid in case exhumation was required later. One of the gravediggers removed his hat. The workers stepped back as Marr, standing over the graves, offered a brief dedication and then recited the Lord's Prayer. A tractor roared to life and the holes were filled swiftly, the ground smoothed. The gravediggers didn't want to talk much about the ritual, which they'd repeated scores of times over the years. It was just a job, said one of the men, named Joe: "It's not personal."

Marr was more reflective. "This is probably the worst part of the job," he offered, after the cemetery workers had gone. "Knowing people and knowing who they are and having the family all there to support each other—that's the way to do things. That's what we don't have here."

With a stick, Marr scraped the thick Imperial County mud from his brown dress shoes and then he drove off, too. Around the graves, bees swarmed the sugar faces of little skulls.

EPILOGUE

When the images of the World Trade Center's collapse played out on the television screen, I was watching in a Tijuana living room. I had gone across to ride to work with a U.S. citizen, Nestor Moran, for a story about the rigors faced by the thousands of workers, like him, who cross to the U.S. side legally every day. We pulled ourselves away from the ghastly televised spectacle to make the cross-border trip.

Fifteen minutes later, we arrived at the port of entry at San Ysidro to a sight unlike any I'd seen in scores of crossings during the previous three and a half years. The line of traffic was long, as always, and surged with the customary jostling of line-hopping drivers looking for a shorter wait. But what was different was what motorists were required to do before entering the United States. More than a hundred yards short of the inspection booths—the gateways where drivers and passengers normally are asked to declare their citizenship and list any goods they are bringing across—the cars were being ordered to stop one by one. Drivers were told to get out of their vehicles as INS and customs inspectors searched under the car hoods, inside trunks and beneath seats. In inspection parlance, the border was under a "Level One alert"—a heightened level of vigilance meant to ensure maximum protection against this apparent new terrorist threat. The heightened security extended to the areas outside of the ports of entry—all the countryside border zones falling under the responsibility of the Border Patrol. That meant agents were working longer hours, making it more difficult to enter unlawfully.

The terrorist attacks of September 11, 2001, marked a turning point, if not a closing chapter, in the border's turbulent recent past. In the months that followed, illegal crossings plunged temporarily to unheard-of lows, accelerating the decline that had begun even before the strikes on the World Trade Center and Pentagon. A combination of factors was responsible for the drop-off, including the blizzard of publicity over the more stringent watchfulness along the border. But an economic downturn in the United States already had dampened crossings as word reached migrant-sending communities in Mexico's interior that there were not many jobs to be had. After September 11, news reports about the discovery of anthrax received wide play in both countries. That prompted some migrants who were in the United States illegally to go home out of fear of being caught up in a terrorist incident and discouraged many would-be migrants in Mexico from starting north at all. By the end of the year, apprehensions of undocumented immigrants had fallen by more than half in some places. By late winter 2002, not a single person had died in the snow-capped mountains of eastern San Diego County.

The extra checks at the border made the waits for legal crossers so onerous—up to four hours at times—that many Mexican shoppers stopped making the trip into the San Ysidro community, whose main boulevard is lined with groceries, automobile insurers and private mail centers patronized by Tijuana residents with binational ways. The drop in cross-border customers brought howls of protest from the San Ysidro shopkeepers, whose dependence on Tijuana customers now competed with the newest preoccupation over keeping the borders secure. Even before September 11, Operation Gatekeeper had ushered significant changes at the border at San Ysidro. Homes were being built and sold on fields where border agents once vainly chased migrants. On what had been a grim vacant lot next to the rattling border gate stood a shiny new shopping center, called Las Americas, that seemed to embody Americans' ambivalence toward Mexico. Its advertising wooed Mexican shoppers to outlets like Old Navy and Banana Republic, while just outside the back door stood the rusting steel fence, in case anyone needed reminding that the border was intended to be a barrier as much as it was a bridge. The new concerns about terrorism brought that longstanding duality into starker relief.

By the summer of 2002, life had changed considerably along the border—and, at the same time, not much at all. The reality of terrorism on U.S. soil significantly raised the stakes around border enforcement, thrusting national security to the forefront of the debate over what should be done at the problematic boundary. But in return visits to border spots during this post-terror era, I could see that many of the previous anxieties lingered, even with the dwindling of illegal crossings following the attacks. People who already viewed the border as a poorly guarded sieve had even more reason to worry as they surveyed a frontier that in many places remained as naked as it ever was. Those who lamented the deaths among migrants waited for the fatalities to return to their rate before the attacks—about one person a day, on average.

In Douglas, Arizona, Roger Barnett had buried more than a dozen sensors in the gravel around his Cross Rail Ranch to detect intruders. In his bedroom, a receiver the size of a small suitcase sounded whenever one of the sensors was set off. Readings showed up on a spool of tape similar to a cash register's; a day's worth could produce five feet or more of tape. Barnett calculated that he and his brother had shelled out somewhere between $30,000 and $50,000 in gear and gas money to patrol the ranch land. The year before, they detained 2,063 border crossers, Barnett said. By late May 2002, the total had reached around 1,200, though the year was not yet half over. On the other side of Douglas, Larry Vance had taken to videotaping groups of migrants who continued sneaking north through the scrub near his family land along the border. "Anyone that tells you the border is under control is a goddamned liar," he said. (By year's end, a citizens' militia in Tombstone, Arizona, called Civil Homeland Defense was organizing its own armed, and unsanctioned, patrols at the border. Another southern Arizona group, calling itself American Border Patrol, had taken the battle to the Internet by uploading live video clips of migrants as they crossed the border illegally. By 2003, the group was promoting plans to keep watch over the border with an unmanned aerial drone mounted with a camera.)

Elsewhere along Arizona's border, the Tohono O'odham continued to press for a change in federal law that would convey U.S. citizenship on the basis of tribal membership. The tribe had persuaded more than a dozen Arizona counties to lend their support to the legislative initiative, which enjoyed the backing of a growing number of state officials and members of the U.S. House of Representatives. But the chaotic scene at the border had prompted the tribe on the U.S. side to end its cross-border shuttle service, the one for which Betty Antone drove. The tribe's stretch of border had grown increasingly scary as immigrant smuggling escalated. Henry Ramon, the tribe's vice chairman, estimated that 1,200 to 1,500 undocumented migrants were moving through the reservation lands daily, and many of their escorts carried weapons. To add to the menacing atmosphere, Mexican soldiers wandered across the U.S. border on tribal land briefly in the spring of 2002 and, for reasons that were unclear, fired in the direction of a Border Patrol agent, Ramon said. As he had two years earlier, Ramon was again describing his people's land as a war zone. The besieged tribe called upon the federal government to end Operation Gatekeeper.

In the Yuma desert, the deaths a year earlier had given impetus to new lifesaving efforts by border agents. Along some of the most perilous areas near Wellton, the Border Patrol was trying an unorthodox approach: it had erected a half-dozen emergency beacons topped with flashing strobes to attract the notice of migrants in distress. Each thirty-foot tower was equipped with a panic button that would summon border agents when activated. The idea for the beacons had been under consideration before the 2001 tragedy, but that incident prodded officials to move without delay. In addition to erecting the light towers, by late summer 2002 the Border Patrol was posting teams of agents deep in the desert near the Camino del Diablo for two weeks at a time. It was just one of the ways the agency hoped to rescue migrants in distress. The teams were shuttled by helicopter to their remote encampment: a twenty-seven-foot travel trailer that was powered by a generator and equipped with a four-hundred-gallon tank to supply water for washing dishes and bathing. The agents had two trucks for patrolling the desert zone. It was reminiscent of the long-ago days when border guards on horseback rode the line for weeks at a time.

The civilian humanitarian efforts also picked up steam, as if no one believed that the slowdown in migrant crossings would last long. By the spring of 2002, Robin Hoover and his Humane Borders alliance were tending a dozen or so water stations scattered over the southwestern

Arizona desert. Hoover had outfitted a heavy-duty Chevrolet pickup with a water tank for replenishing the desert canisters. Earlier in the spring, the Border Patrol had credited the water stations with helping to save a group of thirty-three migrants who managed to find one before being rescued south of Gila Bend, Arizona.

The Yuma tragedy had angered and emboldened the pastor and his volunteers. Hoover continued to believe the tragedy would have been prevented if the federal government had not denied permission for water tanks in the Cabeza Prieta wildlife refuge near where the migrants perished. In May 2002, Humane Borders filed a legal claim against the federal government in U.S. District Court on behalf of the families of the deceased migrants. A year later, the families followed through with a lawsuit, claiming that federal officials acted negligently by not allowing water stations in a zone known to present mortal danger to migrants who had been steered there by the Gatekeeper strategy. The lawsuit claimed that by permitting similar water stations in other desert areas outside Cabeza Prieta, the government made clear that it knew they were needed.

In California, John Hunter, the pioneer behind the Imperial County water stations, had also expanded his efforts. During the winter of 2001–2002, he and a partner, Enrique Morones, also began setting out bins of warm clothes, blankets and food for wayward migrants in the sage-dotted canyons of eastern San Diego County. It was the same section of the Cleveland National Forest where eight people had died in the unexpected snowstorm in April 1999. They made an odd pairing— Hunter, the Republican-leaning brother of a conservative congressman, and Morones, a die-hard Democrat who considered himself equal parts American and Mexican—but the two shared a commitment to take what steps they could. Hunter also was pushing a plan to run rescue lines across the All American Canal in Imperial County to prevent drownings. The proposal had already been rejected by irrigation district officials, but Hunter was determined. He and Morones talked, too, of creating a website that would carry the names and photographs of deceased and missing migrants as a way to mark their loss and perhaps to help families locate loved ones who never completed the journey.

By summer, coroner officials in Imperial County were witnessing another morbid year in the desert, even though fatalities along the full length of the border were falling due to fewer crossings and more aggressive rescue efforts by the Border Patrol. (Agents were rescuing more than a hundred people per month along the entire border.) By late summer 2002, more than fifty migrants had died in Imperial County since the previous October—the start of the federal fiscal year—and it appeared that the toll by year's end could top the record number of ninety-five reached during the 2001 fiscal year. (It did not; the final twelve-month tally was sixty-three, as counted by the Border Patrol.)

Meanwhile, several of the chief protagonists in the recent border drama were moving on. The ubiquitous Johnny Williams, who had taken over the San Diego Border Patrol at the outset of Gatekeeper and then moved up the INS hierarchy, was promoted to the immigration service's headquarters in Washington as the agency prepared for an anticipated overhaul. Williams was proud of what had been achieved during his border tenure, especially the visible turnaround in San Diego. When we spoke in May 2002, he noted that a hospital now stood near the border on a spot where gun battles had raged not long before; the no-man's-land near the Tijuana River now was home to a children's playground. But Williams knew he could not win the debate over whether Gatekeeper was responsible for a greater number of deaths. He doubted that there were more deaths now, but had no hard numbers to prove that, as the INS had not systematically tracked fatalities before 1998.

A study of border deaths by University of Houston researchers, released in March 2001, concluded that while deaths of migrants due to environmental exposure rose sharply after 1994, there was a decline in other causes, such as murders and people being struck by cars. Overall fatalities appeared to have risen modestly as the migration pattern shifted, according to the report, which covered the period from 1985 through 1998. This, of course, was the moment when exposure deaths increased even more dramatically, so a completely up-to-date picture is unavailable.

One of the INS's most persistent critics was stepping aside: Roberto Martinez, the enduring watchdog of the Border Patrol in San Diego, retired from his job at American Friends Service Committee. Meanwhile, fellow activist Claudia Smith was still waiting for a decision on the human rights complaint against the Gatekeeper policy filed in 1999. The Organization of American States' Inter-American Commission on Human Rights held a hearing in November 2001, but had not ruled by mid-2002.

But the most abrupt change at the border after September 11 was the sudden disappearance of any meaningful discussion between the United States and Mexico over migration reform. Hopes for change had built for months before the attacks as Presidents Bush and Fox moved their administrations to begin to come to grips with the difficult issues surrounding unlawful immigration into the United States. Fox, who'd been elected as a reformer, had made clear that migration reform was high on his agenda, and Bush seemed to want Fox's presidency to succeed.

The two governments had talked without much specificity about ways to expand the program for temporary workers to come to the United States, as well as whether to "regularize," or provide legal status to, some segment of the estimated 4.5 million undocumented Mexicans already living in the United States. In the United States, business groups and organized labor alike were calling for legalization, though with very different approaches. Even under the best circumstances, any agreement would surely face significant political hurdles in the United States and require Mexico to help out by cracking down on migrant smuggling and improving economic development in regions that sent the most migrants north.

Despite those long odds, there had been almost giddy talk of the onset of a new era in U.S-Mexico relations. During a visit by Fox to the White House in 2001, Bush declared that the United States had "no more important relationship in the world than the one we have with Mexico" and suggested there was an opportunity for building "a new century of the Americas." Fox said the time had come "to give migrants and their communities their proper place in the history of our bilateral relations. Both our countries owe them a great deal." The presidents' remarks came just six days before the terrorist strikes.

Instantly, after September 11, border-security concerns shoved aside any talk of liberalizing immigration rules. Fox would make no secret of his frustration that the issue had vanished from view, but there was no sign it was coming back anytime soon. There was, however, equally little evidence that the quandaries posed by binational migration were going away. The passage of workers from Mexico to the United States had gone on for so long—carrying a river of so many people—that there now seemed an air of inevitability about it, whether the two governments decided to make formal arrangements or not. University of Pennsylvania sociologist Douglas Massey calculated that one in five Mexicans aged fifteen to sixty-four had been to the United States at least once. And of the 6 million to 10 million foreigners living in the United States without papers, more than half of them were from Mexico, according to a 2001 study by the Pew Hispanic Center. The center also estimated that 3.5 million Mexicans had lived north of the border for five years or more, and about 2.3 million had done so for at least a decade. The figures underscored just how many people had made their way north and made clear that any legalization bid promised to be a huge undertaking. The center's findings included one with relevance to many American families: about one in four people working in private households was undocumented.

The long, particular history of migration between the two countries had some policy experts suggesting that Mexico should be treated as a special case when it came to opening the door to the United States. In any event, there seemed little chance of stuffing the genie back in the bottle. The same forces of globalization that had made Wal-Mart bargain shoppers of so many Americans were also at work in the way Mexican laborers were showing up all over, from the chicken houses of the Southeast to the apple orchards of New England. NAFTA had lowered the barriers for the cross-border movement of goods and capital; the market for a cheap and pliant labor force was taking care of itself. What's more, the migratory trend was strengthening worldwide: the United Nations estimated that at least 185 million people lived in countries different from where they were born, more than double the figure of thirty years earlier.

In the face of such powerful forces, how could a policy built on fortifying the Southwest border alone effectively control the flow of migrants into a thirsty American labor market? Or produce humane conditions for those who did cross? To many along the border, conservatives and liberals alike, U.S. policy seemed blatantly hypocritical. At the time the government was unfurling Operation Gatekeeper and similar strategies along the frontier, enforcement of immigration laws in the nation's interior had fallen to almost zero. Workplace crackdowns were always unpopular. For example, growers loudly complained that they couldn't get their crops in if agents disrupted their operations by hauling off workers who turned out to be carrying false papers. By 2000, raids had become so rare that even top INS officials acknowledged there was little risk of arrest for an undocumented worker, once across the border, unless he happened to get turned in by an employer.

Did the border crackdown begun in 1994 work? In some ways, yes. The get-tough approach, especially in San Diego, did much to quell the political anger over illegal immigration in California. There was no question that it converted the border area in San Diego from a lawless free-fire zone into a more normal and healthy community, and achieved similar effects in a handful of other spots where the defenses were beefed up. The change in San Diego was so complete that Wayne Cornelius, an immigration scholar at the University of California at San Diego who often criticized Gatekeeper, came to label the border there "a living museum of immigration control."

But Cornelius and other analysts, including the U.S. General Accounting Office, Congress's investigative arm, found serious shortcomings in the nearly decade-old border strategy, whose annual cost had surpassed $2.5 billion. Not least among the criticisms was the unanticipated rise in deaths among migrants due to crossing at desolate points. The GAO concluded in an August 2001 assessment that while migrants were now denied entry in the urban areas, there was "no clear indication" that fewer people were trying to cross. The report noted that apprehensions had risen across the border from 1994 to 2000, suggesting that, overall, unlawful entries continued unabated. A 2002 study by the Public Policy Institute of California went a step further: by making it more difficult to cross the border illegally, the government may have unwittingly encouraged migrants to remain in the United States longer, rather than go home and then face the rigors of a return trip north later. In other words, a policy meant to reduce the number of illegal immigrants residing in the United States may have had the opposite effect. And Cornelius argued that U.S. labor data show no signs of the tightening that would accompany a reduction in the arrival of Mexican workers.

It seems clear from this extraordinary time along the border that simple-sounding solutions are doomed to fall short of solving the exceedingly complex challenges confronting it. This is especially true at a time when terrorism has drawn the nation's gaze to its borders. The country will need more control—not less—over who enters. Paradoxically, the need for greater security may provide a push for creating more legal channels for workers to enter, as long as that can be shown to produce a border that is more orderly. But doing so promises to be costly and complicated, just as it would be to fund enough new border agents to achieve hoped-for coverage over the whole southern flank. The 2001 GAO study estimated it would take five to nine years to hire the 3,200 to 5,500 additional agents needed to bolster the 8,500 already poised along the Southwest border. A government-commissioned study by University of Texas scholars in 1998 estimated the Border Patrol would need about 16,100 agents—nearly double the existing force.

Regardless of border enforcement, the many causes of unsanctioned entries—yawning wage differentials, disaffection with Mexican governments, globalization and village tradition—are far removed from the frontier, geographically and in terms of decision making. Any real solutions to illegal immigration must reflect those realities if the border is not to continually end up in the crossfire of a distant fight, victimized not only by poverty and neglect but by policy, too.

For all its intrigue and often-deserved romance, the border is made up of ordinary communities composed of workaday people—noble and not. I found a measure of sympathy for virtually everyone encountered on the journey recounted here. The Arizona ranchers did not ask that their lands become a human highway, nor did the Indians seek the disruptions and dangers to their way of life. The humanitarians were clearly moved by mercy for the migrants, who may have broken the law by entering but remained human beings, above all. The migrants pulled me in competing directions. I felt pity for those who never considered the possibility that their trek could kill them, and admiration for those who did and came anyway—all for the privilege of plucking our chickens, mowing our lawns, parking our cars. As well, I gained great respect for the border agents, serious men and women assigned to a task that seemed Sisyphean as long as Mexicans found reason to flock to a U.S. job market so eager to hire them, and few legal routes by which to do so.

In the meantime, the border remained a dangerous place. In the spring of 2003, tragedy was again in the news. In May, word came that nineteen immigrants had perished in Victoria, Texas, after they and more than fifty-five others were crammed into a tractor-trailer amid suffocating heat and without ventilation. The migrants, most of them Mexican, were being ferried north from Harlingen after finding their way across the border. The death toll surpassed that of the Yuma tragedy, making the truck case the nation's deadliest migrant-smuggling episode. Among the victims was a five-year-old boy joining his father on the trip. Authorities soon arrested the truck's driver, a man from Schenectady, New York, who told investigators he had been paid $5,000 by smugglers to transport the migrants.

U.S. and Mexican officials expressed outrage, vowing to prosecute to the full extent of the law anyone involved in smuggling. And they said they were already preparing new steps to make the border safer. A few weeks later, authorities unveiled that stepped-up safety push, focusing on what officials now were calling the "corridor of death" in the Arizona desert. U.S. officials said they would assign more than 150 new Border Patrol agents and surveillance aircraft to the desert campaign, aided by the desert beacons. On the day of the press conference in Arizona, three more migrants were found dead—this time in a railcar in Texas. No one expected they would be the last.

A Note on Sources

As a work of journalism, this book derives largely from my own reporting of scenes and events, plus interviews. I have relied upon other works—scholarly and journalistic—in the areas of immigration, border history and politics in order to help the reader understand that reporting. The book is not an academic inquiry into U.S. immigration policy and does not seek to be. In most instances where I have drawn upon published works, I have indicated so in brief fashion by mentioning the authors, whose works are listed in the accompanying bibliography.

A few words about some sources are warranted here. Apprehension figures cited throughout the work come from the U.S. Border Patrol, which maintains a remarkably up-to-date tally of arrests its agents make each day, sector by sector. Unless otherwise indicated, I have opted to use Border Patrol statistics when citing fatalities. I have done so out of a desire for uniformity, since deaths are counted in a variety of ways and by several agencies along both sides of the border.

Reports on the Southwest border by the U.S. General Accounting Office provided information on Border Patrol staffing levels and costs.

Borderwide population projections in Chapter One come from an unpublished 1998 report by James Peach and James Williams of New Mexico State University.

The account of the drawing of the border is based upon John Russell Bartlett's own firsthand narrative of the work, whose introduction by Odie B. Faulk provides a good description of the botched-map affair, and from William H. Emory's voluminous report on the border survey. The works of Richard Griswold del Castillo and Carey McWilliams were helpful in learning about the aftermath of the war between Mexico and the United States.

The section on the history of Mexican immigration to the United States is grounded in a wide variety of sources, including works by George J. Sanchez; Kitty Calavita, whose study of the bracero program was especially useful; and McWilliams, the source of the quote by J. Fred Rippy about the two countries lacking "natural barriers." Historical counts of Mexicans living in California came from a 1930 report by California governor C. C. Young's Mexican Fact-Finding Committee.

The letter to the editor of the *New York Times* cited in Chapter Two, describing a feared takeover of California by Mexican immigrants, is quoted in an article by Leo Chavez in Juan Perea's *Immigrants Out!: The New Nativism and the Anti-Immigrant Impulse in the United States.*

My description of hypothermia in Chapter Four borrowed from the separate works of James Wilkerson, William Forgey and Lawrence Armstrong.

Widely published material on the history of the Border Patrol is limited. The section in Chapter Five profited from two documents providing historical overviews—shared with me by the Immigration and Naturalization Service—as well as from an informal chronology of the agency prepared by the INS staff. The immigration service also helped by sharing historical newspaper articles, job postings and other documents. A brief chronicle of the agency by border historian Leon Metz also yielded helpful information. Mary Kidder Rak's *Border Patrol* includes some diverting accounts of life on the line in the early part of the twentieth century.

The history of the sanctuary movement in Chapter Eight was derived from news accounts from that period, as well as from published works by Miriam Davidson, Ann Crittenden and Gary MacEoin.

Bibliography

BOOKS

Andreas, Peter. *Border Games: Policing the U.S.-Mexico Divide.* Ithaca, N.Y.: Cornell University Press, 2000.

Annerino, John. *Dead in Their Tracks: Crossing America's Desert Borderlands.* New York: Four Walls Eight Windows, 1999.

Armstrong, Lawrence E. *Performing in Extreme Environments.* Champaign, Ill.: Human Kinetics, 2000.

Bahti, Tom, and Mark Bahti. *Southwestern Indian Tribes.* Flagstaff, Ariz.: KC Publications, 1968.

Barrera, Mario. *Race and Class in the Southwest: A Theory of Racial Inequality.* Notre Dame, Ind.: University of Notre Dame Press, 1979.

Bartlett, John Russell. *Personal Narrative of Explorations and Incidents in Texas, New Mexico, California, Sonora and Chihuahua, Connected with the United States and Mexico Boundary Commission During the Years 1850–1853.* Chicago: Rio Grande Press, 1965.

Brimelow, Peter. *Alien Nation: Common Sense About America's Immigration Disaster.* New York: Random House, 1995.

Calavita, Kitty. *Inside the State: The Bracero Program, Immigration, and the I.N.S.* New York: Routledge, 1992.

State of California, Governor C. C. Young's Mexican Fact-Finding Committee. *Mexicans in California.* Sacramento: California State Printing Office, October 1930.

Campbell, Federico. *Tijuana: Stories on the Border.* Berkeley: University of California Press, 1995.

Cornelius, Wayne A., Philip L. Martin and James F. Hollifield, eds. *Controlling Immigration: A Global Perspective.* Stanford, Calif.: Stanford University Press, 1994.

Crittenden, Ann. *Sanctuary.* New York: Weidenfeld & Nicolson, 1988.

Davidson, Miriam. *Convictions of the Heart: Jim Corbett and the Sanctuary Movement.* Tucson: University of Arizona Press, 1988.

Dinnerstein, Leonard, and David M. Reimers. *Ethnic Americans: A History of Immigration,* 3rd ed. New York: HarperCollins, 1988.

Emory, William H. *Report on the United States and Mexican Boundary Survey Made Under the Directions of the Secretary of the Interior.* Austin: Texas State Historical Association, 1987.

Feagin, Joe R., and Clairece Booher Feagin. *Racial and Ethnic Relations,* 5th ed. Englewood Cliffs, N.J.: Prentice-Hall, 1996.

Forgey, William W. *The Basic Essentials of Hypothermia.* Merrillville, Ind.: ICS, 1991.

Gray, Andrew Belcher. *The A. B. Gray Report: Survey of a Route on the 32nd Parallel for the Texas Western Railroad, 1854.* Los Angeles: Westernlore, 1963.

Green, Timothy. *The Smugglers: An Investigation into the World of the Contemporary Smuggler.* New York: Walker, 1969.

Griswold del Castillo, Richard. The *Treaty of Guadalupe Hidalgo: A Legacy of Conflict.* Norman: University of Oklahoma Press, 1990.

Hartmann, William K. *Desert Heart: Chronicles of the Sonoran Desert.* Tucson, Ariz.: Fisher, 1989.

Lavin, Patrick. *Arizona: An Illustrated History.* New York: Hippocrene, 2001.

Maciel, David R., and Maria Herrera-Sobek, eds. *Culture Across Borders: Mexican Immigration and Popular Culture.* Tucson: University of Arizona Press, 1998.

Martinez, Oscar J. *Border People: Life and Society in the U.S.-Mexico Borderlands.* Tucson: University of Arizona Press, 1994.

———, ed. *U.S.-Mexico Borderlands: Historical and Contemporary Perspectives.* Wilmington, Del.: Scholarly Resources, 1996.

Martinez, Ruben. *Crossing Over: A Mexican Family on the Migrant Trail.* New York: Metropolitan, 2001.

Massey, Douglas S., Jorge Durand and Nolan J. Malone. *Beyond Smoke and Mirrors: Mexican Immigration in an Era of Free Trade.* New York: Russell Sage Foundation, 2002.

McCarthy, Kevin F., and Georges Vernez. *Immigration in a Changing Economy: California's Experience.* Santa Monica: RAND, 1997.

McWilliams, Carey. *North from Mexico: The Spanish-Speaking People of the United States.* New York: Praeger, 1990.

Meyer, Michael C., and William L. Sherman. *The Course of Mexican History.* New York: Oxford University Press, 1979.

Miller, Tom. *On the Border: Portraits of America's Southwestern Frontier.* New York: Harper & Row, 1981.

———. *Arizona: The Land and the People.* Tucson: University of Arizona Press, 1986.

———. *Jack Ruby's Kitchen Sink.* Washington, D.C.: National Geographic Society, 2001.

Nevins, Joseph. *Operation Gatekeeper: The Rise of the "Illegal Alien" and the Making of the U.S.-Mexico Boundary.* New York: Routledge, 2002.

Perea, Juan F., ed. *Immigrants Out!: The New Nativism and the Anti-Immigrant Impulse in the United States.* New York: New York University Press, 1997.

Proffitt, T. D., III. *Tijuana: The History of a Mexican Metropolis.* San Diego: San Diego State University Press, 1994.

Pumpelly, Raphael. *Pumpelly's Arizona: An Excerpt from Across America and Asia by Raphael Pumpelly, Comprising Those Chapters Which Concern the Southwest.* Tucson: Palo Verde Press, 1965.

Rak, Mary Kidder. *Border Patrol.* Cambridge, Mass.: Riverside Press, 1938.

Rotella, Sebastian. *Twilight on the Line: Underworlds and Politics at the U.S.-Mexico Border.* New York: Norton, 1998.

Saldivar, Jose David. *Border Matters: Remapping American Cultural Studies.* Berkeley: University of California Press, 1997.

Samora, Julian. *Los Mojados: The Wetback Story.* Notre Dame, Ind.: University of Notre Dame Press, 1971.

Sanchez, George J. *Becoming Mexican American: Ethnicity, Culture, and Identity in Chicano Los Angeles, 1900–1945.* New York: Oxford University Press, 1993.

Sheridan, Thomas. *Arizona: A History.* Tucson: University of Arizona Press, 1995.

Suarez-Orozco, Marcelo M. *Crossings: Mexican Immigration in Interdisciplinary Perspectives.* Cambridge, Mass: Harvard University Press, 1998.

Walker, Henry P., and Donald Bufkin. *Historical Atlas of Arizona.* Norman: University of Oklahoma Press, 1986.

Wambaugh, Joseph. *Lines and Shadows.* New York: Bantam, 1984.

Wild, Peter, ed. *The Desert Reader.* Salt Lake City: University of Utah Press, 1991.

Wilkerson, James, ed. *Hypothermia, Frostbite, and Other Cold Injuries.* Seattle, Wash.: The Mountaineers, 1986.

ARTICLES

Gonzalez, Gilbert G., and Raul Fernandez. "Empire and the Origins of Twentieth-Century Migration from Mexico to the United States," *Pacific Historical Review* 71 (2000).

Hing, Bill Ong. "The Dark Side of Operation Gatekeeper," *U.C. Davis Journal of International Law & Policy*, Spring 2001, pp. 2–38.

Rodriguez, Nestor P. "The Battle for the Border: Notes on Autonomous Migration, Transnational Communities, and the State," in *Immigration: A Civil Rights Issue for the Americas.* Wilmington, Del.: Scholarly Resources, 1999.

ARCHIVES

Amnesty International. *USA: Human Rights Concerns in the Border Region with Mexico.* May 1998.

Cornelius, Wayne. *Deaths at the Border: The Efficacy and "Unintended" Consequences of U.S. Immigration Control Policy, 1993–2000.* Center for Comparative Immigration Studies, Working Paper No. 27, November 2000.

Pew Hispanic Center. *Estimates of Numbers of Unauthorized Migrants Residing in the United States: The Total, Mexican and Non-Mexican Central American Unauthorized Populations in Mid-2001.* November 2001.

———. *How Many Undocumented: The Numbers Behind the U.S.-Mexico Migration Talks.* March 21, 2002.

Public Policy Institute of California. *Holding the Line?: The Effect of the Recent Border Buildup on Unauthorized Immigration.* 2002.

U.S. Border Patrol. *Border Patrol Strategic Plan 1994 and Beyond.* July 1994.

U.S. Commission on Immigration Reform and Mexican Secretería de Relaciones Exteriores. *Binational Study on Migration Between Mexico and the United States.* 1997.

U.S. General Accounting Office. *Illegal Immigration: Status of Southwest Border Strategy Implementation.* May 1999.

———. *INS's Southwest Border Strategy: Resource and Impact Issues Remain After Seven Years.* August 2001.

Acknowledgments

This book exists because I had the good fortune to be in the right spot when news happened. I owe thanks to a number of editors at the *Los Angeles Times* for seeing fit to send me to the border and, four years later, for allowing me the chance to weave the strands I had gathered along the way into a book.

Thanks go to Paul Feldman, one of my border-stint editors, whose eye for the unconventional made it easier to get some of those stories into the paper. I am grateful as well to Dean Baquet, the managing editor, and Scott Kraft, national editor, for granting me time off to get a jump on the writing.

The book exists also because some very supportive and sharp-eyed people helped me figure out how to envision it, then make it better. My agents, Todd Shuster and Scott Gold, of Zachary Shuster Harmsworth, showed keen instincts and uncommon patience as I fumbled to produce a coherent outline. My editor, Andrew Miller, was an early believer. His discipline and superb ear resulted in uncountable improvements throughout, and his deft touch made sure the seams didn't show. Thanks also to Amber Hoover for smart editing suggestions in the late going.

I will never find enough places to thank my parents—Wayne, who taught me to work, and Sylvia, to care. Doing one is pointless without the other.

Thanks also to Myra McLarey, who many years ago spurred me to write, and not to stop at five paragraphs.

Demetra Avery, Kevin Sack, Gerry Boyle, and Steve Carroll proved the depth of their friendship by reading the manuscript and offering observations that gave me cheer and spared me embarrassment. Gladdys Uribe provided crucial research assistance. James Metcalf deserves thanks for sharing reams of court transcripts. Faye Taylor allowed me writing quarters with an ocean view.

My work on the border was made easier by too many people to list here. My San Diego bureau mates, Tony Perry and Chris Kraul, helped me stay sane. The job would have been immeasurably more difficult without the assistance of Virginia Kice and Lauren Mack at the former INS, and of the Border Patrol's San Diego office.

Agents and migrants alike showed me respect and patience as I sought to understand their interlocking worlds. The indulgence of government officials, everyday residents, clergymen, ranchers and all the others who populate this book made it better than it would have been otherwise. I owe gratitude to each.

My deepest thanks go to Monique, who saw this book long before I did and, once it came into our lives, never treated it as an intruder.

Index

About the Author

Ken Ellingwood is a staff writer for the *Los Angeles Times*, for which he covered the U.S.-Mexico border from 1998 to 2002. His journalism has won several awards. He is currently based in the newspaper's bureau in Jerusalem, where he lives with his wife and daughter.